THE MYSTERY OF IDENTITY

The Mystery of Identity

LUKE BELL O.S.B.

Angelico Press

First published in the USA
by Angelico Press 2022
Copyright © Luke Bell O.S.B. 2022

Scripture quotations are from *The ESV® Catholic Edition with Deuterocanonical Books*, copyright © 2017 by Crossway, a publishing ministry of Good News Publishers. Used by permission. All rights reserved.

All rights reserved:
No part of this book may be reproduced or transmitted, in any form or by any means, without permission

For information, address:
Angelico Press, Ltd.
169 Monitor St.
Brooklyn, NY 11222
www.angelicopress.com

ppr   978-1-62138-832-6
cloth 978-1-62138-833-3
ebook 978-1-62138-834-0

Book and cover design
by Michael Schrauzer
Cover Image: Joel Whybrew

For Sam Davidson, Poet

CONTENTS

Introduction   1
1: Identity & Identification   5
2: Money & Meaning   35
3: Relationships & Reality   67
4: Christ & Conquering   101
5: Desert & Devils   133
6: Universe & Universality   165
7: Loss & Love   199
Bibliography   233

ACKNOWLEDGEMENTS

I AM MOST GRATEFUL TO THOSE WHO have helped with this book, both by discussing its theme with me and by subjecting drafts of it to scrutiny and making suggestions. I won't say, "You know who you are" since identity is a mystery! You are: Clare Asquith, Mark Asquith, Julian Bell, Sam Davidson, Blake Everitt, Sunman Ho, Leo Maidlow-Davis O.S.B., Neil McEwan, Xavier Perrin O.S.B., Carew Reynell, the Sisters of Saint Cecilia's Abbey, Julia Trahair, Travis Sun, Katherine Tulloch, Julian Van Eyken, Joel Whybrew, Andrew Wye.

INTRODUCTION

IN DOSTOEVSKY'S NOVEL *THE IDIOT*, A DRUNKEN orator maintains that it is possible for a single person to eat sixty monks. In defense of this proposition, he argues that "a Catholic monk is prying and curious by his very nature" and it would be quite easy to "lure him into a forest or some other secluded place and deal with him in the above-mentioned way."[1] As a Catholic monk, I am vulnerable in this respect. My curiosity has enticed me into a veritable thicket: the mystery of identity. There is a tangle of hotly contested philosophical questions; there the brambles of politics, which is all about identity nowadays; there the unfathomable darkness of psychology. And what is literature about except who we are? All of this is without even touching on theology, which is well known for arousing the strongest passions. And yet I am curious. That curiosity, and this book, began with my being struck by an extraordinary paradox intrinsic to the way we use the word "identity." My first chapter, seeking an identification of identity, explores the implications of this paradox which will resonate throughout the entire book.

In doing this I have not been able to conceal that my thinking about it is within the Catholic tradition of faith, but I do not assume that your thoughts, dear reader, are fashioned by the same influences. Rather, I hope that whatever variations there are in our intellectual history we can look together at questions about identity with the aim of remaining as open-minded as possible to the mystery of it all. The ancient wisdom contained in the realization of what we do not know is something that we can perhaps journey towards together. If we can share that unknowing, we may together get a glimpse, if only from afar, of the gladsome mystery. If you do not share my faith, may I share your lack of presumption about what you know; if you do share my faith, may I share with you how it helps me unlearn the kind of prideful knowing that is an illusion and a lie.

I am also helped in this by works of literature, which at their best undo false assumptions about who we are. Therefore, I invite you to

---

1 Fyodor Dostoevsky, *The Idiot*, translated by Richard Pevear and Larissa Volokhonsky (Everyman's Library, 2002), p. 377

read alongside me literary texts which document the struggle to find and establish human identity. I present these at some length because they articulate experience of life in the double sense of saying what it is for anybody to live and of being personal to me. In the latter sense, they carry particular memories, such as Peer Gynt weeping onstage some half a century ago over his disintegrated onion, or Billie Whitelaw speaking with just her mouth illuminated as Beckett's character in the National Theatre in London. Dostoevsky's characters, desperate for personal dignity, have for me denoted the depths of the human psyche since their author became the literary passion of my young mind. Indeed, it is to him that I owe my first inkling of the attractiveness of the monastic tradition. Shakespeare is a perennial presence in my life, in the national identity of the country in which I live and in speaking for all of humanity about who we are. All of these writers are in this book because they bring us into the presence of mystery. And if, in Shakespeare's words, we are to "take upon 's the mystery of things,"[2] it is not surprising if we find ourselves thinking about what is beyond things, beyond the physical—that is to say, about metaphysics. Hence there is metaphysical thought here and indebtedness to the steady movement of the great current flowing from Plato and beyond.

I also engage with contemporary approaches to the questions raised. People in our age are in quest of identity. Purchasing power is brought to bear on its acquisition; social capital is channeled to its establishment. The second chapter looks at these enterprises, registering both their urgency and their inability to offer true satisfaction of the need for identity, a matter on which the Bible is eloquent. It considers the ultimate futility of trying to construct our own identity: this is received rather than made. People want to go deeper than commerce or politics can take them and they look to personal relationships to find who they are.

Chapter Three explores the hazards, harm and help that come from them. They are vulnerable both to mistrust and to the compulsiveness that would blot out self-knowledge, yet we need them—not least in our growth to maturity. True parenting and spiritual friendship give a context for that growth. Christians find who they truly are in their relation to Christ.

---

2 *King Lear*, Act 5, scene iii, l.16. This and all quotations from Shakespeare are from *The Riverside Shakespeare* (Houghton Mifflin, 1974).

Introduction

The fourth chapter focuses on Him and His identity. It is central, both in the sense of being the middle chapter and in the sense that Christ is central in my thinking and in my life. That Christ walked among us in a human body raises the question of how identity is expressed bodily; that He was tempted to diverge from his appointed destiny indicates that the establishment of identity is something to be won; that He invited recognition of who He is suggests that we can find who we are through Him. Ultimately this is a mystery best expressed through silence.

It might seem as though the book has reached its goal here and, in a sense, it has. However, this is also a starting point: having found a Friend with whom an identity can be won, the winning remains to be accomplished. This is, at least figuratively, a struggle with demons in the desert. Chapter Five is about this. It treats of the discipline of solitude, withdrawal from false affirmation and flattery and getting beyond an illusory sense of identity. It discusses the way in which our body is essential to our identity and also the way in which it cannot encompass it. It argues that we cannot identify even with our spiritual virtues and that our true identity is in God alone. In this identity we are united with all of humanity in Christ.

Again, that might seem a natural stopping point for our journey. Yet, Christian identity is all too easily misunderstood as being exclusive, as though it alone could teach about all-inclusive identity. Chapter Six explores such teaching in other traditions. It maintains that the true nature of every human person is to have an all-encompassing identity and illustrates this by the special gift poets have of identifying themselves with others.

The final chapter distinguishes this identity, our birthright, from a false version of it and looks more fully at the implications of truly identifying with all that is. This involves losing everything that is not what it pretends to be and the utter effacement of the false self in a journey that can be purgatorial. This is a costly work, yet it is in losing the identity that we thought we had that we find our true identity; it is in being stripped that we are clothed in glory; it is in giving that we receive. Our identity is a gift of love, a mystery.

Hamlet, a hero most vexed about his identity, complains to one commissioned to find out where he is coming from, "You would pluck out the heart of my mystery,"[3] pointing out that his interlocutor cannot even get music from a simple instrument. It is no part of my purpose to eviscerate inner being and no part of my talent to notate the music of the spheres. If through my words I can simply open my heart, and perhaps yours, a little more to the mystery and beauty of who we are I will consider my time well spent. The curiosity which took me for a walk in these particular woods, which drew me to look at the foliage and to listen to the fauna, will have been a good prompting if you will be so kind as to stay with me and share my adventure.

Gentle reader, you may not agree with all I have to say, you may find flaws in my arguments or gaps in my evidence, but please read this book to the end before you eat me alive.

---

3   Act 3, scene ii, ll.365–66

I
Identity & Identification

"AM I JUST MY PASSPORT?" AND OTHER QUESTIONS

"Identity" is derived from the medieval Latin word, *idemptitas*. This comes from *idem*, meaning "the same." Yet it is universally used to mean what is different, as in the phrase "unique identity." It is a one-word oxymoron. What are the implications of this? What, if anything, does it mean to say—in the same breath—that I am the same and that I am different? If I am asked for my identity and I produce a passport, does this mean that I am the same as my passport but different to everyone else? Am I just my passport? And if not, why does not having one turn me from a citizen to a suffering refugee? Am I only what the state recognizes me to be? Does paper settle the question? What is an official asking me when he or she says, "May I see your identity, sir?" If the United Nations achieves its declared goal of providing everyone on earth with a legal identity by 2030, will that help?[1] Does "photographic identity" really show who I am? In this day and age, am I just a cyber identity? If my digital identity is stolen, where does that leave me? If I have several digital identities, which—if any—is real? Am I identified by the newspaper I read? If my job is my identity, what happens if I change or lose it? What is who I am, what is my identity? Do I have an identity? And if I do, what is the identity of the person who has an identity?

In a sense questions—and, as will become apparent in this book, there are many more—questions of this sort have been with me all my life, for I am a monozygotic twin. I say "monozygotic" rather than the adjective used in popular parlance ("identical") because as we grew up my brother and I felt a need to be—in some respects at least—different. Viewed from certain perspectives, we have pursued different paths. Does this mean we are no longer identical? Sometimes, when I want to know what my attitude to something is and am feeling too lazy to think it through, I just

---

1   Florian Coulmas, *Identity, A Very Short Introduction* (Oxford University Press, 2019), p. 82

remember what my brother thinks. Does this mean we are still identical? Do people who are not identical twins ever think just like this by reference to some significant other? How could I really know? How could the other be identical, anyway?

GOD'S UNIQUE IDENTITY

Let us look at the *Oxford English Dictionary* definition in quest of a way through the tangle of questions. The first meaning given is: "The quality or condition of being the same in substance, composition, nature, properties, or in particular qualities under consideration; absolute or essential sameness, oneness." If absolute oneness is a transcendent characteristic that only God has, this could only really be true of Him. He has identity in the old, etymological sense of being constantly the same. He also has identity in the sense of being uniquely different. There cannot be any like Him, a truth contained in the etymological meaning of the Archangel Michael's name—"Who is like God?" This is true of God in His transcendence but is also true of God in His immanence. It is precisely because (in Saint Thomas Aquinas's words) *Deus totus est in omnibus et singulis*[2] (all of God is in each and every thing) that there are different things. He *creates* difference by keeping each different thing in being. Every created thing has its being in Him. So His *total* uniqueness is participated in by each thing in creation *on its own level*. So each created thing does not have total uniqueness in the divine sense, but rather a relative uniqueness: it is different from other created things in that its space and time coordinates are different, not in the sense that it is totally different. So it has a unique existence on the level of creation: its particular relation to the remainder of creation is not shared. If it were shared by anything, then by the law of the identity of indiscernables, that would be the same thing. That characteristic of being in a unique space and time (or more precisely, since space and time are abstractions from them, of having particular relations within creation) is not shared by God. Each thing, so to speak, identifies with Him—that is why it exists at all—yet God in one sense disidentifies with everything in creation. He does not share the characteristic of created things to block out other created things from a particular time or space. In that sense, He

---

2 Thomas Aquinas, *Summa Theologiae*, 1.8.2

identifies with all creation. If we can say (and the next chapter will look at this) that a person draws identity from belonging to a people and a land, God gives identity to all peoples and lands. He does not fail to be present in time and space. It is only in a metaphorical sense that we can say that any time or place is godless. As Meister Eckhart put it, He is distinguished by His indistinction. He is identically present in all of creation. We can't say—for example—that He is in one country but not another. He doesn't have created difference, only utterly transcendent difference. That difference is His unique sameness which is transcendently in Himself and immanently throughout creation.

This does not say everything about the mystery of God's identity, however. It is in the nature of theology that we have to unsay as well as say what we say about God, who transcends our categories, on pain of falsifying who He is. God communicates and in communicating He has a particular identity. He is not limited to a universal identity. So He can identify Himself with a particular people, the Jewish people, to speak to the world. Furthermore, He can identify with a particular land, as evidenced when Elisha the prophet is asked for soil from it when he cures Naaman the commander from leprosy.[3] Yet that, too, is transcended with the destruction of the temple and the dispersion of the Jews in the context of His identifying Himself as a particular person, Jesus Christ. Yet this identification spreads out to include all of suffering humanity, everybody in need, and is manifest sacramentally in every celebration of the Eucharist.

WHO AM I?

God's identity is mysterious. And the mystery of identity is the mystery of God. In Him identity is both absolute oneness and absolute difference. He is completely the same and completely different, the two characteristics that identity denotes. The mystery of His identity lies like a mist over creation. The ambiguity of identity speaks of the mystery of creation. Everything in it is the same in having being. Without identity in this sense of sameness, nothing can have identity in the sense of being different. Having the same being enables difference. The human heart, the heart of creation, longs to belong and longs to be different. It longs for

---

3   2 Kings 5.17

identity, an identity that is rooted in a shared life and an identity that marks the special uniqueness of the individual. This longing for a stable identity, now crying out in our world with an almost anguished plangency, is at root a longing for God.

In what sense can I say that I have an identity? In the sense that I am made in the image of God: I am a tangle of matter and ghost in whom identity is a paradox insofar as I belong to the passing creation but in whom there is a spark of the life of the One in whose image I am made, calling me to a transcendent identity which is beyond paradox. What this calling is begins to be apparent from the second definition of identity given by the *Oxford English Dictionary*: "The sameness of a person or thing at all times or in all circumstances; the condition or fact that a person or thing is itself and not something else; individuality, personality." It is the sameness of the One who is "the same yesterday today and forever."[4]

THE DIFFICULTIES OF CONSISTENT IDENTITY

Difference and sameness: these are the parameters of identity. Uniquely, and with absolute consistency, they characterize God, in whom they are one. The human quest for identity, for a true self, is the quest for God. It takes place along a path leading up a precipice at whose summit is a celebration of divinization, a realization of being truly in the image of God. To the side of this path is an abyss where the self condemns itself to the attempt to replace the One who transcends place, to dominate the One who is Lord of Time. It would be merely a faint adumbration of the quest simply to say, let God be God and you will find who you are. That simply points us to mystery, for we cannot see God and live. Yet it does tell us that the quest involves allowing mystery, being open to mystery, not insisting on deciding what is there. The mystery is the coming together of difference and sameness. The mystery is the goal. Yet to follow the path, we need to know distinctly what difference and sameness are in this mystery of identity. And we need to know how in common practice they are sought before we think about how they are truly to be found, lest in reflecting on the true path we ignore wrong turnings from which steps need to be retraced before we tread that path. Hence in the first two chapters of this book and the first part

---

4 Hebrews 13.8

of the third chapter, the emphasis will be on tracing how people try to grasp identity, alert to the kernel of truth in the questing of their hearts and to the misapprehension in the imagination of their minds. Later chapters will be about how we receive identity.

This chapter will focus on sameness, the second rather on difference. We don't have to go back very far, if at all, in human history to see that a sense of who you are depends on being reliably the same. If you are a person of your word, you will do tomorrow what you promised today. If you are not, your word has no credibility and in a sense you cannot say who you are; you cannot articulate an identity. There can even be a question about the value of your life: certainly a question about your social life. If your failure to speak truly amounted to fraud, you could be separated from society in a prison. It is a question of honor, that is to say, the respect due to a person. Yet it is not only a question of respect *due*, of a person being in reality constant in character; it is also a question of being seen to be such. This implies that identity tends in practice to have a social dimension. If you are not a saint, or *mutatis mutandis* have that sort of commitment to the work of the devil, you are liable to have your sense of who you are influenced by what other people say. This could literally be a matter of life or death. An insult—which is to say, an imputation of negative identity—was of yore to be answered only by a duel which would either nullify the naysayer or end the challenger's life. So was Pushkin lost to poetry, Galois to mathematics, and Hamilton to American politics.[5] The implication is that you don't really have a life if you have been labeled as dishonorable. Duels may be out of fashion now, but people can still turn even deadly violence against their own lives if they are not socially honored. Being trashed on Twitter can be terminal.

There are other problematic aspects to having a consistent identity over time (which, traditionally, is having an identity at all) but before exploring those it will be helpful to say how in principle these ones can be dealt with. I say "in principle" because dealing with them is a whole life work, a more complete exposition of which will be deferred to Chapter Five. The two aspects considered in the above paragraph can be characterized as *moral* and *social*. Accordingly,

---

[5] Kwame Anthony Appiah, *The Lies That Bind: Rethinking Identity* (Profile Books, 2019), pp. 149–50

THE MYSTERY OF IDENTITY

to be someone (or have a credible identity) you have to *be* a good person and *be thought to be* a good person. Both of these are obviously difficult to achieve! Many a life has been shipwrecked attempting to steer between the Scylla of failing to be of true worth and the Charybdis of not being reputed to be truly worthy. It is impossible, except that all things are possible to God. God alone is good; God alone is truly worthy of honor; God alone is consistently who He is. So it is *in relation to God* that we find true identity. Yet, "If we say we have no sin, we deceive ourselves, and the truth is not in us,"[6] so it would seem that we cannot truthfully have an identity. Yet the mercy of God accepts us back when we fail. So *He* is our constancy, He is our consistency, He is our goodness; for He never changes. In relation to Him we have a consistency and an identity. He keeps them in His heart. It is simply a matter of remaining open to His mercy and love, and acknowledging that of ourselves we cannot pilot this ship of our soul. The second, social aspect of having a consistent identity is addressed in the same way. We cannot please all of the people all the time and even if we get near it they may get hold of the wrong end of the stick or be destructively jealous of how far we have come. The only answer is to say with Jesus, "I do not receive my glory from people."[7] That means not living from what people think of us. A kind compliment can be a serendipity, an add-on to the joy of day, an encouragement, but we cannot truly live from it. We can only truly live from God. Only He can tell us who we are; only He can speak that word that strengthens and empowers us; only He can give us an identity.

Yet it is not only the moral and social aspects of identity over time which are problematic. There are philosophical issues. In 1971, the British philosopher, Derek Parfit, published a paper entitled "Personal Identity" in which he argues that personal identity is not a necessary belief. He observes that one could say, "It was not I who did that, but an earlier self."[8] This prescinds from moral and social questions of responsibility rather in the manner of Hamlet saying it was his madness, not himself, that acted in what he did.[9] Parfit, developing his thought in his book *Reasons and Persons* (1984), doubts whether questions about identity should have an answer,

---

6   Cf. 1 John 1.8   7   John 5.41
8   *The Philosophical Review*, vol. 80, No. 1, Jan. 1971, p. 25
9   Act 5, scene ii, ll.230ff.

Identity & Identification

claiming, "Persons are like nations, clubs or political parties."[10] He memorably cites Proust's dictum, "We are incapable, while we are in love, of acting as fit predecessors of the next persons who, when we are in love no longer, we shall presently have become."[11] This has force. One could take issue with Proust and say being in love motivates commitment and commitment becomes enduring friendship, yet if this was all that ever happened there would be no novels, no dramas, no films. Life isn't like that: it is more like Shakespeare's *A Midsummer Night's Dream* where people madly fall in love first with one and then with another, not excluding adoring the weaver Nick Bottom in the guise of a donkey. And Parfit is not the only one to see Proust as pointing up a fundamental philosophical difficulty in the concept of identity over time. Samuel Beckett, in his essay on Proust (1930), wrote, "We are not merely more weary because of yesterday, we are other, no longer what we were before the calamity of yesterday." By this account, discontinuity in identity invalidates the attainment of personal goals:

> We are disappointed at the nullity of what we are pleased to call attainment. But what is attainment? The identification of the subject with the object of his desire. The subject has died—and perhaps many times—on the way. For subject B to be disappointed by the banality of an object chosen by subject A is as illogical as to expect one's hunger to be dissipated by the spectacle of Uncle eating his dinner.[12]

Can you really speak for the person you are going to be when the meal you are ordering in a restaurant arrives?

The answer to this and analogous questions is that *we are not our desires*. Someone in a restaurant who wants, and places an order for, a lamb cutlet is not fundamentally and for all time a lamb cutlet person. He is just hungry. If, while waiting for it to be prepared he nibbles a lot of bread and so on, so that when it does finally arrive he rather thinks he would prefer a cheese salad, he is not a different person. He is simply not very hungry. The reality is helpfully explained by another British philosopher,

---

10 Derek Parfit, *Reasons and Persons* (Oxford University Press, 1987), p. 277
11 Ibid., p. 305
12 Samuel Beckett, *Proust* (Grove Press, 1957), p. 3

THE MYSTERY OF IDENTITY

Robert Bolton. He points out that so much of our life nowadays is focused on getting stuff done and, concomitantly, what we want done. However, meditation techniques which focus on "a simple object or thought, so as to finally exclude all others, and even have no object at all" can make us aware that, "At higher levels of concentration, we have power to control the quantity of our conscious contents, and so to approach the ground and medium of their connection."[13] The person who wants a lamb cutlet or a cheese salad is not the wanting: he *has* the wanting. That disidentification is important and we shall return to it in later chapters in different contexts. Here, though, let us follow through the implications of there being a "ground and medium" in which the contents of our consciousness connect. Essentially this is (to speak metaphorically) a beholding. I am aware that I am hungry; later on I shall be aware that I am no longer hungry. I am the same person, it is just that I am aware of different things within my psyche just as I would be aware of different things around me if I travelled to a foreign place.

So what about Proust? He, of course, is famous for his examination of time. Identity is not to be found in a particular moment of time. It is, as I have argued above, to be found in God. Identity belongs to what is divine and eternal. It is less in the love for a particular person than in the love within that love, the love that is God, the love that moves the stars. Philosophical difficulty occurs if we try to limit identity to the partial and passing. It is in reality all-encompassing. In an earlier, slower age, people could see the stars move—not just because there was no light pollution, but because their attention was not fragmented and their concentration not feeble. The whole of the cosmos over the entirety of a life *and* the whole of the microcosm that is the human person—everything in the psyche—speak more nearly of our identity than the project of the day or the infatuation of the week. This is, in its way, an image or instantiation of God's all-seeing. It is said that at the last moment of their existence people see their whole lives flash before them. Perhaps then they have some sort of hint of who they are.

The practice of meditation referred to above of excluding awareness of many particulars by focusing on one particular, even to the

---

13   Robert Bolton, *Person, Soul and Identity* (Minerva Press, 1994), pp. 176–77

Identity & Identification

point of no longer being aware of this latter, directs the meditator to the seeing rather than the seen, to the perceiver rather than the perceived, to awareness itself. It is worth emphasizing that in practice, especially in our attention-dispersed age, this is a *work*. It doesn't just happen. Without such work we are just carried down the river of time before being discharged into the ocean of eternity knowing nothing but that river. The work is not so much that of fighting time—we cannot abolish the particular in the name of the whole—as of using time in a way that opens us to its source. That source is ultimately the heaven from which falls the rain that makes the river. This work of looking beyond can be taken further than the aforesaid meditation. This is in a sense just a preparation. It removes our attention from the many and varied beckoning to it in order to make us capable of gazing towards what is divine and immutable, unfastens us from time so as to unite us to Him who is its source, enables the inner man to be journeying upstream to the ever-fresh spring of mountain water even as the outer man is carried downstream along a sometimes stagnating river. Saint Paul articulated and enjoined it thus: "Seek the things that are above, where Christ is, seated at the right hand of God. Set your mind on things that are above, not on things that are on earth."[14] So the work goes from cultivating simple awareness to becoming aware of what heaven shows us of what is eternal, through the revelation of Christ. This is the work of realizing identity, for it moves from the fissiparous fragments of time to the wholeness of eternity in which we ourselves can be whole and integrated.

Shelley expressed the difference between the "things that are above" and the "things that are on earth" poetically:

> The One remains, the many change and pass;
> Heaven's light forever shines, Earth's shadows fly;
> Life, like a dome of many-colored glass,
> Stains the white radiance of Eternity...[15]

The many which change and pass are also the subjects A and B and so on of which Beckett writes, in which there is no stable identity.

---

14 Colossians 3.1-2
15 Percy Bysshe Shelley, *Adonais*, stanza 52, *The Norton Anthology of Poetry* (New York, 1983), p. 636

THE MYSTERY OF IDENTITY

The One which remains offers stability and integrity, enabling us to see our wholeness and consistency. It gives the light that shows who we are; the things of earth are, independent of it, evanescent shadows which cannot identify us. Our lives do not radiate who we are: they simply color "the white radiance of Eternity." Our essence comes from the divine, not from the particularities of our circumstances. These are in reality limitations: like stained glass, they limit what can come through them. Yet—beautiful paradox of creation and life—the stains are not in the end sin and shame: they are beauty. We are beautiful people; God makes us so. That is who we are.

KNOWING YOUR ONIONS

But we need to realize who we are. I say "realize" because it has a double sense. We need to realize who we are in the sense that we realize a project by making it happen. That is the work I have spoken of. Yet "realize" also means "become aware of" in the sense of animadverting to something true but hitherto not perceived. And that is the deeper truth about being God's beautiful people. "In this is love, not that we have loved God but that he loved us."[16] His love is already there; to Him we are already beautiful; He knows us in all the radiance we are to have in eternity. We simply need to discover this, that is, to take away the covering, to deconstruct the supposed identities that cannot speak who we truly are. This discovery is the work of a lifetime, the theme of this book, the burden of literature. Many are the explorations of this in fiction, but I want to focus on one: *Peer Gynt*, by the Norwegian playwright Henrik Ibsen, which shows us both the quest for man-made identity and its final failure to satisfy. Ibsen wrote concerning the play's genesis, "in every new poem or play I have aimed at my own spiritual emancipation and purification."[17] The play presents a person who is a serial reconstructer of his own identity. Consistent he is not.

It starts with his mother's accusation: "Lies, Peer, lies!"[18] His "tall tales" characterize him. He is "stuck 'twixt truth and fable,"[19]

---

16 1 John 4.10
17 *Peer Gynt* (Everyman, London, 1950), p. viii
18 Act 1, scene i, p. 168 in *Peer Gynt and Brand: Verse Translations by Geoffrey Hill* (Penguin, 2016)   19 Act 1, scene i, p. 172

yet he is touched by the devout young girl Solveig whom he meets at a wedding feast. At this feast he ignobly makes off with the bride who is pledged to another man. Yet he has aspirations:

> I so desire to soar—higher!—
> to bathe in keenest winds, plunge
> to redemption, to become pure,
> naked in keeping with my heart's pledge.[20]

He would be "clean of heart."[21] Yet he finds himself engaged to a troll. If he marries her, he must never leave the trolls' land. Her father explains the difference between the troll world and what is beyond it:

> Out there—remember?—under the sky's high-gleaming vault,
> 'be thyself, be thyself, even to thy most inward fault'
> is the great injunction. Down here, with the race of trolls,
> 'be to thyself sufficient' is the motto that appeals.[22]

The light of "the sky's high-gleaming vault" would show who he truly is; the troll motto "be to thyself sufficient" points to an identity constructed for an interested purpose, after the manner of modern-day online trolls. Peer refuses squinting "troll-vision."[23] He is set free by the ringing of church bells. In pitch darkness, he is confronted by a voice saying, "I am what I am./ Can you say the same?"[24] He is saved from the ensuing confrontation because, "The prayers of good women were keeping him safe."[25] He is disinherited and outlawed for taking the bride, but Solveig comes to him, bringing her "divine grace."[26] She enters the cabin he has built, but he is confronted by the troll woman with his troll child. He goes, leaving Solveig waiting for him in his house, and returns to his mother who is on her death bed. She departs this life to the sound of Peer's tales.

When we next see him, he has made his fortune. He has also made his self, taking as his principle, "I am the law/ unto myself and to no other." Money makes what he calls "The Gyntian *self*—that iron brigade/ of wishes, passions and desires,/ a massive

---

20   Act 2, scene iv, p. 204
21   Ibid.
22   Act 2, scene vi, p. 209
23   Act 2, scene vi, p. 213
24   Act 2, scene vii, p. 216
25   Act 2, scene vii, p. 219
26   Act 3, scene iii, p. 227

THE MYSTERY OF IDENTITY

flood that know no shores,/ vortex of impulse, need and claim,/ the world that I entirely am."²⁷ Losing his fortune as a shipping magnate, he finds himself in a desert "totally unsupportive of humanity's self-belief."²⁸ Here he reinvents himself as an Arab emperor, for whom life

> means to glide
> along time's river still dryshod;
> to be oneself at each extreme
> of agency in space and time.
> The very core, the I am I,
> Of selfhood's self, such potency!²⁹

As the words "agency" and "potency" imply, he sees his identity as being what he does and what he can do. He means to establish what he calls, "the caliphate/ of my grand Selfhood"³⁰ in the heart of Anitra, the Arab woman he has taken as his own. He is to become "Peer as two in one self-reigning."³¹ She gets his money and leaves him. Yet he still believes in "Gyntism, alias/ Imperialism of the New Humanity,"³² although Solveig is waiting for him,³³ and manifests it "in the guise of an Egyptian gent."³⁴ Questioned at the site of the Sphinx as to who he is, he replies, "I have always sought to be myself./ You may examine my passport."³⁵ He finds himself in a madhouse, emperor of the insane for having solved the Sphinx's riddle, "Who is selfhood's self?"³⁶ He is "bunged in the barrel of himself, fermenting,/ hermetically sealed-in with self-cementing."³⁷ He sees himself as "a sheet of paper on which nothing is written."³⁸ Crying, "What am I?" he loses consciousness.³⁹

In the final act of the play we see him old and returning to Norway,⁴⁰ on whose shore he is shipwrecked.⁴¹ Seeing the funeral of one who "to his own self was true" he reflects, "being unshakeably for yourself is where I always stand."⁴² He finds he

---

27 Act 4, scene i, p. 248   28 Act 4, scene v, p. 258
29 Act 4, scene vii, p. 269   30 Ibid.
31 Act 4, scene vii, p. 270   32 Act 4, scene ix, p. 276
33 Act 4, scene x, p. 276   34 Act 4, scene xi, p. 277
35 Act 4, scene xii, p. 280   36 Act 4, scene xiii, p. 283
37 Act 4, scene xiii, p. 284   38 Act 4, scene xiii, p. 289
39 Act 4, scene xiii, p. 290   40 Act 5, scene i, p. 290
41 Act 5, scene ii, pp. 298–302   42 Act 5 scene iii, p. 305

is still remembered as "a damnable fabricator."[43] Finally he sees himself as "an onion, in need of peeling."[44] On his knees in the heart of a forest, he peels an onion. Each layer is one of the selves of his life. The outermost layer is "the shipwrecked man" that he recently was. He works his way down the many layers of his life, including, among others, "gold-digger" and "the wealthy man of the world." Seeking to "uncover the core" he pulls the whole onion apart and finds "it doesn't have a heart."[45] Such is the emptiness of the Gyntian, self-constructed self. He sees the cabin he built where Solveig is singing and comparing himself to her at last understands:

> Ah! One who remembered and one who forgot.
> One who lost faith while the other did not.
> Dire gravitational pull of things never to be reversed.
> Here was my right true empire but I was self-deposed.[46]

Nature reproaches him for the life he has led.[47] He meets a button molder who says he is "to be melted down."[48] He was "meant for a shining button/ on the world's waistcoat; but somehow a loop broke."[49] The button molder rejects his protests, saying

> Never in the past,
> even for a moment, have you been yourself,
> so what does it matter? And on whose behalf
> do you bewail this lost identity?[50]

To Peer's claim to an "irreducible entity/ indissoluble to mere quantity" the button molder opposes his defiance of the "determination for his road."[51] He is nonetheless allowed "some time of grace."[52] He tries to get the Troll King to witness for him, but is told that he left with the trolls' commandment, "Troll, to yourself be sufficient!" stuck in his soul and has lived according to it.[53] He meets the button molder again and asks him what it means to "be oneself," to be told that he has done away with himself by misusing God's gifts. To "be oneself" in the Gyntian sense is "to

---

43 Act 5, scene iv, p. 310
44 Act 5, scene v, p. 312
45 Act 5, scene v, p. 313
46 Act 5, scene v, p. 314
47 Act 5, scene vi, pp. 315-17
48 Act 5, scene vii, p. 318
49 Act 5, scene vii, p. 320
50 Act 5, scene vii, p. 322
51 Ibid.
52 Act 5, scene vii, p. 323
53 Act 5, scene viii, p. 326

treat as pelf/ the master's treasures, and to smear with glue/ his best intentions, plaster them on the wall of...self-adulation and the desire to sell."[54] Yet he is granted "further time of grace."[55] Looking for a priest, he meets the devil who doubts if his identity is clear enough for hell. It seems he is to "return/ to pristine nothingness in the dense grey."[56] He is told by the button molder to set his house in order.[57] Returning to the forest cabin, he says to Solveig, "I am lost." She replies, "But surely to be found/ in Him who holds all things at His command."[58] He asks, "Where has it been, my true self, all this time?" She answers, "In my faith, in my hope, and in my love you have been carried."[59] Solveig is Peer's true life, his soul whose faith, hope, and love unites him to God where he finds his identity. His "true empire"[60] is outside the grasp of his self. He can only receive it as a gift, accepting "full forgiveness."[61]

IDENTITY CRISIS

Only in the divine mercy can identity survive the fragmentation that human willfulness inflicts upon it. God's sameness heals our inconstancy. Yet it is not only time that is problematic for identity: it is also space. We long to be the same, we long for identity. That raises the question: the same as what? What do we identify with? Psychology speaks of this. In his highly influential book, *Identity, Youth and Crisis* (1968), Erik H. Erikson argues that, essentially, the answer is: the culture of the society. What is around gives us identity. As the title of the book suggests, he does not see this as unproblematic. His approach to the question is too intelligent for him to claim to rob identity of its mystery. "The more one writes about this subject," he acknowledges, "the more the word becomes a term for something as unfathomable as it is all-pervasive."[62] Part of the difficulty of identity, he argues, is that although one looks to the culture around to find an identity, this changes. Giving psychological help to people who had experienced the convulsions of the Second World War or its aftermath, Erikson saw how critical

---

54 Act 5, scene ix, p. 329   55 Act 5, scene ix, p. 330
56 Act 5, scene x, p. 337   57 Act 5, scene x, p. 338
58 Act 5, scene x, p. 339   59 Act 5, scene x, p. 340
60 Act 5, scene v, p. 314   61 Act 5, scene x, p. 340
62 Erik H. Erikson, *Identity, Youth and Crisis* (Norton, 1994), p. 9

Identity & Identification

for people's identity is the identity—in the sense of sameness—of the surrounding into which they emerge as young adults. When that changes in the double sense of being a new country because of immigration and the culture of that country itself changing, the effects are especially critical. The first usage of the phrase "identity crisis" recorded in the *Oxford English Dictionary* is from 1954. It emerges from the upheavals of the age.

And it threatens who we are. Erikson goes so far as to say, "In the social jungle of human existence there is no feeling of being alive without a sense of identity."[63] He identifies identity with life. He considers "a sense of identity" best described by these words of the nineteenth-century psychologist William James:

> A man's character is discernible in the mental or moral attitude in which, when it came upon him, he felt himself most deeply and intensively active and alive. At such moments there is a voice inside which speaks and says: "*This* is the real me!"[64]

This recalls the promise of Christ, "I came that they may have life and have it abundantly."[65] Erikson, however, links the experience of having "a coherent identity" (with its sense of being alive) to an Old Testament text:

> No quantifiable aspect of this experience can do justice to its subjective halo, for it means nothing less than that I am alive, that I *am* life. The counterplayer of the "I" therefore can be, strictly speaking, only the deity who has lent this halo to a mortal and is Himself endowed with an eternal numinousness certified by all "I"s who acknowledge this gift. This is why God, when Moses asked Him who should he say had called him, answered: "I AM THAT I AM." He then ordered Moses to tell the multitude: "I AM has sent me unto you." And, indeed, only a multitude held together by a common faith shares to that extent a common "I," wherefore "brothers and sisters in God" can appoint each other true "You"s in mutual compassion and joint veneration. The Hindu greeting of looking into another's eyes—hands raised close to the face with palms

---

63 Ibid., p. 130
64 Ibid., p. 19
65 John 10.10

joined—and saying "I recognize the God in you" expresses the heart of the matter.[66]

Erikson is aware of the difficulty involved when man "tries to remake himself in the blueprint of a manufactured identity,"[67] but since he wrote this has become more acute. The accentuating factor is precisely the particular societal identity that he describes: "the technological super-identity in which even the American dream and the Marxist revolution come to meet"[68] where there is a "common language only in the workings of science and technology."[69] He gives an account of a Native American whose tradition is not one of acceleration to a technically empowered future and the concomitant difficulty of claiming an identity in the context of the latter, but is writing at a time when this difficulty was not so widely recognized. Heidegger had already raised concerns about technology and Romano Guardini had already raised a prophetic voice in *The End of the Modern World,* but it is in our own time that identifying human persons with the manipulation of nature has come to be seen more fully as what it is: dubious and insubstantial to a critical degree. Pope Francis in his encyclical letter *Laudato Si'* articulates the questionability of the project of prioritization of potency over purpose. And Extinction Rebellion, the protest against the biodegrading of the planet even to the prospect of death, is an adamant refusal of this once hegemonic identity. Identity concomitantly becomes fraught, fragmented and fought over.

Erikson admits to not having any better explanation of man's true identity than that implied by the narrative of God creating Adam, but argues that God's expulsion of Adam from the Garden of Eden "tied man's identity forever to the manner of his toil and of his co-operation with others, and with technical and communal pride."[70] That leaves open the question of whether paradise can be regained and with it a primordial identity. Utopian substitutes along the lines of transhumanism—technology making man more or different than he was made to be—abound, but the Christian tradition has always held out the prospect of paradise regained, of redemption. And a socially and culturally mediated identity with

---

66   Erik H. Erikson, *Identity, Youth and Crisis* (Norton, 1994), pp. 220-21
67   Ibid., p. 40   68   Ibid., p. 259
69   Ibid., p. 260   70   Ibid., p. 40

Identity & Identification

this teleology is offered by the Church. We can become sons and daughters of the Most High. Yet if identity needs that to which to be identical, there is the practical problem of as it were germinating as a seed of wheat in a field full of tares. If a society is radically untrue to its Christian or God-given identity, how can youth growing up into it find a true identity? While there have always been tares in the wheat field, if it is now a tare field where is the support for the fresh shoot of wheat? We can answer that it is the Church of all ages, militant and triumphant, which can speak to the one who reads and prays, but that is not what tare-dominated society immediately presents. Finding that supra-temporal ecclesial context for identity formation is analogous and concomitant with finding God in an ungodly society. It is a quest. And to undertake that quest one needs a sense of oneself as not defined by the society into which one is emerging. One needs some sort of autonomy of identity and this needs to be protected from the social pressure to conform to ungodly norms.

HAMLET THE DANE

Shakespeare's *Hamlet* dramatizes this mission to protect identity. The eponymous hero is in a corrupt society, ruled over by his uncle, the fratricidal king, Claudius. He is, as Erikson acknowledges in his own reflection on what the play teaches us about identity, "inscrutable."[71] That is true for the theatre-goer and critic, for this is on one level a play about the mystery of identity; but it is also true within the play, for Hamlet deliberately hides himself from those around him. When he learns that his uncle is a "smiling, damned villain,"[72] he decides "to put an antic disposition on."[73] In acting out madness he conceals his fidelity to his father in his opposition to his uncle who murdered him. I say "acting out" as the phrase has the ambiguity of denoting both behavior driven by a disturbed psyche and the deliberate playing of a part. To safeguard his inner self he refuses a public identity. When Ophelia returns the love tokens he has given her, he denies it was he who gave them: "No, not I,/ I never gave you aught."[74] He refuses ownership of words as well as deeds: when the king, expressing his lack of understanding of Hamlet's speech says, "these words are not mine,"

---

71 Ibid., p. 236
72 Act 1, scene v, l.106
73 Act 1, scene v, l.172
74 Act 3, scene i, ll.94–95

Hamlet's response is, "No, nor mine now."[75] The same deliberate denial of consistent identity is evident in his telling Ophelia first, "I did love you once"[76] and then "I lov'd you not."[77] Those given the task of finding the real Hamlet have to admit that he "with a crafty madness keeps aloof/ When we would bring him on to some confession/ Of his true state."[78]

From the beginning, even before he has been given his mission of avenging his murdered father, he has "that within which passes show."[79] The customary mourning clothes—"suits of solemn black"[80] and so on—cannot denote him truly. He needs to separate himself from the conventions of society to follow the advice given to another son by his father, "to thine own self be true."[81] Yet this separation becomes a disconnection from action, for "the native hue of resolution/ Is sicklied o'er with the pale cast of thought."[82] Hamlet, through "thinking too precisely on th'event [outcome],"[83] fails to identify himself by action, in contrast to the strong-armed Fortinbras who does. His hesitation threatens his identity, in the sense of consistent purpose, for (as the King in the play he stages says), "What to ourselves in passion we propose,/ The passion ending, doth the purpose lose."[84] The difficulty of being true to the resolution of love inversely reflects that articulated by Proust (cited above) of being fit predecessors of the persons we shall have become when no longer in love, for when things happen, as another son who would revenge the death of his father says, "this 'would' changes."[85] Hamlet's admiration for his friend Horatio who is "not a pipe for Fortune's finger/ To sound what stop she pleases"[86] reveals his yearning for a purposeful identity not knocked off course by events. Similarly, he indicates his contempt for those who seem what they are not in his outburst, "God hath given you one face, and you make yourselves another."[87] As for Hamlet himself, he says, "I know not 'seems.'"[88] He seeks a true identity.

---

75 Act 3, scene ii, ll.97-98
76 Act 3, scene i, l.114
77 Act 3, scene i, l.118
78 Act 3, scene i, ll.8-10
79 Act 1, scene ii, l.85
80 Act 1, scene ii, l.78
81 Act 1, scene iii, l.78
82 Act 3, scene i, ll.83-84
83 Act 4, scene iv, l.41
84 Act 3, scene ii, ll.194-95
85 Act 4, scene vii, l.119
86 Act 3, scene ii, ll.70-71
87 Act 3, scene i, ll.143-44
88 Act 1, scene ii, l.76

Identity & Identification

He finds it. Significantly, this is after he is sent to England where "the men are as mad as he."[89] This line always gets a laugh (at least in England) but it suggests the serious point that in journeying towards a place where he is not concerned by the difference between himself and those around him, he finds who he truly is. For on his return, he boldly announces, "This is I,/ Hamlet the Dane!"[90] The earlier ambiguity is gone: he says emphatically, "I lov'd Ophelia."[91] He has no patience with people, like the courtier Osric, who depend on another's opinion even to say whether it is hot or cold[92] and have "only got the tune of the time."[93] With less than half an hour to live, he kills Claudius. Fortinbras has Hamlet's "dying voice"[94] to become King of Denmark. This soldier is "with divine ambition puff'd" and unswayed by what might happen.[95] He, too, knows who he is.

FIGHTING THE FIRST PERSON

Hamlet finds his identity through not letting a corrupt society tell him who he is. In a sense, that is possible for him because he is "most royal"[96]—he is a central figure who can call himself "the Dane" because it is his role, as leader, to *give* Denmark its identity. He is, by birth and destiny, a safeguarder of integrity for his country. Identity is very much more problematic when the person occupies a position of receiving, rather than giving, identity. That can mean that the person concerned looks at the given identity and can only say, "This is not I." This dynamic is an acting out of the question raised above: if I have an identity, what is the identity of the person who has an identity? It is a confronting of the inconsistency of encountering oneself as another and being unable to accept this other as "I."[97] It is dramatized in its extreme form in Samuel Beckett's play *Not I*. The speaker is an old woman of whom Beckett said, "I knew that woman in Ireland. I knew who she was—not 'she' specifically, one single woman, but there were so many of those old crones, stumbling down the lanes, in the ditches, beside the hedgerows. Ireland is full of them. And I

---

89   Act 5, scene i, l.154-55
90   Act 5, scene i, l.257-58
91   Act 5, scene i, l.269
92   Act 5, scene ii, ll.94-101
93   Act 5, scene ii, l.189-90
94   Act 5, scene ii, l.356
95   Act 4, scene iv, ll.49-50
96   Act 5, scene ii, l.398
97   Cf Florian Coulmas, *Identity, A Very Short Introduction* (Oxford University Press, 2019), p. 120

heard 'her' saying what I wrote in *Not I*. I actually heard it."[98] The play presents her as a waif coming into the world with "no love of any kind."[99] Only her mouth is seen. Five times in the course of a long and disconnected monologue she says, "what?..who?..no!..she!..."[100] An authorial note characterizes this as a "vehement refusal to relinquish third person" and explains how in response an auditor ("sex undeterminable")[101] in a djellaba raises his or her hands "in a gesture of helpless compassion" which "lessens with each recurrence till scarcely perceptible at third."[102] There are four such movements so the last needs must be diminished in the extreme. The fifth refusal to relinquish the third person is even more emphatic—"What?..who?..no!..she!..SHE!.."[103]—and no gesture of compassion accompanies it. Various biographical incidents—such as a court appearance—can be gleaned from the monologue, but the key one is the battle to disidentify with her voice which "she did not recognize...at first" and "then finally had to admit...could be none other...than her own..." although "she began trying to...delude herself...it was not hers at all...not her voice at all..."[104] The struggle to escape her identity with the voice (which, in a sense, *is* her identity, her "I") is motivated by the "awful" possibility of "feeling coming back!"[105] She cannot bear to feel the lack of love in her life; she prefers to disassociate herself from her identity.

People suffering from what psychologists call Dissociative Identity Disorder can actually refuse to accept an identity with the (possibly multiple) person(s) that they sometimes are. As with Beckett's character, a defective nurturing can leave the psyche so wounded that the sufferer does not wish to inhabit it, leaving it to act out compulsively its need for love and attention. Sometimes this will show itself by the unaccepted and unacknowledged identity seeking attention by extraordinary behavior. This is an extreme version of a very common psychological type so often depicted by Dostoevsky which hates being ordinary and which acquires "a kind of

---

98 James Knowlson quotes Beckett in his biography of him, *Damned to Fame* (Bloomsbury Publishing, 1996), p. 590.
99 Samuel Beckett, *The Complete Dramatic Works* (Faber, 2006), p. 376
100 Ibid., pp. 377, 379, 381, 382   101 Ibid., p. 376
102 Ibid., p. 375   103 Ibid., p. 382
104 Ibid., p. 379   105 Ibid., pp. 379-80

Identity & Identification

typicality—as that ordinariness which refuses to remain what it is and wants at all costs to become original and independent, but has not the slightest means of achieving independence."[106] For these folk, identity with everyone else (being the same as everyone else) is unacceptable. Ironically, escape from this is sometimes sought by identifying with (being the same as) a particular social subgroup (perhaps one not generally approved of) with a passion that excludes any personal difference. The driving force is to escape from the identity that society as a whole would give them. While Hamlet does this by claiming his royal identity, they can only do it by submitting to another perhaps more exacting socially determined identity. This evasion of identity that society in general would impose is a milder form of that of Beckett's character who would evade the identity that parental absence and concomitant lack of love imposed on her: an identity which is in a sense a non-identity, characterized by an absence of speech till she was "coming up to seventy."[107] Yet, with a pathos only intensified by the diminution of the auditor's response, the very act of speech articulates the identity of not having an "I," not being loved into being. The refusal of the given (untrue because unlovingly given) identity is its acceptance. She is, her speech would indicate, *not* the "I" that the lack of nurture said she was not. Yet the true "I" is there implicitly in that against which she struggles so vehemently, as also in the beginning of speech although, implicitly comparing it to vomit ("nearest lavatory...start pouring it out...steady stream..."),[108] she uses speech against finding the voice of her "I."

DOUBLE TROUBLE

The dearth of love and truth in her begetting is an absence of the Divine. Those who should instantiate it for her—her "parents unknown"—are not there for her. Her father "vanished" into "thin air...no sooner buttoned up his breeches" and her mother "similarly...eight months later" and "so no love."[109] She can only laugh at the idea of God,[110] in whom love and truth

---

106 Fyodor Dostoevsky, *The Idiot*, translated by Richard Pevear and Larissa Volokhonsky (Everyman's Library, 2002), p. 462
107 Samuel Beckett, *The Complete Dramatic Works* (Faber, 2006), p. 376
108 Ibid., p. 382   109 Ibid., p. 376
110 Ibid., p. 377

THE MYSTERY OF IDENTITY

are one, whose love gives being and whose truth gives identity. There can be a similar absence in a society which has no love for the insulted and the injured at the bottom of its hierarchy and which maintains its structures through mendacity. In his story, *The Double*, Dostoevsky depicts a clerk, Mr. Goliadkin, responding in the same way as Beckett's woman to such a society. To try to be somebody he hires a carriage and goes out in it with a liveried servant. He is spotted by the head of his office, Andrei Filippovich, and "in indescribable anguish" wonders if he should recognize him or "pretend it's not me but someone else strikingly resembling me, and look as if nothing has happened? Precisely not me, not me, and that's that!" He nonetheless tips his hat, whispering, "I'm quite all right, it's not me at all, Andrei Filippovich, it's not me at all, not me and that's that."[111] He cannot acknowledge the identity given him by his relationship of subservience. As though to establish a different one, he gate-crashes a social event given by his office superior, saying "This has more to do with my domestic circumstances and my private life, Andrei Filippovich...this is not an official event..."[112] After various embarrassments he is removed from the party. The narrator observes, "Mr. Goliadkin was destroyed—fully destroyed, in the full sense of the word." His loss of social identity is equivalent to death. A "disinterested observer" seeing him fleeing through the streets of St. Petersburg, the narrator observes, would have said, "Mr. Goliadkin looked as if he wanted to hide somewhere from himself, as if he wanted to escape somewhere from himself!... Mr. Goliadkin now wanted not only to escape from himself, but to annihilate himself completely, to be no more, to turn to dust."[113] He is desperate to escape the identity society has given to him, even at the cost of obliteration. He is "so bewildered" that several times he stops "motionless, like a post, in the middle of the sidewalk" and at those moments he dies, vanishes.[114]

His social identity, however, does not. He sees, in a snowstorm, a passer-by: "He, too, was walking hastily, he, too, like Mr. Goliadkin, was dressed and wrapped from head to foot and, just like

---

111 Fyodor Dostoevsky, *The Double and The Gambler*, translated by Richard Pevear and Larissa Volokhonsky (Everyman's Library, 2005), p. 8
112 Ibid., p. 37   113 Ibid., p. 44
114 Ibid., p. 44

Identity & Identification

him, pattered and minced down the sidewalk of the Fontanka with scurrying little steps, trotting slightly."[115] Ten minutes later he sees him again and the distance between them is "quickly diminishing."[116] His reaction to him is ambivalent: "Mr. Goliadkin did not even nurse any hatred, or hostility, or even the slightest animosity for this man, even the contrary it would seem—yet (and the greatest force lay in this circumstance), yet he would not have wanted to meet him for all the treasures in the world and especially to meet him as he had now, for instance."[117] He refuses to identify him: "not for anything, and again not for all the treasures in the world, would he have wanted to name him, to agree to recognize, say, that he was called such-and-such, that such-and-such was his patronymic, and such-and-such his last name."[118] A "forsaken little dog, all wet and shivering" recalls to him "the remembrance of circumstances that had occurred long ago" which will not leave him alone.[119] The stranger precedes him into his flat. Finally, he faces the truth: "His night companion was none other than himself—Mr. Goliadkin himself, another Mr. Goliadkin, but perfectly the same as himself—in short, what is known as his double in all respects."[120] He has disidentified from and fled his horribly humiliating social identity so there are now two of him: his social self and the one who is looking at it. What follows is Dostoevsky's unsparing exploration of the question, "What is the identity of the person who has an identity?" and its fellow, "Can the latter be separated from the former?"

The next day Mr. Goliadkin's double turns up at the office and "no one, decidedly no one, would have undertaken to determine which was the real Goliadkin and which was the counterfeit, which was the old and which the new, which was the original and which was the copy."[121] His original self suffers from the copy, which is the identity he has in society. He is "oppressed and tormented" by anguish.[122] His double comes home with him and the next morning his servant treats *him* as the visitor. Arriving at the office, he finds his double already there, usurping his position and the respect due to him. He feels "annihilated" by being "laughed at and

---

115 Ibid., p. 47 116 Ibid.
117 Ibid., p. 48 118 Ibid.
119 Ibid., p. 49 120 Ibid., p. 50
121 Ibid., p. 55 122 Ibid., p. 56

THE MYSTERY OF IDENTITY

spat upon in the presence of strangers" by his double.[123] His social identity is destroying his true self. He wants to assert his dignity, but decides, like Beckett's character, to distance himself from his public persona: "I'll be on my own, as if it's not me... I'll let it all pass; it's not me, that's all."[124] However, he has to pay for pies his double eats and is otherwise grieved and humiliated by him. He dreams that his double "thoroughly blackened his reputation, right there, almost in front of Mr. Goliadkin's eyes, trampled his pride in the mud and then immediately took over his place at work and in society"[125] and that, by flattering people, "Goliadkin Jr. destroyed all the triumph and glory of Mr. Goliadkin Sr., eclipsed Goliadkin Sr., trampled Goliadkin Sr. in the mud, and, finally, proved clearly that Goliadkin Sr., the real one at that, was not the real one at all but a counterfeit, and he was the real one."[126] His waking relationship with his double is no less nightmarish. Neither indicating that he is ready to meet him with pistols nor being conciliatory makes it any better. When he tries to make representations to his superiors at the home of one of them, he gets thrown out, apparently at his double's prompting. At his final attempt to establish himself socially, he becomes almost "oblivious," losing "both memory and feeling."[127] Then a doctor comes and goes with him to a lunatic asylum. He has lost all identity.

The ambivalence of Hamlet's madness, the third-person life of Beckett's character and the actual madness of Mr. Goliadkin all raise the same question: if the social milieu one has to live in is inimical to love and truth, can one have a truthful identity, or does madness that way lie? In a traditional society, theocratically structured, one can say that the identity given each soul by God can be socially mediated, whatever individual failings there may be in the society. If the society as such no longer acknowledges God, what hope is there of an authentic *and* sane identity? In Hamlet's case that hope comes from what he remembers (and is enjoined to remember) of his father: a royal nobility. That enables him to give leadership. Something similar was at work in the leadership Churchill gave during World War II: although many could not see things his way, he drew strength from the values of those who went

---

[123] Ibid., p. 84
[124] Ibid., p. 88
[125] Ibid., p. 96
[126] Ibid., p. 109
[127] Ibid., p. 166

Identity & Identification

before him, especially (as he saw it) his father—though he had in fact very little contact with him. But what of those who are aware that their society lacks authentic values and seek through the stand they take themselves to find a true identity in which to live without the compromise of insincerity? The question is explored by the literary critic Lionel Trilling in his book, *Sincerity and Authenticity* (1972).

WHAT WE FEEL

He considers at length the maxim cited above (from *Hamlet*), "to thine own self be true,"[128] and focuses on the difficulty of following it, quoting Matthew Arnold's poetic expression of the depth to be plumbed in quest of one's own self:

> Below the surface-stream, shallow and light,
> Of what we *say* we feel—below the stream,
> As light, of what we *think* we feel—there flows
> With noiseless current strong, obscure and deep,
> The central stream of what we feel indeed.[129]

The implication of "central" in the last line is that there is a core of personal identity to be found in our true feelings. The difficulty with this of course is that our deepest feelings may not be true in the sense of corresponding to reality—they may just be *folie de grandeur*, for example—though they may be true in the sense that we really have them. Before they can, as it were, be educated, though, they have to be known. Trilling traces the cultural thread of the quest for that knowledge. The key difficulty is Mr. Goliadkin's: society is saying something else. This is explicit in Diderot's dialogue, *Rameau's Nephew*, in which (Trilling explains):

> The theory of society advanced by the Nephew rests on his recognition of the systematic separation of the individual from his actual self. The social being, he tells us, is a mere histrionic representation—every man takes one or another 'position' as the choreography of society directs.[130]

It follows, then, that "the dialogue passes a direct and comprehensively adverse moral judgment upon society" whose insincerity

---

128 Act 3, scene iii, l.78
129 Lionel Trilling, *Sincerity and Authenticity* (Oxford University Press, 1974), p. 5   130 Ibid., pp. 30-31

entails a "loss of personal integrity and dignity" for its members whom it gives parts to play.[131] This offers liberation from corruption and falsehood in society, but it also takes away any educative influence the latter may have for the individual who is left with the burden of a virtually solitary quest for true being.

This autonomy can have its tragic aspect. Trilling draws attention to the eponymous hero of Goethe's novel, *The Sorrows of Young Werther*, who wants to remain true to "his own passions" which "verge upon insanity."[132] He expresses his commitment to "the image of a one true self" by always wearing the same costume: "dark blue coat, yellow waistcoat, and boots."[133] He dies by his own hand wearing this, unable to reconcile his fidelity to "the simplicity of the honest soul" with the reality of "a disintegrated consciousness."[134] His sincerity is not life-giving. In his stand against "the attenuation of selfhood that results from impersonation"[135] as required by society, he has not found in the "central stream" of what he feels "indeed" a firm place to put his feet. His defeat is no less complete than Mr. Goliadkin's. Yet, the mechanisms of society are equally "inimical to the authenticity of experience and being."[136] What Blake called "dark Satanic Mills"[137] of industrialization enslave to the false god of quantity any quality that identifies the craftsman. The individual is caught between the rock of technical system and the hard place of the struggle to find the heart of his being. The futurist manifesto of 1908 which celebrated the automobile for its speed and its facility in enacting human will is adequately answered by the traffic jam.[138] Mere enactment of will as identity fails because others also enact their wills. Moving the struggle of wills from highways to cyberspace merely makes the will as identity less real because enacted only virtually. No technology as such gives identity.

Trilling's final consideration of the quest for a sincere identity in contradiction of society's demands looks at a psychologist in intellectual fashion at the time he was writing[139] who argued that schizophrenia is caused by "a pressure exerted by society through

---

131 Ibid., p. 31
132 Ibid., p. 50
133 Ibid., p. 52
134 Ibid., p. 50
135 Ibid., p. 64
136 Ibid., p. 128
137 https://www.poetryfoundation.org/poems/54684/jerusalem-and-did-those-feet-in-ancient-time
138 Ibid., pp. 128-30
139 R. D. Laing

the agency of the family." Accordingly, the difficulty of finding one's identity is caused by "the demand of parents that one have a self which is not one's true self, that one be what one is not."[140] This hypothesis "inculpates society in an ultimate degree"[141] without offering any path by which individuals may find a true identity other than the withholding from them of any "prescriptive influence" in their upbringing.[142] The consequence is "the view that insanity is a state of being in which an especially high degree of authenticity inheres."[143] Trilling's final sentence (in both senses) on this view deserves quotation in full:

> The falsities of an alienated social reality are rejected in favour of an upward psychopathic mobility to the point of divinity, each one of us a Christ—but with none of the inconveniences of undertaking to intercede, of being a sacrifice, of reasoning with rabbis, of making sermons, of having disciples, of going to weddings and to funerals, of beginning something and at a certain point remarking that it is finished.[144]

CENTER AND PERIPHERY

What this rightly excoriated view misses is that true identity for all of us is to be found in the *same* Christ: not in the insanity of thinking oneself, as opposed to others, God. In Him, "the way, and the truth, and the life,"[145] is found the real self, not in the lunatic asylums visited by Peer Gynt or inhabited by Mr. Goliadkin even before such alienation became fashionable. Each personal identity is a spoke in a bicycle wheel, fastened to the still, turning center who is God among us and stretching out to the rim whose extension is the space and time co-ordinates of individual lives. Identity in the sense of uniqueness is on the circumference where one position is not another; identity in the sense of sameness is in the center where all are one in Christ. The radiating outward is the creation; the hub, the center, is the Creator. The Creator is identified with being ("I AM WHO I AM")[146] and He shares

---

[140] Lionel Trilling, *Sincerity and Authenticity* (Oxford University Press, 1974), p. 160
[141] Ibid.
[142] Ibid., p. 161
[143] Ibid., p. 167
[144] Ibid., pp. 171-72
[145] John 14.6
[146] Exodus 3.14

THE MYSTERY OF IDENTITY

that identity with us who have being; He is unique ("the LORD our God, the LORD is one")[147] and He shares that identity with us who have our differences. Yet God's identity is not God. God is being but being is not God; God is one, but one is not God. The same is true of other scriptural identifications of God: God is light, but light is not God; God is love, but love is not God. And so on. It follows that at the heart of the turning wheel, at the point that is so central that it is beyond movement, there is an eternal stillness that transcends the being which radiates out, a beauty that transcends the play of many and one that characterizes the earthly aesthetic, a mystery that cannot be spoken. But this also is true: we are made in the image of God. Our identity is not who we are. For example, I am a writer, but the writer is not me. I am a monk, but the monk is not me. I am a brother, but the brother is not me. And so on. Each of us is touched by the eternal stillness that transcends being, the beauty that transcends what can be seen in this life, the mystery that cannot be spoken. But how do we come into the presence of this mystery, in ourselves and in others?

There are two hazards: the centrifugal and the centripetal. Spinning on this wheel we can lose our binding to the center (for which "religion" speaks etymologically) and fly off into chaos where there is no stillness, no beauty and in the place of mystery only the despairing crudeness of an epistemology that would kill enigma, reducing all quality to quantity. Or we can undertake the perilous journey within toward the center, risking the dislocation from the lateral (the social, the earthly) to which we have reached out and which we have held by the hand for the sense it gives us of who we are. The examples from literature given above make it clear that dislocation from what is around us, even if that be corrupt and mendacious, is not necessarily the same as relocation in the purity of truth. It can simply make us *loco*—mad. Is there a way to the central truth that does not deny the sanity of which adhering to what is around us gives us at least a version? Can we come near enough to the mystery within to begin to see the mystery around us? How can we respond to the Delphic injunction "know thyself" without a premature and false closure of the question? As Adam and Eve knowing their nakedness in their self-conscious separateness, do we have to clothe ourselves in an

---

147 Deuteronomy 6.4

identity that hides us? Or will God clothe us as He did them? What is our destiny? What is our identity? How do we find it? Where is it to be sought?

At the end of a chapter that began with questions, we come back to questions. This can only be a quest. If you think you have a mystery nailed down, you haven't. Yet you can journey further into a mystery. You can be unafraid of the cloud of unknowing. You can refuse to close yourself to the transcendent. That journey, that fearlessness, that openness requires that we eschew false resolutions. The quest for identity is so primal, so strong an urge that we can be tempted to think it settled by things that are partial—even by partiality itself—before it truly is. These divagations from the narrow way which leads to absolute plenitude, from the refusal of false comfort which leads to bliss, from the claiming of nothing which is the true self, are so prevalent and so seductive that we need to see them for what they are to map our journey. We need to touch the yearning for the divine that sources their compulsion and channel it to where alone it will not destroy our peace. We need to know who we truly are.

2
Money & Meaning

BUYING IDENTITY

Mr. Goliadkin, before he begins to be troubled by his double, goes on a shopping trip. Accompanied by a liveried servant, he visits "a silver- and goldsmith's shop."[1] He arranges a purchase that includes a complete dinner and tea-service for fifteen hundred roubles, but resists the pressure of the shopkeeper on him to give a small deposit. Multiple other shops are visited where similar arrangements are made, with no more than a promise of a deposit. In reality, he only purchases "one pair of gloves and a flask of scent for a rouble and a half."[2] He has, however, gone "into a money-changer's shop" and broken "all his big notes into smaller ones," albeit at a cost.[3] Both the fantasy shopping and the fattening of his wallet have a single purpose: to bolster his sense of who he is. Dostoevsky (in his notebook of 1880) described money as "an intensification of personality, a mechanical and spiritual embodiment."[4] Marx made a similar point about the purchasing power of money giving its possessor a sense of having "its properties and essential powers" and a recent study links the growth since the mid-eighteenth century of the idea of the independent self with the rise of the concept of money.[5] It is a theme widely explored in Dostoevsky's works. For example, his penultimate novel, *The Adolescent* (also called *The Raw Youth*), develops the idea of a person looking to money for a sense of identity. The titular character, Arkady, cherishes an "idea"—"to become Rothschild," that is, "as rich as Rothschild."[6] It is not for the trappings of wealth that he wants this. On the contrary, he explains:

---

1 Fyodor Dostoevsky, *The Double and The Gambler*, translated by Richard Pevear and Larissa Volokhonsky (Everyman's Library, 2005), p. 21
2 Ibid., p. 22 3 Ibid., p. 21
4 Yuri Corrigan, *Dostoevsky and the Riddle of the Self* (Northwestern University Press, 2017), p. 108
5 Ibid., p. 108 and note 12, p. 202
6 Fyodor Dostoevsky, *The Adolescent*, translated by Richard Pevear and Larissa Volokhonsky (Everyman's Library, 2003), p. 78

> If I were Rothschild, I'd go about in an old coat and carry an umbrella. What do I care if I am jostled in the street, if I'm forced to go skipping through the mud so as not to be run over by cabs? The awareness that it was I, Rothschild himself, would even amuse me at that moment. I know that I can have a dinner like nobody else, and from the world's foremost chef, and it's enough for me that I know it. I'll eat a piece of bread and ham and be satisfied with my awareness.[7]

Dostoevsky had read confirmation of this as a possibility in a newspaper article about a clerk "retired and living in the direst poverty, who was found at his death to be worth a half-million roubles."[8] Arkady's reflections about being a Rothschild offer an explanation of this strangeness. His "awareness" of being such is the sense of who he is: he looks to money to give him "solitude" and "power"—that is to say an autonomous identity, independent of others so as not to be vulnerable to self-blaming in his relation to others and suffer from a lack of reciprocity.[9] Money, he fancies, would give him an identity that can't be stared out of countenance by the prying eyes of others. He is an illegitimate child, still in quest of a father figure; and his sense of self is fragile.

These fantasies chronicled by the novelist are unrealistic in more than one sense: not only can Mr. Goliadkin not afford what he asks shopkeepers to put to one side for him and Arkady not really be able to save up the sort of money he is dreaming of—they wouldn't in truth gain substantial selves through the acquisition of genuine purchasing power. This is obvious if we think of the opposite transaction: exchanging who one is for money. This is what is commonly called prostitution, or selling one's honor. If money is identity, identity is only money if it is in some way a questionable identity. It is not identity in the sense of being true, of reflecting the highest values. The antithesis between identity as money and identity as reflecting truth is the antithesis between serving mammon and God: you cannot serve both. The money

---

7   Ibid., p. 88
8   Joseph Frank, *Dostoevsky, A Writer in His Time* (Princeton University Press, 2010), p. 300
9   Fyodor Dostoevsky, *The Adolescent*, translated by Richard Pevear and Larissa Volokhonsky (Everyman's Library, 2003), p. 85

Money & Meaning

and identity nexus cannot be a closed system. It necessarily is open to honor, to glory, to the transcendent.

Dostoevsky is also a chronicler of people's instinctive sense that something more valuable than money is being lost if they allow themselves to be bought. For example, Captain Snegiryov in *The Brothers Karamazov* is in desperate need of money, not least for medical care for his sick little son Ilyusha—who has minutes before asked him the rhetorical question, "Is it true that the rich are stronger than anybody in the world?"[10]—but when given it by Alyosha, the brother of a man who has insulted him, he seizes the banknotes "in some kind of rage" crumples them and throws them "with all his might on the sand." His negative reaction is as great as his need:

> And suddenly raising his right foot, he fell to trampling them with his heel, in wild anger, gasping and exclaiming each time his foot struck:
> "There's your money, sir! There's your money, sir! There's your money, sir! There's your money, sir!" Suddenly he leaped back and straightened up before Alyosha. His whole figure presented a picture of inexplicable pride.[11]

His pride—his need to be someone—is greater than the desperate need of the family he dearly loves. The sense of self having precedence over monetary gain has an even more dramatic illustration in the famous scene in Dostoevsky's novel *The Idiot* in which Nastasya Filippovna wants it to be seen what is in the heart of Ganya, who has been offered seventy-five thousand roubles to marry her by a man who took advantage of her youth. She throws a hundred thousand roubles on the fire, telling him that if he plucks it out it is his to keep. The novelist tells us:

> He could not take his eyes off the fire, off the smoldering packet; but it seemed something new had arisen in his soul; it was as if he had sworn to endure the torture; he did not budge from the spot; in a few moments it

---

10 Fyodor Dostoevsky, *The Brothers Karamazov*, translated by Richard Pevear and Larissa Volokhonsky (Everyman's Library, 1997), p. 207
11 Ibid., p. 211

THE MYSTERY OF IDENTITY

became clear to everyone that he would not go after the packet, that he did not want to.[12]

Nastasya comments, "He didn't go in after it, he held out! So his vanity is still greater than his lust for money."[13] As with Captain Snegiryov, this response is the opposite of the expected one: in both cases Dostoevsky is dramatizing the power of the urge to an honorable identity. When he has Arkady (in *The Adolescent*) continually staking his money in roulette on zero (like "Grandmother" in *The Gambler*), it is as if he is saying that money cannot give any real identity. Looking to money for identity is, like gambling, an addiction since addiction is the craving for something that does not deliver true satisfaction. It is the yearning of the unsatisfied heart for God, trying to find the infinite in the finite. Our only true identity is in God, seek it as we will in the merely terrestrial or monetary, in the tawdry glory that is all that man without God can offer.

That of course does not stop it being sought there. In fact, it is sought so frenetically that there is little pause for the silence in which the truth of God's blessing—love—can be received, making redundant any other putative source of ontological security. The quest is pervasive, the invitation to join in seductive, the noise of barking up the wrong tree deafening. Remaining in Russia, but in this rather than the nineteenth century, we can find it exemplified in a literally spectacular way. Peter Pomerantsev chronicles it in an event in honor of the wedding of a plutocrat called Grigory:

> He has taken over a mini-Versailles-like palace for the occasion. Near the entrance to the park teams of make-up artists from Moscow's film studios dress up the guests in motion-picture costumes: tonight's theme is 'A Midsummer Night's Dream'. The same crowd follows Grigory around from week to week, recreating itself for his latest whim. Inside the park trapeze artists on invisible ropes swoop down and through the trees; synchronized swimmers dressed as mermaids with shining silver tails flip and dive in the dark lake. Geysers shoot up from the water: as the droplets fall they're lit up to create a rainbow in

---

12   Fyodor Dostoevsky, *The Idiot*, translated by Richard Pevear and Larissa Volokhonsky (Everyman's Library, 2002), p. 172
13   Ibid., p. 174

38

> the night. Everyone wonders: where are the bride and groom? A spotlight illuminates the lake. Grigory and his bride appear on opposite sides, on separate little boats made up like tortoiseshells, both dressed in white. The tortoiseshells move magically towards each other (pushed, I later learn, by frogmen). The boats meet in the middle; the lovers join hands and step barefoot on the water. They do not sink. Suspended on the lake, they turn and walk across the water towards us, their path illuminated by lasers. We gasp at the miracle and all applaud. The effect is achieved with a secret walkway installed specially under the lake, but is still divine.[14]

It is rather a simulacrum of the divine: an effort to make for oneself what only God can truly give—an identity. Different effects are achieved by Grigory on different occasions and they are photographed—"all the rich have their own photographers. They take them on holidays, to parties, to family gatherings; you've made it only when your life becomes a magazine."[15] A magazine offers only glory from people, not glory from God; and so, although practically limitless amounts of money are available, the spectacular self-presentations do not satisfy. Pomerantsev tells us:

> Grigory seems to need rebirths ever more intensely. Every time I see him he is wearing a new costume, transforming himself for another of his fancy-dress evenings—one night an elf, then Hitler, Rasputin—escaping, changing and mutating, clipping his hair short, growing it longer, brushing it to the side, then forwards.... When the moon is new the theme of the party is 'White'. Grigory, carrying a white rabbit in a cage, announces, 'Tonight is all about my rebirth, a new me.'[16]

Finally, after many more Muscovite transformations, he begins to settle for the more ordinary life of England, where "though he has all the money in the world he likes to travel across west London in big red public-transport buses."[17] The identities that

---

[14] Peter Pomerantsev, *Nothing is True and Everything is Possible: Adventures in Modern Russia* (Faber, London, 2017), p. 152
[15] Ibid., p. 156   [16] Ibid., p. 158
[17] Ibid., p. 159

money could buy were not really him. Like Peer Gynt, he leaves behind the self that money makes. And indeed, money cannot really buy identity because it is only quantity, not quality. It does not signify because it does not discriminate: it can purchase anything indiscriminately. Identity is not simply size: laying up funds is a wrong turning in the quest to find who we are, although one our society has mostly gone down. "Getting and spending" do not make us who we are: rather they "lay waste our powers."[18] Our true life, our true self, is always a gift, never an accomplishment.

Yet anxious hands close themselves on what is at hand rather than open themselves to beg, to pray, to respond to the invitation, "he who has no money, come, buy and eat! Come, buy wine and milk without money and without price."[19] Milk and wine are life and joy, feeling oneself (as William James, cited in Chapter One, put it) "most deeply and intensively active and alive," hearing "the voice inside which speaks and says: 'This is the real me!'" Buying who one is (just to phrase it like that indicates the inescapable frustration of the project) is an attempt to realize this liveliness, to hear the real self speaking. It is the quest for glory—that is to say affirmation. As in Arkady's aspiration, there can be a sense of being owed something by virtue of being a fund holder. One can, albeit briefly, command a kind of respect. One can have a sense of autonomy from society. There is the difficulty however that there is a limit to how much in the way of goods and services is really of use. If one has half a grapefruit and a boiled egg for breakfast, one is not going to be happier or even feel more important by having a whole grapefruit and two boiled eggs. And so, money is spent for the sake of status. In restaurants this may take the form of food that is designed to have a certain appearance. There will not be vegetables recognizable as such, or chunks of meat but instead artistic shapes decorated with little trails of sauce running across largely empty, and perhaps strangely shaped, plates. What is written on the menu about the food may not give a clear indication of what to expect, substituting perhaps more general statements, such as, "we offer an experience that goes beyond food and drink. Just being here is a statement about who you are...." But one thing will be clear: the food will cost more than one needs to pay

---

18   William Wordsworth, https://www.poetryfoundation.org/poems/45564/the-world-is-too-much-with-us   19   Isaiah 55.1

to get a properly nourishing meal. Glory, in the attenuated sense of being not as other men are, is for sale.

Cars are another form in which people buy status. They have acknowledged currency as bearers of human glory. A model in one manufacturer's range will have a recognized equivalent in another manufacturer's range. A certain level of seniority in management corresponds to a particular level in the range of car models. Cars are sold and bought not just for transport but also for human glory, so that people can use them to say who they are. It is even clearer that money is spent for the sake of status when it comes to clothes. A pair of trainers, for example, made to a high quality may even be cheaper than trainers that are of a poorer quality but which carry a brand name. And people wear clothes that advertise the marketers of those clothes. Instead of being paid for providing this advertising, they pay more in order to do the advertising. It is done for the sake of the name. Just to phrase it this way points to what is going on. Christians through the ages have suffered "for the sake of the name"—the holy, sacred name of God made Man who won the victory over death.[20] They suffer and are willing to die for the glory of God. Unnecessarily large amounts of money are paid for clothes "for the sake of the name." This expense is undergone for the sake of being associated with the human glory of "the name" of a particular brand: an identity—of sorts. Yet let the buyer beware: whatever the advertisements say, there will lurk the intuition that this glory is not the real thing. Fashion is seasonal identity and the glory of a brand tawdry.

THE BIBLE'S ACCOUNT OF TRUE GLORY

The Bible compares this kind of glory to the true glory of God. The psalmist sets the omnipotence of God alongside the powerlessness of idols:

> Our God is in the heavens;
> he does all that he pleases.
>
> Their idols are silver and gold,
> the work of human hands.
> They have mouths, but do not speak;
> eyes, but do not see.

---

20 Cf. Acts 5.41

THE MYSTERY OF IDENTITY

> They have ears, but do not hear;
> noses, but do not smell.
> They have hands, but do not feel;
> feet, but do not walk;
> and they do not make a sound in their throat.[21]

These idols—and their modern equivalent—belong only to time and so death will take away even the shadow and pretense of glory that people seek by association with them:

> Those who make them become like them;
> so do all who trust in them.[22]

The spiritually healthy attitude, that associates itself with true glory, is that proclaimed at the beginning of the psalm quoted:

> Not to us, O LORD, not to us, but to your name give glory,
> for the sake of your steadfast love and your faithfulness![23]

To be associated with true glory like this is to participate in it. Giving glory is receiving it: the dynamic is the opposite of zero-sum. That is because it is infinite. In acknowledging an infinite glory, an undying life, an unbounded identity, we find who we truly are: people whose glory is worship, whose being is a participation in the One who says I AM THAT I AM, whose identity is mystery beyond telling, beyond ken, transcending this earth.

The Lord gives the prophet Jeremiah a word that similarly compares the true Creator with idols:

> Thus shall you say to them: "The gods who did not make
> the heavens and the earth shall perish from the earth and
> from under the heavens."
>
> It is he who made the earth by his power,
> who established the world by his wisdom,
> and by his understanding stretched out the heavens.
> When he utters his voice, there is a tumult of waters
>   in the heavens,
> and he makes the mist rise from the ends of the earth.
> He makes lightning for the rain,
> and he brings forth the wind from his storehouses.

---

21 Psalm 115.3-7   22 Psalm 115.8
23 Psalm 155.1

> Every man is stupid and without knowledge;
> every goldsmith is put to shame by his idols,
> for his images are false,
> and there is no breath in them.
> They are worthless, a work of delusion;
> at the time of their punishment they shall perish.
> Not like these is he who is the portion of Jacob,
> for he is the one who formed all things,
> and Israel is the tribe of his inheritance;
> the LORD of hosts is his name.[24]

The idols referred to here have more qualitative substance than the idols of our time: they are made of gold. Today's idols share this with them, however: "they are worthless, a work of delusion." The delusion is that any real life, any real sense of being "deeply and intensively active and alive," of being who one is, can come from the idols given honor, that is to say, worshipped. The delusion is kept going sometimes by the use of drugs, which may be associated with a life that depends on the idea that there is some glory to be had from mere fashion. The "images" of the brand names "are false," that is they have no real life. The status attributed to them is a merely human construct that will pass away. They do not make anything, as the Creator does. This disjunction between creativity and branding is particularly clear where companies, who own a brand name for which people will pay high prices, outsource the actual manufacturing of their product to a poor country and concentrate their own efforts on the promotion of the image. To actually buy a product that can be purchased more cheaply without loss of quality, albeit with the loss of a name, is to be, as the prophet says, "stupid and without knowledge," even in terms of worldly prudence. It is to try to find oneself in the wrong place, an error that is corrected by the understanding that "Not like these is he who is the portion of Jacob, for he is the one who formed all things." The eternal, the creative, is not profitably substituted by that which only passes for it, the unbounded by the branded, a divine identity by a factitious one. Indeed, the very idea of branding suggests the painful burning in of ownership by another that animals undergo. To allow ourselves to be identified by brands is beneath human dignity.

---

[24] Jeremiah 10.11-16

THE MYSTERY OF IDENTITY

In order to persuade people to make this substitution (so as to make money to buy human glory) it is necessary to promote an image belonging to one's particular brand. To promote the image, it is necessary to advertise. This advertising takes the place of what in an earlier age would have been an important means of turning the attention to the source of glory: preaching. The difference is that the preaching would have aimed to turn attention to the real source of glory, the eternal God. This advertising aims to turn attention to "a work of delusion," the human glory coming from the respect given by people to a name, a respect belonging to time, that, unlike God's glory, passes away. Such advertising is lying about death. It is saying that what fades away can be a substitute for the eternal. It invites us to ignore that, in the light of eternity (the only enduring reality), what it offers us is worthless. The whole chain of promoting an image to others so as to make money to be able to buy an image for oneself depends on haste. If time is taken out to reflect on what all this ultimately adds up to, a sense of real values—values that have eternal validity—can emerge. So the devil has an interest in keeping things moving swiftly. Haste forgets eternity, forgets where we belong, forgets who we truly are. It mangles time, stopping it from opening to eternity.

Time will never be eternity; quantity will never be quality; money will never be identity. There is a sense, though, in which these—that belong to what is below—can take us to what is above: a sense in which our time on earth wins transcendence; in which what we have is enough; in which we can buy what is beyond price. It is told in this parable:

> The kingdom of heaven is like a merchant in search of fine pearls, who, on finding one pearl of great value, went and sold all that he had and bought it.[25]

"All that he had" is the same as the widow's mite: it is all, everything, the whole. In giving that—whatever time we have, whatever amount we have, whatever money we have—we buy the "pearl of great value," the citizenship of the kingdom beyond limit, the identity that has everything. We receive not because of a certain amount, but because of a certain love—certain because it will not hold anything back for itself by way of precaution or insurance.

---

25 Matthew 13.45-46

Money & Meaning

By keeping nothing back we do not keep control, by handing over control we accept what is beyond our control, our ken, our imagining—what eye has not seen, nor ear heard, nor the tongue of man spoken: a self that is radiant with all the luster of the divine light. The parable of the manager of the rich man's goods gives the same teaching about love of others as the parable of the pearl of great value gives about love of God. It urges, "Make friends for yourselves by means of unrighteous wealth."[26] The teachings of the two parables converge, since "God is love" and so subordinating wealth to friendship amounts to subordinating it to God. In loving God and neighbor we find who we truly are; only a false simulacrum of this can be actually bought. It is no accident that those giving their lives to God take vows of poverty.

Ersatz personal identity is sold as well as bought. This happens when famous people endorse products, rewarded either by the products themselves or by money (or "sponsorship" as it is more delicately put). They can do this because they are famous and fame *appears* to be a sort of identity. It is the sort of identity that the attention of other people gives, the opposite of the divine identity personified in the one who said, "I do not receive glory from people."[27] Those who buy the products are invited to identify with these famous people and consider themselves as having this "glory from people." The names of these people are as it were sold to the purchasers of the products who are invited to feel they are very "so-and-so"—whatever the name of the famous person is. A more hidden (though not unperceived) trade in apparently positive identity is through "charitable" donations. A company whose managers would like to be liked will give money to a charity whose declared aim corresponds to what the company would like to be liked for. Of course, this can be a straightforward benefit for the charity's official cause, but it can also serve simply to conceal what the company is doing (for example, ecological damage) by buying a reputation (for example, for caring for the planet) from a charity that is officially involved in work that would give it. This can be corrupting for the "charitable" organizations themselves if their policy becomes perverted by the realization that the big money is to be had for laundering reputations. A true identity is found

---

26 Luke 16.9   27 John 5.41

in openness to the all-loving presence of God, but some of the people can be fooled some of the time into thinking that a group of folk have such an identity if another group of folk say that they are being supported in their loving work by the former group.

All of this is trading, of course. It is not God, but mammon that is speaking who people are and therefore speaking untruthfully and—ultimately—unconvincingly. Money is the agreement of others to give stuff, as in the traditional British banknotes on which could be read, "I promise to pay the bearer..." and in the cases considered here what is given is attention and respect. That can be untruthful respect, as in Shakespeare's observation: "Plate sin with gold,/ And the strong lance of justice hurtless breaks."[28] If this comes to light, yet more money can be brought to bear on burnishing reputation, but it can never fool the infinite knowing of God or buy an eternal identity, a place in the heavens. At best it buys the turning of some heads with deludedly glad eyes towards an individual for a time. The merely human does not replace the divine. Nonetheless, these are real eyes and if they do not meet others in which they can see the depths of a truthful soul at least there is a human presence. The trading in reputation as a substitute for true identity can go much lower than that. In our day much is supplied algorithmically. At the opposite end of the spectrum from that of the monarch awarding medals, machines can give online badges of merit. And much nearer the latter than the former end of the spectrum, folk can offer their approval online through the click of a mouse rather than a pat on the back. Even if genuine approbation is here being truly given to a truly loved friend for a true deed, the nexus is trading: trading in attention. Saint John of the Cross says that God alone is worthy of a thought of man[29] —such is its true value—but here the price of sending even such a true message is the exposing of the attention to clickbait. One can resist it (and any concomitant purchase), but the forum of exchange would close down unless many didn't. And one undergoes the hazard of diversion from one's eternal purpose (that is, squandering attention) not simply in the cause

---

28 *King Lear*, Act 4, scene vi, ll.165-66
29 *The Collected Works of St. John of the Cross*, translated by Kieran Kavanaugh, O. C. D. and Otilo Rodriguez, O. C. D. (Institute of Carmelite Studies, 1979), p. 676

of acknowledging truth but all too often in the giving of meaning to what has no meaning but is simply a construct, divorced from what is healthy and human, of a mendacity craving an identity. All of this would be laughable were it not that it can lead to suicidal desperation as the brittle shell of highly attenuated reality cracks (in the case of positive feedback) or as the nugatory, even if highly quantified and viciously expressed, presence of disapprobation is mistaken for a substantial reality. The sadness of it is that the craving for the attention that is traded on the internet (as well as through old-fashioned cash) can be satisfied to overflowing by that infinitely available from the gaze of the all-loving God if only that were animadverted to for some minutes of quiet each day. Yes, it is a terrible thing to fall into the hands of the living God, but it is worth it. It is indeed the only way to be straightened out so as to be worthy, so as to have a true identity.

SOCIALLY DISTRIBUTED IDENTITY

The pernicious effects of the market in attention may suggest that a more Marxist, or at least socialist, model of exchange would attenuate the diversion from love and truth, from the divine. Yet this too is a field of hazard. Here "social capital" is what is sought. People want meaningful recognition and look to the state, or at least society as a whole, to provide it. Acknowledgment, affirmation of identity, becomes a collective or political matter. That it should become part of the common agenda is an indication of how critical the issue is in our time. The phrase "identity politics" was not recorded in the *Oxford English Dictionary* until 1987. It is as though at around that time the sense of rootlessness and concomitant identity crisis of many an individual following the upheavals of the Second World War reached a critical mass that made it everyone's problem, with the earlier shared firmness of belief and value fading from view. It is critical and problematic because there is vulnerability around identity, a fundamental fragility. You cannot, it seems, source your own identity, since you have to be identical *to* something, but if you identify with something (or someone) that amounts to admitting that, in yourself, you have no identity. You are a beggar of identity. Even the words you have to say who you are have been received as alms. To be different, you have to speak the same language as others, you have to be the same as another: that is, to have an identity you need a model, even if it is one chosen by yourself. The pathos of the unfathered and unmothered cries out that this is so.

Ultimately, in the theological perspective that I have been arguing for, we can only receive our identity from God, Our Father. So, before we consider the various ways in which we people seek identity in a politically or socially validated way, we would do well to acknowledge that we are treading on sacred ground. The longing for identity is in its root a longing for God. It follows that what gives identity is identified with God. This explains why identity can be so non-negotiable. It also explains why it can subsume the mutually contradictory, as in Peter Pomerantsev's witness to the Russian biker whose love for his motherland expressed itself in devotion to God and Stalin and who, when it was pointed out to him that Stalin murdered thousands of priests, said, "When you cut out a disease you have to cut out healthy flesh too."[30] Where people seek identity in this sort of national or social context, God really does take priority over mammon or (at least) precedence over economic considerations is awarded to the national or social identity, which is the object towards which people direct the longing for the divine and the affirmation which the divine alone can give. A sociological model that sees all voter behavior as determined by economic interest cannot explain the longing for identity. If people oft times seek money for the sake of buying an identity, they forswear it too for the sake of identity. Identity, with its kernel of longing for God, is the driver in both free market and statist organization of society. If identity is a live-wire, hot-button, incendiary issue, it is because God is involved; if the commitment to it takes forms that might be considered heretical that is because it is the revenge of a neglected truth: money cannot replace God.

BLOOD AND SOIL

The aura of the divine attaches itself in a particular way to identity when people seek it in nationhood. So there is, for example, the notion that "God is an Englishman," although the loss of empire has made this somewhat outdated, and the concept

---

[30] Peter Pomerantsev, *Nothing is True and Everything is Possible: Adventures in Modern Russia* (Faber, 2017), pp. 216–17

of "Holy Russia," although not everything in that country is true to its sacred tradition. The inhabitants of many countries have this sense of their homeland and tradition expressing the divine purpose in a special way, the Jewish people being a sort of archetype in this respect. Yet a nation cannot in itself have the stability of the eternal and divine. Israel is a case in point, having in its present form only comparatively recently been constituted. Then there is Hong Kong, which is being forcibly integrated into China in contradiction of its own political traditions. And there is Canada, which self-consciously avoids being exclusive in its identity. When Justin Trudeau became Prime Minister in 2015, he declared Canada a "post-national state," saying, "There is no core identity, no mainstream in Canada."[31] This is a country which contends with Denmark over ownership of an island rock (Hans Island) by leaving a bottle of Canadian whisky there for the other side.[32] This is very different from the "little patch of ground/ That hath in it no profit but the name" in *Hamlet* for which the nation hazards "Two thousand souls and twenty thousand ducats."[33] It relativizes the idea that the identity which a country has and gives is so essential to life that it is worth sacrificing life for it. The Vatican is another state that challenges this, for it stands for the Catholic—that is to say, that which includes all.

Professor Kwame Anthony Appiah deftly deconstructs the idea that there is any sort of fixed identity in nationality in his book *The Lies That Bind: Rethinking Identity*. He starts with the example of a person who "lived in an era when nation-states were only gradually becoming the dominant form of political organization around the world"[34] who clearly can't be identified with one particular state. In the nineteenth and twentieth centuries, he explains, the idea that peoples should have nations came to the fore. Yet this has manifold difficulties. How do you decide where, between the whole human family and your nuclear family, to draw the line? How do you "pick

---

31   Florian Coulmas, *Identity, A Very Short Introduction* (Oxford University Press, 2019), p. 60
32   https://www.nytimes.com/2016/11/08/world/what-in-the-world/canada-denmark-hans-island-whisky-schnapps.html
33   Act 4, scene iv, l.25
34   Kwame Anthony Appiah, *The Lies That Bind: Rethinking Identity* (Profile Books, 2019), p. 72

among the many groups of shared ancestry to which you belong?"[35] How do you cope "when political boundaries keep shifting,"[36] as happened last century, for example, in the Indian subcontinent and in Eastern Europe? How do you negotiate differences between how you think of yourself and how others think of you? How do you make your nation homogeneous, so that its people truly share an identity? Do you annihilate, expel, or assimilate those who do not fit? Is a nation constituted simply by what the people who live in it feel about it? Does this depend on songs and poems? Appiah concludes, "As a rule, people do not live in monocultural, monoreligious, monolingual nation-states, and they never have."[37] The self-determination of peoples, albeit "a sacrosanct ideal," can only be dealt with cautiously and inconsistently. "We" can only have a right to self-determination "once we've decided who 'we' are"[38] and that question can have many possible answers.

And of course the answers are contested. There are those for whom a nation is what it has become by people sharing the same government over decades and those who want to limit it to people meeting certain criteria, "dismissing their opponents as inauthentic betrayers of the people, or else foreigners, not part of the people at all."[39] The idea that "the only important thing is the unification of the people" even led one American politician to say, "The other people don't mean anything."[40] Julia Ebner, who undertook an undercover investigation of the more extreme warriors in the battle to impose a homogeneous identity on people, met a leader of "Generation Identity" (GI), a grouping committed to this cause. "To us," he said, "identity is about both culture and ethnicity. The only way to prevent the European civilization from being replaced—ethnically and culturally—is to keep immigrants out." The GI goal is "to create homogeneous societies—societies where different races and cultures do not mix," even if that involves repatriating migrants who have already arrived, including second and third generation migrants.[41] It is an international

---

35 Ibid., p. 76
36 Ibid., p. 77
37 Ibid., p. 88
38 Ibid., p. 90
39 Ibid., p. 99
40 Francis Fukuyama, *Identity: Contemporary Identity Politics and the Struggle for Recognition* (Profile Books, 2018), p. 159
41 Julia Ebner, *Going Dark: The Secret Social Lives of Extremists* (Bloomsbury, 2020), p. 28

organization.[42] It recruits through people's vulnerability around identity. Ebner observes: "A recurring theme among recruits ... is identity—a troubled self-image, a broken self-esteem."[43] It offers to repair this. Properly, this sort of healing is a divine prerogative since only the absolute and divine love can realistically heal our sense of who we are, assure us that we are no less than "children of God."[44] The laying claim to that prerogative goes some way to explaining the fanatical devotion which the organization's cause evokes. However distorted the theology is, for them it is in practice (even if not acknowledged as such) a divinely ordained mission.

The repair work (it would be an exaggeration to call it "healing") on the "broken self-esteem" is wrought by extremist groups (which can have aims far beyond those of GI) through resocialization: people are manipulated to think of themselves as having the identity given to them by belonging to the (often online) group to which they are being recruited. Ebner reports, "Platforms that offer advice on how to deal with hyper-personal questions around identity and anxiety provide common gateways into toxic ideologies." Online forums "not only facilitate recruitment, they also create powerful lock-in effects by establishing close in-group bonds and tying their ideology to the members' identities."[45] Technology is used to give individuals "belonging, self-confidence and identity. Or illusions of that."[46] Such an illusion, a seemingly positive identity established by means of the internet, prompted the massacre of persons at prayer in mosques in Christchurch, New Zealand in 2019. While to people at large gunning down the defenseless is an atrocity, to those with an identity formed by a particular online closed group, it is a matter for applause. Ebner comments on the perpetrator: "His livestreamed shooting was an attempt to draw on the camaraderie within the far-right trolling community in the hope of receiving their applause, praise and respect" and notes "a sense of brotherhood and friendship in the attacker's last message" which tells those following, "You are all top blokes."[47] If one sees the attack as concerned to safeguard an identity that

---

42   Ibid., p. 46   43   Ibid., p. 49
44   1 John 3.1
45   Julia Ebner, *Going Dark: The Secret Social Lives of Extremists* (Bloomsbury, 2020), p. 88
46   Ibid., p. 263   47   Ibid., p. 237

is rooted in a particular religious tradition, one might almost say it was motivated by (a perversion of) the great commandment to love God and neighbor. If that is so, it would explain why life and liberty would be hazarded for it. It also shows how radical is the need for an identity rooted and founded on the divine and nourished in human fellowship.

OTHERING

This need is vulnerable to exploitation in many ways. As Professor Appiah observes, "The assertion of an identity always proceeds through contrast or opposition."[48] That means that politicians or those who are recruiting for an extremist organization who can point to others who are not the people they are speaking to can by this means give their audience a sort of identity and thereby win their support. Peter Pomerantsev reports on the Institute for Strategic Dialogue (ISD) which works to counter extremism:

> The ISD defines extremism as "a system of belief that posits the superiority and dominance of one 'in-group' over all 'out-groups,' propagating a dehumanizing 'othering' mind-set that is antithetical to the universal application of Human Rights." Sometimes they simply refer to it as "othering."[49]

This "othering" is a sort of zero-sum game to win identity: if others do not count, the in-group does and thereby has an identity. I say "game" because the struggle to do down others by influencing opinion is fought on the internet in a mode similar to online gaming: "recruits move from computer games to digital political campaigns that feel like another sort of game."[50] Pomerantsev observes that this "othering" is becoming "ever more pervasive."[51] He is even told by one political operator that "All politics is now about creating identity"[52] and draws the conclusion "to seal this improvised identity one needs an enemy: 'the non-people'"—who are most effectively considered in the abstract so as to gather

---

48 Kwame Anthony Appiah, *The Lies That Bind: Rethinking Identity* (Profile Books, 2019), p. 202

49 Peter Pomeranstev, *This is <u>Not</u> Propaganda: Adventures in the War Against Reality* (Faber, 2019), p. 202

50 Ibid., p. 203   51 Ibid., p. 207

52 Ibid., p. 208

those with multifarious hatreds into one fold of voters. He cites one campaigner as saying, "I believe that a well-identified enemy is probably a 20 per cent kicker to your vote."[53]

If identity is felt to be a vital need and it is created through "othering," can conflict be avoided? Can people so happily own their identity that they can gladly allow others their own identity? Can such disparate identity ownership be united in a higher identity? All of these questions can be answered positively if we think more deeply about the meaning of "other." Traditionally, God is *totaliter aliter*: totally other. The otherness of God is infinitely beyond any otherness in creation which, after all, shares the quality of being in time and space and therefore is open to rivalry for the occupation of these. The otherness of God defines identity, but through friendship, not enmity. Believing that I am not God means that I have a sense of being separate from the Creator, an awareness of being someone by reference to the One, an understanding that I am an image of the unimaginable. Because this other is infinite love nurturing me with joyful delight, I know who I am by yearning and reaching out towards the arms that, like those of the father of the prodigal son, would enfold me in an embrace. I find myself in worship. The beauty of this dynamic is that it includes. The absolute otherness of God is the source of the relative otherness of other people. So it follows that when in loving worship I gratefully acknowledge this otherness as sustaining my identity I am also acknowledging it as sustaining the identity of other people. Receiving affirmation of my identity is receiving affirmation of the identity of others. To put it in terms of traditional piety, knowing God as Father I know others as brothers and sisters.

The atheist model of relationship is non-fraternal. If there is no subsuming reality then there is rivalry and envy because we are all the same. This is more marked in non-hierarchical societies. Apparently identical identity leads to competitive identity or lack of identity: if all are the same only one can truly realize it, the others struggling to be as fashionable, wealthy and famous. Older feudal identities were given, not bought or made, so folk didn't normally even worry whether they had one, any more than they would stop to think if there were air to breathe. Homogenized status creates insecurity hence the political adage

---

53 Ibid., p. 213

THE MYSTERY OF IDENTITY

that your opponents are in the other party, your enemies in your own. In a horizontal, this-worldly, perspective, "Human happiness is oftentimes more strongly connected to our relative than to our absolute status."[54] Only in relation to what is above space and time can we really be free of the struggle to lay hold of something marked out within their limitations: something that has to be at the expense of some other questor for the finite, something that is not from the One who can, and wants to, give infinitely. In relating only to what is here below, we are left to cling desperately to what floats on the tide, the flux that sweeps away what used to be at least points of reference for an identity—such as an employment for life, a partner for life, a hometown for life. The gig economy, replaceable relationships, and global transferability may work for economic growth, but they only weakly anchor our sense of who we are.

It is little wonder, then, that this ontological insecurity is exploited by politicians. The process is documented by Francis Fukuyama in his book, *Identity: Contemporary Identity Politics and the Struggle for Recognition*. The Canadian philosopher Charles Taylor coined the phrase "politics of recognition"[55] to designate the process of deciding which identities should receive public acknowledgment from the state. Professor Fukuyama sees the kernel of this as being "recognition of dignity."[56] Individuals who themselves want to be recognized as exceptional, he argues, exploit in the furtherance of that purpose "the resentments of ordinary people" about the disrespect shown to "their nation or religion or way of life."[57] He summarizes, "Demand for recognition of one's identity is a master concept that unifies much of what is going on in world politics today."[58] He sees this as true for both international and national politics:

> In all cases a group, whether a great power such as Russia or China or voters in the United States or Britain, believes that it has an identity that is not being given

---

54 Francis Fukuyama, *Identity: Contemporary Identity Politics and the Struggle for Recognition* (Profile Books, 2018), p. 84
55 Charles Taylor, *Multiculturalism: Examining the Politics of Recognition* (Princeton University Press, 1994)
56 Fukuyama, *Identity*, preface
57 Ibid.   58 Ibid.

adequate recognition—either by the outside world, in the case of a nation, or by other members of the same society. Those identities can be and are incredibly varied, based on nation, religion, ethnicity, sexual orientation, or gender. They are all manifestations of a common phenomenon, that of identity politics.[59]

He interprets much of what is understood as being "economic motivation" as reflecting "not a straightforward desire for wealth and resources, but the fact that money is perceived to be a marker of status and buys respect."[60] Yet this is not about individual status: identity politics in the absence of a "shared moral horizon" and in the upheavals of industrialization is rather about "the search for a common identity that will rebind the individual to a social group,"[61] whether that group claims a national or a religious identity. It is in some sense a reaction against the trend to simply focus on people feeling good about themselves, without their lives being led according to any particular values.[62] The recognition of identity, so craved in the politics of identity, is sought for the sake of lives being meaningful. As a result, people come to think of "their own aims and objectives" as defined by "the dignity of the groups" of which they are members[63] and identity, formerly "a matter for individuals," becomes "the property of groups."[64] Fukuyama proposes "larger and more integrative national identities"[65] that work against the filtering tendencies of social media, saying "Identity can be used to divide, but it can and has also been used to integrate."[66]

HATEFUL HETERONORMATIVITY

If everybody is happy enough to be identified principally as a member of the human race then the troubles described in Fukuyama's book are as good as dealt with. The difficulty is that people feel oppressed and defend themselves with identities. This oppression can be something that has happened predominantly in the past, bequeathing an identity which was once a tactical maneuver and is now taken for an essential reality. An example

---

59 Ibid., p. 9
60 Ibid., p. 10
61 Ibid., p. 56
62 Ibid., p. 96
63 Ibid., pp. 106-107
64 Ibid., pp. 110-11
65 Ibid., p. 122
66 Ibid., p. 182

is given by Michael W. Hannon in an article entitled "Against Heterosexuality"[67] which refuses to see "straight" and "gay" as "ageless absolutes," seeing them rather as belonging to "a conceptual scheme with a history."[68] Sexual orientation, in this reading, is "nothing more than a fragile social construct, and one constructed terribly recently."[69] If we go back to before the "recent inventions" of heterosexual and homosexual,[70] we find the traditional Christian teaching about chastity, which as it were offers a level playing field. This, of course, has always been difficult and in the nineteenth century it began to be seen as a medical rather than a moral issue. By way of a compromise with traditional standards some, but not all, violations of chastity were stigmatized. To try to keep the ship of sexual morality afloat some of its cargo was thrown overboard. Instead of committing to the age-old quest for holiness, folk were enjoined to at least limit themselves to behavior styled "heterosexual." Thus "straight" became the new "strait gate" and what had hitherto been seen as the primrose path to the everlasting bonfire—that is, all sorts of violations of chastity (albeit between these newly located goalposts)—became the new normal. This had presumed medical sanction as being "healthy." It therefore became a matter of pride, replacing in this respect chastity (which one had never been encouraged to boast about in any case). Any lingering sense of wrongdoing or shame could then be projected on the out-group that did not fly the flag of the in-group. In other words, they were hated for the sins of those doing the hating. One is left with the number one violation of the life of virtue, pride, which even the loosest living can celebrate under color of being "normal," with its shadow, despair, being left for those not flying that flag. These (pride and despair) are of course more dangerous sins than sexual immorality. They come about through thinking that the fire and the earthquake of our desires truly tell us what we are and not listening to the gentle voice of God in the still, quiet breeze saying we are His children. This failure to listen leads to hurt, especially to the stigmatized, and hurt leaves wounds and wounds make one defensive. A classic defense maneuver in battles of identity is to

---

67 Michael W. Hannon, "Against Heterosexuality" in *First Things*, March 2014, Number 241, pp. 27–34
68 Ibid., p. 27   69 Ibid., p. 28
70 Ibid., p. 34

revalue labels. If you act oppressively towards me because I have four legs and you have two, I will say, "Four legs good, two legs bad." Or at the least I will say they are as good as each other. But all this is tactical rather than in the service of finding the most truthful identity, which can only come from the Truth which is God. I have given this narrative in my own version rather than Hannon's, but I certainly agree with him that any "champion of Christian chastity" needs "to dissociate the Church from the false absolutism of identity based upon erotic tendency."[71]

THE FLUIDITY OF TERRESTRIAL IDENTITY

It is indeed very difficult to make absolute any identity, other than that given by God who *is* the Absolute. What people desire, sexually or otherwise, sometimes changes or even comes to an end. When all passion is spent, is there no more identity? And then there is the issue of intersectionality: that is to say a person can have multiple identities—for example, as an Englishman, a doctor, and an uncle. In terms of identity politics, a person can be a member of multiple groups working for social recognition. And identities of this sort can change. For example, someone can change nationality, profession, or family relations—even without doing anything oneself, one can become a grandparent! And an identity can be provisional and only for the sake of the people doing the identifying. For example, when I lived as an expatriate in a country where the great majority of the foreigners the locals came across were French, much of the time I did not think it worth correcting the assumption that I myself was French. It was as convenient an identity as any other.

Some grasp of the French language was of course necessary to this. The very fact that it is possible to learn another language indicates that identity in a this-worldly sense is fluid. Learning the language is indeed often a requirement of being given a new nationality, which in its way is a new identity. Language is in a sense the clothing of identity. A mother tongue gives us a sense of what family we come from and it also is formative of new families. Language is related to identity in both identifying a person with a particular group and, in the particular way it is spoken, marking out the individual. Like identity, it indicates both sameness and

---

71 Ibid, p. 33

difference. The range of that sameness and difference is considerable. I speak English, which links me to people all over the world, yet I have a particular accent which even in England itself considerably narrows the group of those with whom others will identify me. And when I was very young my twin brother and I had an idiolect which only he and I understood—there was no point in us using the full version of the language and its words and structures when fragments selected by us did the job perfectly well. Language reflects in many ways the fluidity of identity given or claimed. Our parents teach us who we are through it and then we use it to say who we are, whether honestly or not. It can even be used temporarily as in technical language used for a specific purpose, as though one were putting on work clothes. And then some things are easier to say in French.

One could say that the language of the Bible is the clothing of a Christian. In a sense this is a God-given identity, yet nothing is so like God as silence. We do not know who people really are except in the reverence of silence. Living in a monastery I have ample opportunity to observe in silence guests whom I haven't met before. And watching how they move often tells me more about them than how they present themselves in words. It is no accident that the word "articulate" refers both to how the body is framed and to how speech is organized. Yet even the body does not say it all for is a person paralyzed nothing but a cripple? That can no more be true than somebody who no longer experiences sexual desire being a non-person.

MAKING YOUR OWN IDENTITY

With all this range of possible identity, it is not surprising that a philosophy scholar can say, "The postmodern self...constructs itself, at least in part, and recognizes this fact. It is inherently fluid, constantly reinventing itself."[72] That of course raises the question of whether such a self or identity can be stable, but it also raises the question of where the idea of the identity comes from. If it comes from outside, then its autonomy is limited to resisting some influences and allowing others. If it comes from within, then the question is how one constructs, or alters, one's

---

72   Florian Coulmas, *Identity, A Very Short Introduction* (Oxford University Press, 2019), p. 14

own consciousness. One answer is through drugs which give the appearance of a freely chosen state of consciousness, that which they induce. But although there may for a time be feelings associated with the transcendent, the result will not tend to be a sense of stable, divinely-given identity. In *Will*, "substantially a work of non-fiction based on the life, experiences and recollections of the author," the tellingly named Will Self recounts his experience of a sunny Tuesday morning in May 1986:

> 'Is this who you are?' he queries aloud—then runs on in a moaning undertone: 'A frightened young man of twenty-four...fraying—no! Fuck it—*falling* apart.' Will fumbles in his sad little grab-bag of received wisdom and comes up with: *When addicts are getting plenty of junk, they look anonymous—but when they start to withdraw, their image sharpens, and then disintegrates.*[73]

This illustrates the citation from Aleister Crowley's *Diary of a Drug Fiend* that precedes the narrative: "I've often thought that there isn't any 'I' at all; that we are simply the means of expression of something else; that when we think we are ourselves, we are simply the victims of delusion." All of this—from a context of an extreme attempt to direct one's own consciousness—suggests that identity construction as a solitary affair has a poor track record.

Shakespeare dramatizes this in *Coriolanus*, the tragedy of a man who tries to maintain an identity apart from his people. The eponymous hero is strongly identified with Rome, particularly through his mother, Volumnia, from whom he has imbibed its martial virtues. He is famed for his military service to Rome, though the word in the street is that "he did it to please his mother."[74] His mother confirms that she is the originator of his renown, saying, "To a cruel war I sent him, from whence he return'd, his brows bound with oak."[75] We see him in a war against Rome's enemy, the Volsces, entering their city Corioles and being shut in, where "he is himself alone,/ To answer all the city."[76] He is triumphant and wins the name "Coriolanus" in honor of his victorious conduct of the siege. Thus he can claim

---

[73] Will Self, *Will* (Viking, 2019), p. 1
[74] Act 1, scene i, ll.38-9   [75] Act 1, scene iii, ll. 13-15
[76] Act 1, scene iv, ll.51-52

THE MYSTERY OF IDENTITY

to have made a name for himself; he can say, "Alone I did it."[77] This self-won identity is not as autonomous as it seems, however. There are vulnerabilities. Firstly, of course, this identity comes from his mother who brought him up to fight. How much this is so is clear from her words of welcome as he returns to Rome:

> I have lived
> To see inherited my very wishes
> And the buildings of my fancy...[78]

Secondly, and less obviously, it depends on his relationship with his enemy, the chief Volscian warrior, Aufidius, the man of his "soul's hate,"[79] "a lion" he is "proud to hunt."[80] His hatred is also a kind of love. He asks an envoy who has parleyed with him, "Spoke he of me?"[81] wanting to know details, and finding out that Aufidius lives in Antium he comments, "I wish I had a cause to seek him there," adding by way of explanation, "To oppose his hatred more fully."[82] He receives his identity from Aufidius in antagonism, but even in the first scene of the play his speech makes clear that a straightforward identification is not beyond his imagining:

> I sin in envying his nobility;
> And were I any thing but what I am,
> I would wish me only he.[83]

His "what I am"—his identity—is not as stable as he imagines. His mother wants him to be not only a warrior but also a consul. To become this he has to put on a "gown of humility"[84] to beg the voices of the people of Rome. To do this is for him to "stand naked"[85]—it is just not who he is. He nevertheless does so, but it is only when he has taken the gown off that can he speak of "knowing myself again."[86] It is not difficult for his opponents to stir up the people against him. He is reluctant to give the "fair speech"[87] that would calm them. His mother asks this of him, reasoning, "My praises made thee first a soldier" and insists: "To have my praise for this, perform a part/ Thou hast not done before."[88]

77	Act 5, scene vi, l.116	78	Act 2, scene i, ll.198-200
79	Act 1, scene v, l.10	80	Act 1, scene i, ll.235-36
81	Act 3, scene i, l.12	82	Act 3, scene i, ll.19-20
83	Act 1, scene i, ll.230-32	84	Act 2, scene iii, l.40
85	Act 2, scene iii, l.40	86	Act 2, scene iii, l.147
87	Act 3, scene ii, l.96	88	Act 3, scene ii, ll.108-10

They argue. She lays claim to his valor: "Thy valiantness was mine, thou suck'st it from me."[89] He gives in, pleading "Chide me no more."[90] Nonetheless, his mother's sway over his identity does not extend with any steadfastness to the move "from th'casque to th'cushion,"[91] that is, from the military to the political, for it is not his nature to be "other than one thing"[92]—a man of war. A politician he is not, and it is not difficult for the tribunes of the people to get them to revoke their decision and his relationship with them collapses. Since (as they are persuaded by a tribune) "the people are the city"[93] his relationship with Rome is also broken. He is banished. He refuses to let the people define him as one who is banished, however, retorting, "I banish you!"[94] He now looks beyond Rome, telling the people:

> Despising,
> For you, the city, thus I turn my back;
> There is a world elsewhere.[95]

His parting promise to his family and friends is that he will remain who he is:

> While I remain above the ground, you shall
> Hear from me still, and never of me aught
> But what is like me formerly.[96]

Yet he can neither remain a Roman nor have an independent identity. So he goes to the "goodly city"[97] of Antium and switches sides:

> My birthplace hate I, and my love's upon
> This enemy town.[98]

He seeks out Aufidius. Five times his enemy asks, "Thy name?"[99] Coriolanus' delay in answering is of course caused by an awareness of the hostility its pronouncing will cause, especially since his "surname, Coriolanus"[100] comes from his conquering of a Volscian city, yet it may also reflect a deeper sense of struggle to find a sure

---

89 Act 3, scene ii, l.129
90 Act 3, scene ii, l.132
91 Act 4, scene vii, l.43
92 Act 4, scene vii, l.42
93 Act 3, scene i, l.199
94 Act 3, scene iii, l.123
95 Act 3, scene iii, ll.133-35
96 Act 4, scene i, ll.51-53
97 Act 4, scene iv, l.1
98 Act 4, scene iv, ll.23-24
99 Act 4, scene v, ll. 53, 54, 57, 59, 64
100 Act 4, scene v, l.68

THE MYSTERY OF IDENTITY

identity. When he says, "Necessity/ Commands me name myself"[101] he could as well be talking about his quest for an autonomous identity as about the immediate exigency. His intuition that he may find a point of reference in his relationship with Aufidius is true. The latter responds with a passion verging on the erotic:

> That I see thee here,
> Thou noble thing, more dances my rapt heart
> Than when I first my wedded mistress saw
> Bestride my threshold.[102]

He tells Coriolanus that since their battles, he has:

> Dreamt of encounters 'twixt thyself and me;
> We have been down together in my sleep,
> Unbuckling helms, fisting each other's throat…[103]

Coriolanus becomes to him "more a friend than e'er an enemy" though "that was much."[104] He sets about getting himself a new name and joins forces with Aufidius to attack Roman territory. A Roman general sent to parley with him reports:

> Coriolanus
> He would not answer to; forbade all names;
> He was a kind of nothing, titleless,
> Till he had forged himself a name a' th' fire
> Of burning Rome.[105]

He is "a kind of nothing" because he has forsworn his identity as a Roman and as victor over Corioles; he is "titleless" because he has not yet accomplished the martial deeds which would give him a new identity. To achieve this he has to steel himself against his family. He tells his old friend Menenius (who loved him "above the measure of a father"[106] and was his "belov'd in Rome"),[107] "Wife, mother, child I know not."[108] Rome, on which he wills to take revenge, becomes for him what Aufidius was, the identity-giving antagonist. This steeling of himself is in the presence of Aufidius. The latter acknowledges his "constant temper"[109] but the friendship is already beginning to

---

101	Act 4, scene v, ll.56–57	102	Act 4, scene v, ll.115–18
103	Act 4, scene v, ll.123–25	104	Act 4, scene v, ll.146–47
105	Act 5, scene i, ll.11–15	106	Act 5, scene iii, l.10
107	Act 5, scene ii, l.93	108	Act 5, scene ii, l.82
109	Act 5, scene ii, l.94		

Money & Meaning

crack: although Aufidius keeps the alliance for the sake of winning Rome, he has already seen the influence his new friend has over his own soldiers and is looking to redress the balance.[110]

And Rome, the new antagonist, includes his mother, wife, and child. Even before they come onto the stage he has to struggle to keep fast to his new identity:

> Shall I be tempted to infringe my vow
> In the same time 'tis made? I will not.[111]

When he sees them, his will begins to weaken. An identity free from the soil in which one grows is hard to defend and he falters, saying, "I melt and am not/ Of stronger earth than others."[112] He gives eloquent expression to what is involved in taking his stand:

> Let the Volsces
> Plough Rome and harrow Italy, I'll never
> Be such a gosling to obey instinct, but stand
> As if a man were author of himself,
> And knew no other kin.[113]

A gosling instinctively bonds with its mother and follows where she goes. Coriolanus claims to be different. He wants his identity to be self-constructed "as if a man were author of himself." These last words speak the project of his life: to define himself—first against Aufidius, then (less successfully) against his political enemies (the tribunes) and finally (and most perilously) against his own flesh and blood. They resonate in our own age in which it is so often assumed that we can simply be who we decide to be, irrespective of those from whom we drew life, those with whom we share life and, indeed, our own body. This assumption is finally an ignoring of God who made us and who alone can give us true identity. This latter point would not be part of the mind-set of the Rome in which the play is set, but it would not have been news to Shakespeare. He sets before us the tragedy of mankind seeking to live without God. That is not to say that Coriolanus is simply in error in wanting independence from his mother: it would not be a tragedy if there were not something noble in this. There is potentially the highest nobility in it, for the Lord Himself

---

110 See Act 4, scene vii
111 Act 5, scene iii, ll. 20-21
112 Act 5, scene iii, ll. 28-29
113 Act 5, scene iii, ll. 33-37

THE MYSTERY OF IDENTITY

said, "If anyone comes to me and does not hate his own father and mother and wife and children and brothers and sisters, yes, and even his own life, he cannot be my disciple."[114] The tragedy is that of a nobility that does not reach out to the divine, to a relationship that can give the only true identity.

The tragedy is not slow in coming. Coriolanus finds it difficult to "perform a part"[115] written by his mother; he finds it even more difficult to perform one that she does not want him to play. Despite—or perhaps because of—the fact that he wrote it himself, he cannot remember his lines:

> Like a dull actor now
> I have forgot my part, and I am out,
> Even to a full disgrace.[116]

He kneels to his mother. She kneels to him, violating his sense of the ordained order. She calls him "my warrior"[117] and tells him, "There's no man in the world/ More bound to 's mother."[118] He is silent while she pleads. Finally, he gives way and, pathetically, asks Aufidius (whom he has deliberately made a witness) if he would not have done the same. Shortly after this, Aufidius reveals that he feels himself to be a "follower, not partner"[119] and conspires to have his former enemy killed.

The final dialogue between Aufidius and Coriolanus is a devastating destruction of first his identity and then his life. Far from being the martial hero he hoped to be, he is a "traitor."[120] He is not going to be called "Coriolanus"—the first name he made for himself—in Corioles. He is even forbidden to invoke Mars, the god of war for whom he was named, for he is "a boy of tears."[121] This insulting reference to his yielding to his mother is more than he can take and he resorts to boasting about his exploits in Corioles, clinging to the shred of autonomy this gives him: "Alone I did it."[122] In the uproar this causes, the conspirators are soon able to kill him. Having been stripped of his Corioles name, he dies before he can make another for himself. He has not been able to forge an identity on his own.

---

114 Luke 14.26
115 Act 3, scene ii, l.109
116 Act 5, scene iii, ll.40-42
117 Act 5, scene iii, l.62
118 Act 5, scene iii, ll.158-59
119 Act 5, scene vi, l.38
120 Act 5, scene vi, l.84
121 Act 5, scene v, l.100
122 Act 5, scene v, l.116

OTHER OTHERING

It seems you cannot do that. You need a relationship of some kind. This is the conclusion that Peter Pomerantsev comes to at the end of his book, *This is Not Propaganda: Adventures in the War Against Reality*. He writes of another sort of othering from the one he had considered earlier in the book, that in which an outsider group is given a negative identity. This is the sort in which one *receives* an identity by being another for another. He makes the point by reference to a novella written by his father, a dissident in the Soviet Union. "Early in the story," he explains, "the author is trying to work out where his sense of self begins." He asks whether identity begins with politics, or with religion and creed and answers both questions: no. He concludes that "identity only appears when it recognizes the presence of someone else." This is his experience:

> A girl, on the shore of you. How high the sky. How deep the kiss. We do not say 'you' to each other but 'I.' I swim far out into you—past buoys, past—horizons; glancing back could not see the rim of the shore and was glad.[123]

This finding of identity in relationship with another is given a brilliant and profound expression in Jewish philosopher Martin Buber's seminal book, *I and Thou*. He identifies two "primary words": "*I-Thou*" and "*I-it*." They are different attitudes and each articulates a different "I" or identity. The difference is that "The primary word *I-Thou* can only be spoken with the whole being" and "The primary word *I-it* can never be spoken with the whole being."[124] The difference between the whole and the fragmented identity is the difference between the unbounded and the bounded:

> When *Thou* is spoken, the speaker has no thing for his object. For where there is a thing there is another thing. Every *It* is bounded by others; *It* exists only through being bounded by others. But when *Thou* is spoken, there is no thing. *Thou* has no bounds.

---

[123] Peter Pomeranstev, *This is Not Propaganda: Adventures in the War Against Reality* (Faber, 2019), pp. 249–50
[124] Martin Buber, *I and Thou*, translated by Ronald Gregor Smith (T. & T. Clark, 1966), p. 3

THE MYSTERY OF IDENTITY

> When *Thou* is spoken, the speaker has no *thing*; he has indeed nothing. But he takes his stand in relation.[125]

Relationship is so critical to identity that Buber, understanding "*It*" to include all third person pronouns, can say, "He who lives with *It* alone is not a man."[126] This *aperçu* is given contemporary expression in Kazuo Ishiguro's novel *Klara and the Sun* in which the eponymous heroine, who is an AF (artificial friend) designed to stop a teenager being lonely, speaks to the humans among whom she operates in the third person.[127] Being able to say "you" belongs to being human.

---

[125] Ibid., p. 4   [126] Ibid., p. 34
[127] Kazuo Ishiguro, *Klara and the Sun* (Faber, 2021)

3
Relationships & Reality

TRUTH AND TRUST

It makes more sense to seek identity through personal relationships than to seek it through money or through a politically recognized identity. There is relationship of a sort involved in the latter, but it does not reach the mystery of who someone is, some reified notion doing duty for this. Each person is in the image of God and so of the absolute Other which gives each of us our true identity. It follows that being in relationship with another person tells us who we are, but in a qualified sense. The qualification comes, of course, from the other not actually being God, not being the Truth in person. How much we know who we are in our relationships depends on their quality. It depends on how truthful they are. Only in real relationships do we know who we really are. If they feed illusions, they take us away from our true selves. And even if our relationships do not feed illusions, illusions (such as those springing from paranoia or mistrust) can damage them. To know oneself in a relationship requires a great deal of trust. It is easier to act "as if a man were author of himself" than to entrust who one is to another, but that too is acting on an illusion. Illusions make unhealthy relationships: illusions break healthy relationships. The quest to find who we are through relationships is a quest for truth.

It is a quest for the truth of identity. The very language we use to relate to others reflects the ambiguity of identity: that is both being the same and being different. It is remarkable that in any relationship with another we are both "I" and both "you." We are the same in this. We are the same in our human nature; our DNA is not very far off being identical. The more we plumb the depths of who we are, the more we find that we are like others. That is why writers, such as Shakespeare, who have sounded the depths of human nature have a universal appeal in a way that more superficial writers do not: the greater the interiority, the greater the connection with those who are exterior to ourselves.

THE MYSTERY OF IDENTITY

This makes sense in view of the presence of God in the deepest part of the human soul, since in Him all things are one. Yet God is also totally other and this too is reflected in other people who are often referred to as living on another planet if not indeed in another universe. The words of the prophet Isaiah through which God speaks of his utter difference could be understood as being spoken by each person made in His image. He says:

> My thoughts are not your thoughts, neither are your
> ways my ways, declares the LORD.
> For as the heavens are higher than the earth,
> so are my ways higher than your ways
> and my thoughts than your thoughts.[1]

Between people there is sameness and difference; identity in the sense of being very much in the same boat and identity in the sense of being so personally characterized as to be an utter mystery to each other. We couldn't be different if we were not the same: without the connection we couldn't perceive the difference; we couldn't perceive the other at all. In our connectedness and difference we make each other other, make each other unique, reflecting the work of God, who as Creator remains the very source and root of our being while making us other than He is. That is why our relationships matter so much and why it matters whether they are truthful or not, whether they participate in the truth of God. It is why it matters whether they are trusting or not, whether they participate in the reckless self-giving of God, in His love. Truth and trust, these two: truth is first in the sense of being the goal, the truth of God which is also love; but trust is first in the sense of being a prior requirement for the journey into truth and love. Theologically, this trust is faith in the God of truth and love, but the theological dynamic also plays out on the simply human level in which trust of another person gives us some sense of who we are in relation to that person.

OTHELLO'S OCCUPATION

The critical nature of that trust is dramatized by Shakespeare in *Othello*, a tragedy of a man whose trust in his identity-giving relationship is undermined. Martin Lings, in his book *Shakespeare*

---
1   Isaiah 55.8-9

in the Light of Sacred Art, has identified Othello's wife, Desdemona, as a symbol of his soul: that which is spiritual, noble and life-giving in him. That identification is made explicit in another Shakespearean couple who, like Othello and Desdemona, are separated by mistrust. Their story, told in *Cymbeline*, by contrast ends happily: Posthumus Leonatus says to Imogen when they are reunited and she has her arms around him, "Hang there like fruit, my soul,/ Till the tree die!"[2] He calls her "my queen, my life, my wife!"[3] The soul is a person's true life, a life that the body cannot express without the soul, so it is in a sense the person's identity. Just as the body if soulless (i.e., dead) lacks human identity, so the identity of Othello collapses with the failure of the spousal connection born of trust.

How central that connection can be to the sense somebody has of personal being is illustrated in a Shakespearean comedy, *The Two Gentlemen of Verona*. In it, Valentine, who loves Silvia, feels the wrath of her ducal father who banishes him on pain of death. He responds:

> To die is to be banish'd from myself,
> And Silvia is myself: banish'd from her
> Is self from self, a deadly banishment.
> What light is light, if Silvia be not seen?
> What joy is joy, if Silvia be not by?
> Unless it be to think that she is by,
> And feed upon the shadow of perfection.
> Except I be by Silvia in the night,
> There is no music in the nightingale;
> Unless I look on Silvia in the day,
> There is no day for me to look upon.
> She is my essence, and I leave to be,
> If I be not by her fair influence
> Foster'd, illumin'd, cherish'd, kept alive.[4]

His beloved is his "self" and his "essence." It is significant that without her he is deaf to harmony ("There is no music") and unable to look ("There is no day"). In other words, she makes possible

---

2 *Cymbeline*, Act 5, scene v, ll.263-64
3 Act 5, scene v, l.225
4 *The Two Gentlemen of Verona*, Act 3, scene i, ll.171-84

his hearing and seeing; she gives him the ability to know; she is his means of knowing. That is psychologically apt, for we tend to perceive the world through the ears and eyes of those we love, but the verse is saying more than this. It is telling us that who we are depends on how we listen and look; furthermore, another's hearing and seeing shapes this listening and looking and so shapes us. Of course it need not be a fiancée or a spouse; it need not be only one person, it could be several friends; it could even be people we know through their singing and writing. But another pair of ears, another pair of eyes are a significant or even necessary catalyst to the finding of significance in the world, and therefore to our take on the world, and so to who we are. Marriage is a common and fruitful way of finding such significance.

The one flesh of the Bible and the marriage service is hardly an exaggeration or a flight of fancy: the oneness is such that mistrustful division between the spouses entails a shattering of meaning, a tearing apart of the self. This happens to Othello. Initially, he has great trust. When accused of dishonorably abducting Desdemona, he stakes his life on her witness to him:

> If you do find me foul in her report,
> The trust, the office I do hold of you,
> Not only take away, but let your sentence
> Even fall upon my life.[5]

Her testimony justifies his confidence. It tells how her soul became his:

> My heart's subdu'd
> Even to the very quality of my lord.
> I saw Othello's visage in his mind,
> And to his honors and his valiant parts
> Did I my soul and fortunes consecrate.[6]

The "quality" of her lord is both his nature and his military profession. She identifies with his valor, confident that his face truly reflects his thinking. Desdemona shows Othello who he is: a military leader at the service of the Venetian state. As long as he trusts her, he has an identity. His trust is absolute: when her father says, "She has deceiv'd her father, and may thee" he retorts,

---

5 Act 1, scene iii, ll.117-20   6 Act 1, scene iii, ll.250-54

Relationships & Reality

"My life upon her faith!"[7] This trust of one worthy of trust is destroyed by Othello's trust of one unworthy of trust: "honest Iago,"[8] as he calls him, whose machinations persuade him that Desdemona is unfaithful. So persuaded, he will lose both his identity and his life. Desdemona is his "soul's joy,"[9] its principle of life. His love for her stands between his identity and its dissolution, as is evidenced by his exclamation:

> Perdition catch my soul
> But I do love thee! and when I love thee not,
> Chaos is come again.[10]

Chaos comes when Iago's insinuations cause Othello's trust to begin to fray. Imagining Desdemona no longer consecrated to his "valiant parts," he bids farewell not only to a "tranquil mind" and "content" but to all the apparatus of war:

> Farewell the plumed troops and the big wars
> That make ambition virtue! O, farewell!
> Farewell the neighing steed and the shrill trump,
> The spirit-stirring drum, th' ear piercing fife,
> The royal banner, and all quality,
> Pride, pomp, and circumstance of glorious war!
> And O you mortal engines, whose rude throats
> Th' immortal Jove's dread clamours counterfeit,
> Farewell!

All of these things gave him his identity as a soldier. Without the love and trust which bond him with Desdemona, who as it were validates his soldier's status by her loving attention to it, he bids farewell to them, concluding, "Othello's occupation's gone."[11] This is more than a job loss: the very soul that inhabits his body is gone, leaving him a prey to murderous passion; the noble calm which characterized him as a soldier is gone; the primordial chaos that was there before the creating spirit of God hovered over the waters is come again. When Desdemona meets him again, she can only say, "My lord is not my lord."[12] His identity is gone. Taunted by Iago, he loses the calm for which he is famed and

---

7 Act 1, scene iii, ll.293-94
8 Act 1, scene iii, l.294
9 Act 2, scene i, l.184
10 Act 3, scene iii, ll.90-92
11 Act 3, scene iii, ll.348-57
12 Act 3, scene iv, l.124

THE MYSTERY OF IDENTITY

is hardly recognizable as the man he was. The emissary of the Duke of Venice asks:

> Is this the noble Moor whom our full Senate
> Call all in all sufficient? Is this the nature
> Whom passion could not shake? Whose solid virtue
> The shot of accident nor dart of chance
> Could neither graze nor pierce?[13]

Othello, believing Iago's slandering of Desdemona, feels rejected from the very source of his life:

> There, where I have garner'd up my heart,
> Where either I must live or bear no life;
> The fountain from the which my current runs
> Or else dries up: to be discarded thence![14]

His being depends on the dynamic of trust between himself and Desdemona. He has chosen this in the sense of making it the safe-keeping place for his heart, but he is not free to revise that decision. The only way out is through the destruction of who he is. Killing Desdemona does that. Even as he prepares to do this, there is a recognition that there is something at least potentially holy and light-giving about her, for he urges her to be reconciled to God saying, "I would not kill thy soul."[15] That soul was consecrated to him and when he has laid violent hands on her, even before he knows the truth about her innocence, he knows that to say, "I have no wife" is to acknowledge not only an intolerable grief but also the extinguishing of spiritual light from his life:

> O insupportable! O heavy hour!
> Methinks it should be now a huge eclipse
> Of sun and moon, and that th' affrighted globe
> Did yawn at alteration.[16]

The withdrawal of the light of sun and moon from the earth is the proper expression of his loss of his way of seeing the world, which is through his wife, Desdemona. She gave the world its value for him. He acknowledges:

---

13 Act 4, scene i, ll.264–68
14 Act 4, scene ii, ll.57–60
15 Act 5, scene ii, l.32
16 Act 5, scene ii, ll.97–101

Relationships & Reality

> had she been true
> If heaven would make me such another world
> Of one entire and perfect chrysolite,
> I'd not have sold her for it.[17]

Of course she was true and he has lost what was the perfection of the world for him: sharing it with her, seeing it through her eyes. When he knows this, he sees he has reached his "journey's end," the "butt/ And very sea-mark" of his "utmost sail."[18] There is no point in any soldierly defense of himself, for "Where should Othello go?"[19] When the Duke's emissary asks, "Where is this rash and most unfortunate man?" he replies, "That's he that was Othello; here I am."[20] He is he that *was* Othello: he no longer has an identity. He has no *raison d'être*, no fountain from which can spring the current of his life, no world to live in for there is no one to tell him how to see it. There is indeed no one to tell him who he is. He ends his life.

Leonatus in Shakespeare's *Cymbeline* also finds his identity through his wife. He says to her, "I my poor self did exchange for you."[21] Their marriage is an exchange of identities. It is an instinct of an intense love to say to the loved one, "Call me by your name." Indeed, a procreative love is a genetic sharing of identities, these merging in the new life that is born. It is the other who gives identity—identity in name as, traditionally, in "Miss" becoming "Mrs."; identity in the oneness of flesh; identity in the child that is the offspring of both. This identity is an escape from the narrowness of an egotistical identity. Being in love is as it were a booster rocket to get out of the gravitational pull of the egoism that would center everything on itself. Love is the entry into a realm beyond ownership, the gift of the entire world received anew because it has the freshness of another perspective, the bliss of dying to self. It is stepping towards the utter generosity of God's love which allows the other to be other while at the same time identifying with the condition of the other even unto death, the death of the cross. It is identity in the double sense of being different and being the same, giving the other both freedom to be and solidarity in being. Love is in its way the gift of identity to another.

---

17 Act 5, scene ii, ll.143-46
18 Act 5, scene ii, ll.267-68
19 Act 5, scene ii, l.271
20 Act 5, scene ii, ll.283-84
21 *Cymbeline*, Act 1, scene i, l.119

THE MYSTERY OF IDENTITY

Leonatus receives this gift from Imogen, but like Othello he is falsely persuaded that his wife is false. His response is a tirade against all women, whom he now trusts so little as to believe, "We are all bastards." A bastard is of course someone without a respectable social identity. Leonatus pursues the metaphor of false coinage to articulate his sense that all is counterfeit—identity as such has been destroyed:

> And that most venerable man which I
> Did call my father, was I know not where
> When I was stamp'd. Some coiner with his tools
> Made me a counterfeit.[22]

Identity is linked to faithful and trustworthy love, but also (which is not possible if mothers are not faithful and trustworthy) to knowing the identity of one's father. In the general restoration in the last scene of the play, identity is revealed: Imogen is shown to be a woman and not, as was thought, a man; her fidelity is vindicated, giving Leonatus back his true life; those who gave her hospitality in her time of distress are made known as her brothers, offspring like her of King Cymbeline. The latter reflects that she is thereby disinherited, saying, "O Imogen,/ Thou has lost by this a kingdom." She responds, "No, my lord;/ I have got two worlds by't. O my gentle brothers."[23] Each new world is the world as it is for one of her brothers. Her knowing now includes their knowing. As Sylvia does for Valentine in *The Two Gentlemen of Verona*, they shape how she hears and sees; they fashion how she is; they help create her identity. That fashioning helps bring her nearer to the ultimate identity, which is beyond this world, of which we can say with Saint Paul, "Then I shall know fully, even as I have been fully known."[24] That is the divine identity, a sharing in God's knowing and in that sense identity with Him, while yet—through some miracle which is a mystery—retaining an identity in the sense of being uniquely different. That unique difference itself is of course an imaging of the absolute uniqueness of God, dispersed and refracted through the creation of heaven and earth and yet gathered back to Him in the fullness of time in what is essentially the same movement as its going out from Him, since it is eternal and beyond time.

---

22 Act 2, scene v, ll.2-6
23 Act 5, scene v, ll.372-74
24 1 Corinthians 13.12

We give something of, something from, that eternal and divine knowing to each other as spouses and siblings; yet it does not come first of all from us, even humanly speaking. As Imogen and her brothers receive it from King Cymbeline, so do we receive it from our mothers and fathers. That is true not only in the sense that we share their genes: they teach us what the world is by transmitting their knowing of it; they articulate our being by giving us words to speak; by showing us how to know and speak of the world they lead us to realize who we are. They are progenitors not of bodies only but also of identities.

IMPRINTING

The Austrian ornithologist, Konrad Lorenz, made famous "imprinting," the process by which some nidifugous birds such as geese bond instinctively with the first moving object entering their field of vision in the hours immediately after their emergence from their shells. In normal conditions this would be their mother, but Lorenz showed that it could be his boots. I have myself been attacked by a (grown) goose for coming between him and the wearer of the boots with which he had bonded. Patrick Bateson, a distinguished scientist who developed Lorenz's work, called this "filial imprinting" to distinguish it from bonding relating to mating, but questioned whether the process was as instantaneous and irreversible as the metaphor implies.[25] The philosopher Robert Bolton also questions the implication of the metaphor, in this case as indicating that the granting of identity to progeny is a one-way process:

> Typically, each animal and bird identifies itself with the first thing it sees after it is born or hatched, which is normally an adult member of its own species. This form of self-identification is so automatic that for some species even an inanimate object can be substituted with the result that it relates to the object as to a parent. What this has in common with the way in which human beings understand their world is an absorption in what is perceived

---

25 Patrick Bateson, "Is imprinting such a special case?" in *Philosophical Transactions: Biological Sciences*, August 29, 1990, Vol. 329, No. 1253, Behavioural and Neural Aspects of Learning and Memory, pp. 125-31

which blinds the perceiver to something essential about himself.[26]

Bateson, too, draws attention to the avian-human parallels:

> Analogies between imprinting in birds and the developments of attachments in humans have been drawn, particularly by the great psychiatrist John Bowlby. The day-old baby is affected by her auditory experience before birth and she prefers the sound of her mother's voice to that of other women.[27]

This observation of the scientist about the plasticity of the process and that of the philosopher about being absorbed in the perceived at the cost of being aware of the perceiver both point to the truth that identity is not just a given received from parents as a newspaper receives its content from a press: there is an active involvement of the one receiving the identity. That is to say: identity is not simply being the same (as a parent), it is also (as parents learn, sometimes painfully) being different. Identity is sameness and difference. It is not simply given and it is not simply chosen: it is created in the pain and the glory of relationship.

Avian science gives some pointers to the scope and nature of this relationship. The bonding happens at a particular time:

> Filial imprinting occurs just before the stage in the life cycle when, for its own safety, the young animal needs to discriminate between its parents and other members of its own species that might attack it. In precocious species this occurs shortly after hatching or birth.[28]

This is called the "sensitive period" which, Bateson observes, seems "to be brought to an end by the formation of a social attachment."[29] Human development is analogous, but more sophisticated. Very young children identify with and identify as safe their own parents,

---

26 Robert Bolton, *Person, Soul and Identity* (Minerva Press, 1994), pp. 130–31
27 Patrick Bateson, *Behaviour, Development and Evolution* (Open Book Publishers, www.jstor.com/stable/j.ctt1sq5tz0.5), p. 21
28 Patrick Bateson, "Is imprinting such a special case?" in *Philosophical Transactions: Biological Sciences*, August 29, 1990, Vol. 329, No. 1253, Behavioural and Neural Aspects of Learning and Memory, p. 125
29 Ibid., p. 126

Relationships & Reality

but there are further periods which are "sensitive" in other ways. Children are naturally relatively biddable during their first decade, when they receive their primary schooling. The frustration expressed by Shakespeare's shepherd in *The Winter's Tale* sums up the change that follows:

> I would there were no age between ten and three-and-twenty, or that youth would sleep out the rest; for there is nothing in the between but getting wenches with child, wronging the ancientry, stealing, fighting—[30]

However—and this distinguishes the human from the avian—after this insensitive period (the timing of which is not necessarily exactly that of the Shakespearean text) there is a further "sensitive period." We might call this the time of formation of spiritual identity. It has been my privilege to have care of people at this stage in their development in my capacity as the monk responsible for interns who come to spend a couple of months in our monastery engaged with our spiritual routines and practices. This period (the age parameters we set are 18–25) is characterized in my experience by a particular openness to tradition. On one level this is evidenced in an enthusiasm for the retro—manual typewriters, the Beatles and so on: which my generation but not theirs knew directly—but more fundamentally by a longing to engage with a deeply rooted spiritual tradition, specifically that of Saint Benedict. This is felt by emerging adults—like goslings emerging from their shells—rather than either school children or people who have already settled on a course of life. There is an interesting further parallel with avian maturation. Bateson notes that, in the context of presenting chicks with various visual stimuli to see what will most readily stimulate imprinting, "Strong evidence suggests that the features of the jungle fowl, the ancestral fowl, are particularly attractive to chicks."[31] Even in the animal kingdom, this suggests, there is an instinct to go back beyond the lives of their progenitors to their ancient source. The domestication of the fowl parallels the taming of the human spirit by the state's systemization of human aspiration: as

---

30 *The Winter's Tale*, Act 3, scene iii, ll.59-63
31 Patrick Bateson, "Is imprinting such a special case?" in *Philosophical Transactions: Biological Sciences*, August 29, 1990, Vol. 329, No. 1253, Behavioural and Neural Aspects of Learning and Memory, p. 126

THE MYSTERY OF IDENTITY

with the fledgling birds, so with the young of our day—they are drawn to something wilder, freer, and more ancient than what is presented to them by their immediate social context.

Barack Obama found that something wilder, freer and more ancient at the site of ancestral graves in Kenya. There he learnt that identity comes through knowing tradition, not from ourselves alone. "Oh Father," he cried:

> There was no shame in your confusion. Just as there had been no shame in your father's before you. No shame in the fear, or in the fear of his father before him. There was only shame in the silence the fear had produced. It was the silence that betrayed us. If it weren't for that silence, your grandfather might have told your father that he could never escape himself, or re-create himself alone. Your father might have taught these same lessons to you.

In the strength of this tradition, Barack Obama's father might have understood something about the power of western technology:

> That this power could be absorbed only alongside a faith born of hardship, a faith that wasn't new, that wasn't black or white or Christian or Muslim but that pulsed in the heart of the first African village and the first Kansas homestead—a faith in other people.

Weeping at the graves, at this particular place, the future president of the United States has an intuition of his identity:

> I realized that who I was, what I cared about, was no longer just a matter of intellect or obligation, no longer a construct of words. I saw that my life in America—the black life, the white life, the sense of abandonment I'd felt as a boy, the frustration and hope that I'd witnessed in Chicago—all of it was connected with this small plot of earth an ocean away, connected by more than the accident of a name or the color of my skin.[32]

DYSFUNCTIONAL DEVELOPMENT

As with the course of true love, there is no guarantee that these three stages in the development of identity—the bonding

---

32 Barack Obama, *Dreams from My Father* (Canongate Books, 2004), pp. 429-30

Relationships & Reality

with parents, the learning of the early years, and the young person's quest for the wild and the free—will run smoothly. It was an occasion for laughter (at least for the onlooker) when I was attacked by the goose who had bonded with boots, but it is no laughing matter when people are wounded during the sensitive periods when identity is emerging. Being orphaned is a loss that being in an orphanage does not mend. People in this situation are vulnerable to the human equivalent of "imprinting" happening with those who are in fact not available to commit to a parental role. It can be gratifying for those visiting as emotional tourists to receive the unconditional love of a child, but for the child it may be an experience of abandonment since the love reaches out to a source of care which proves unreliable when the visitor is unable to stay. Ultimately, this reaching out is to the One who said, "I will not leave you as orphans; I will come to you."[33] It is a seeking "to become children of God."[34] God never fails those who trust Him to adopt them, but trust becomes very much more difficult if it is humanly betrayed. And the instinct of imprinting becomes weaker the more objects it is exercised on. With a proper first object it distinguishes friend from potential foe; betrayed, it can end up seeing all as potential foes.

Here is a particular example which I have personally encountered. In order to protect the identity(!) of the person concerned, I will change the specifics but the psychological dynamic remains true. Esmeralda was the illegitimate daughter of a prominent South American politician. In order to protect the latter's reputation, she was placed in an orphanage run by religious sisters. She was adopted from there into a family which she thought was her own blood. She bonded closely with the person she imagined to be her mother. The latter died—in her arms—and immediately those she thought to be her brothers revealed to her that she was not truly a member of the family and, furthermore, was no longer welcome in their home. Esmeralda changed her name more than once over the decades that followed and her country of residence many times. She found it painfully, almost impossibly difficult to receive love: for her, to open up to it was tantamount to opening up to betrayal. The nurturing love of a family that she had relied

---

33 John 14.18   34 John 1.12

on had come—in one sense, anyway—to seem unreal, or at least a prelude to abandonment. And that, of course, was on top of the weakening of the capacity to bond that the moves into and out of the orphanage would have effected. Avoiding the dangers of investing trust in more directly personal relationships, she sought love and respect by pretending to be someone in a calling which normally evoked them for its members. Her social situation of course became considerably worse when this came to light. She has not despaired, she has not given up on God's love; but her path in life has been of singular difficulty.

There is a special vulnerability around the time when people are looking to bond with parents, but there is also danger in the spiritually sensitive period when young people are looking for a guide who can open up meaning and purpose for their lives. Moses (a good guide) says, "See, I have set before you today life and good, death and evil"[35] to encourage his hearers to choose the former, but there are guides who direct the young to the latter and that in the most literal sense. *Corruptio optimi pessima*: it is only through the corruption of the highest and most noble spiritual aspirations—the urge to do something extraordinarily generous for God—that people can be persuaded to blow themselves up to wreak murderous havoc on others. No one would do such a thing out of some sort of minor vice, like being lazy or eating too much. Little virtuous habits, like being polite or helping the frail to cross the road, could never promote such behavior. Only the most extreme urge to self-transcendence could ever be the material from which such evil is fashioned, for evil is always parasitic on good. It seeks the good but unformed on which to imprint its identity. That is not to say that people led astray like this have no responsibility for what happens, only that the older generation are co-workers in the development of the identity of the young. Those who have lived beyond the identity-sensitive periods have the task of helping those who have not. As Erik Erikson observes: "The problem of adulthood is how to *take care* of those to whom one finds oneself committed as one emerges from the identity period, and to whom one now owes *their* identity."[36]

---

35 Deuteronomy 30.15
36 Erik H. Erikson, *Identity, Youth and Crisis* (Norton, New York, 1994), p. 33

LONGING FOR A FATHER

The young can, for their part, long intensely for this. Dostoevsky gives artistic expression to this in *The Adolescent*. In that novel, Arkady (the adolescent in question) lets slip his initial idea of finding identity through money, to give himself to a passionate quest to relate to the father with whom he has had only one brief meeting. The first step is to get a sense of his father's identity. Arkady says to someone who knows about his life: "I beseech you to tell me the whole truth. I precisely want to know what kind of man *he* is."[37] What he learns is "like dreams and delirium," he says, and his interlocutor responds with deep sympathy, "Is this man very dear to you?"[38] Reflecting on how his image of his father differs from the reality, he asks himself, "And why had I fallen in love with him, once and for all, in that little moment when I saw him while still a child?" He thinks "that 'for all' has to go."[39] However, although Arkady is initially uncertain whether his father is worthy of the role his imagination has given him, when he finally meets him again, the effects of the sensitive period imprinting do not vanish. It is not just that he wants his father's name to escape from the stigma of being illegitimate: all his life he has "needed Versilov himself, the whole man, the father."[40] This longing for a connection is so intense that on one occasion when his father looks at him angrily, he reflects:

> "He finally looked at me *seriously!*" I thought, and my heart stood still. Oh, if I hadn't loved him, I wouldn't have been so glad of his hatred![41]

Yuri Corrigan, in his remarkably insightful book, *Dostoevsky and the Riddle of the Self*, gives an account of how Versilov becomes central to his son's quest for identity:

> When Versilov subsequently renounces an inheritance and thus demonstrates, through his noble action, that he indeed resembles his son's idealized image of him, Arkady discards his defenses and allows his father to "grasp and conquer [his] soul": "'Now I have no need to

---

37 Fyodor Dostoevsky, *The Adolescent*, translated by Richard Pevear and Larissa Volokhonsky (Everyman's Library, 2003), p. 66
38 Ibid., p. 71   39 Ibid., p. 73
40 Ibid., p. 133   41 Ibid., p. 168

fantasize and dream, now it is enough to have you! I'll follow you!' I said, giving myself over to him with my whole soul." Having found an apparently robust, attractive, mysterious, and secure location into which he can displace his identity, Arkady attempts to blend himself into his father's personality as he continually insists on confusing the boundaries between them: he resolves to fight a duel on Versilov's behalf, borrows money in his name, falls passionately in love with the object of Versilov's desire, fastidiously protects Versilov's reputation and image in the eyes of others, repeats the latter's thoughts as his own, and longs for his father to "invade his conscience."[42]

Arkady's love for his father means so much to him that he seeks to protect it by avoiding knowing his secrets, confessing to him, "I'm afraid that your secrets will tear you out of my heart completely, and I don't want that."[43] In Arkady's heart, his father is placed "extremely high, in the clouds" and Arkady clothing his father's destiny "in something mysterious" helps to keep him there.[44]

The longing for a father who is a reliable guide can be so intense that it can distort perceptions, even in a somewhat willful way, as with Arkady. The very young, of course, need to trust their parents completely and in the course of normal development they will adjust to their parents' failures as they become more mature. If the parents have been good enough when the children were little, a more adult perspective will not make them resentful, simply more clear-sighted. However, a parent like Versilov who is absent during a critically sensitive period is liable to be viewed with the naivety of that period even when the offspring is old enough to make a critical assessment. If the longing has not done its work of bonding, it remains and will color what it sees to achieve the imprinting that the fledgling lacked. This is brought out with great poignancy in Kazuo Ishiguro's tellingly titled novel, *When We Were Orphans*. This narrates the story of a famous London detective, Christopher Banks, who seems to have

---

42 Yuri Corrigan, *Dostoevsky and the Riddle of the Self* (Northwestern University Press, 2017), p. 111
43 Fyodor Dostoevsky, *The Adolescent*, translated by Richard Pevear and Larissa Volokhonsky (Everyman's Library, 2003), p. 412
44 Ibid., p. 481

acquired his investigative skills from the urge to find the father who disappeared from his life when he was young and known as "Puffin." As his story progresses, it becomes obvious to the reader from its unrealistic aspects that it is being distorted by the teller, Banks himself, to give an importance to the quest and a nobility to the parent that they do not really have. The full pathos of the capacity of longing to distort perception emerges in this climactic interview that Banks has with his uncle, who has just told him that his father is dead:

> "Tell me, Christopher. What do you believe happened to your father?"
> "Is it any business of yours what I believe? I came here to hear it from you."
> "Very well. But I was curious to know what you'd worked out for yourself. After all, you've made quite a name for yourself for such things."
> This irritated me, but it occurred to me he would be forthcoming only on his own terms. So in the end, I said: "My conjecture has been that my father made a stand, a courageous stand, against his own employers concerning the profits from the opium trade of those years. In doing so, I supposed he set himself against enormous interests, and was thus removed."
> Uncle Philip nodded. "I'd supposed you believed something like that. Your mother and I discussed carefully what to have you believe. And it was more or less what you've just said. So we were successful. The truth, I'm afraid, Puffin, was much more prosaic. Your father ran off one day with his mistress."[45]

The longing is so powerful because another is essential to identity.

Even if one is "a chip off the old block" in relation to a progenitor, however, difference is involved in identity. Identity is sameness and difference. As we grow into our identity we move from reaching out to one who is different so that we might be the same towards autonomy, to becoming ourselves different in our sameness: indeed, as with any tradition, there has to be change to maintain the sameness. That longing, which motivates the reaching towards

---

45 Kazuo Ishiguro, *When We Were Orphans* (Faber and Faber, 2001), p. 286

THE MYSTERY OF IDENTITY

sameness, will not be deflected by imperfection in the one who fathers or mothers identity, but in time it will seek beyond what they offer, for ultimately it is a longing for God. It is a longing for His perfect identity: perfect in itself, perfect in its omniscient and loving identity with all that is and perfect in its absolute and transcendent uniqueness. It is mediated through the generations, carried through the ages from the Primordial Man who knew the touch of God in his fashioning from clay, who was created in His image, who was blessed by Him. That touch, that creation, that blessing, is a universal heritage, but one obscured by the divagations of history, marred by the sin of the past, flawed by the infidelities of forefathers. Longing reaches towards it through the veneration of ancestors, through research into olden times, through receiving spiritual tradition. Ultimately, it is a wanting to have God in His perfection as our Father and to share with Him Mary His Immaculate Mother. Our identity, at its deepest, comes from belonging to this Father who invites us to the same perfection that He has, and to this Mother who loves us in our frail flesh which separates us and makes us different.

Every other quest mirrors the quest to find this identity, comes from the heart's longing that only this identity can satisfy, echoes this primal need to be birthed into eternal perfection. Ishiguro's famous detective speaks for all of humanity when he asks, "My parents. Where are they?"[46] Having found out the truth about his father and met his mother, who can no longer recognize him, he returns from the Far East. At the end of the novel he walks "down a winding lane in Gloucestershire"[47] with his niece, who is, like him, "an orphan, with no one."[48] Afterwards, he reflects, "Our fate is to face the world as orphans, chasing through long years the shadows of vanished parents."[49] Such is the particular destiny of those, like them, separated prematurely from parents, but such too is the common lot of us who live in an age that godlessness, war and frenzy have separated from the truth about who we are. We chase shadows, not simply shadows of our parents, but shadows of who we are. We seek, sometimes compulsively and tragically but sometimes realistically and hopefully, to know who we are through our relation with others. They can reflect either what is accidental

---

46 Ibid., p. 285
48 Ibid., p. 308
47 Ibid., p. 306
49 Ibid., p. 313

Relationships & Reality

in us or what is essential. The relation can be spousal, filial or one of friendship; it can be concentrated on a single individual or extend to a group; its effect can be benign or malign.

TAKING OVER OTHER SELVES

Yuri Corrigan (in the book cited above) considers "the haunting presence of unwanted memory"[50] in Dostoevsky's fictional characters and how, rather than face the story of their lives, they latch passionately onto those of others. Characteristically, "the protagonist appropriates his interlocutor's memories as a form of replacement for his own erased interior life."[51] This is not so much discovering an identity through another as denying it. The other enables the pretense that the hard-to-bear things of one's own life are not one's own but the other's. The passionate engagement with the other is a making of the other's life into one's own rather than a dialogue recognizing the presence of someone else in the context of which who one truly is can appear. The relationship becomes the dramatization of unresolved trauma: the other person is not allowed an independent identity but clung to as embodying the pain that cannot be faced directly. This can be framed as being a reaching out in compassion while in reality being a dragging of the other into a solipsistic abyss of destruction.

Such ambiguity is present in the character of Prince Myshkin, the "idiot" in Dostoevsky's novel of that name. On one level, he is simply the ideal Christian who is free of egoism and always ready to accept the other's point of view, even when that places himself in a bad light. Yet he arrives on the St. Petersburg scene from abroad, where he has been treated for "some strange nervous illness"[52] with a past he cannot remember and seems terrified of facing. Corrigan describes him as "the apotheosis of Dostoevsky's traumatized protagonists"[53] and "a wounded individual who struggles to distinguish between a projective world, populated with reflections of his own psyche, on the one hand, and the actual

---

50 Yuri Corrigan, *Dostoevsky and the Riddle of the Self* (Northwestern University Press, 2017), p. 8
51 Ibid., p. 38
52 Fyodor Dostoevsky, *The Idiot*, translated by Richard Pevear and Larissa Volokhonsky (Everyman's Library, 2002), p. 6
53 Corrigan, *Dostoevsky and the Riddle of the Self*, p. 69

THE MYSTERY OF IDENTITY

world of people, on the other."[54] He is one who is characterized as "a personality tormented by some sequence of painful, submerged memories which he confronts outside of himself in the arresting face of a suffering woman."[55] He first hears of this woman on the train into St. Petersburg from a merchant's son called Rogozhin, who talks feverishly about how he bought her diamond ear-rings. Not long after, Myshkin sees her portrait and is convinced that "she has suffered terribly."[56] When he meets her, she seems to belong to his memories as this dialogue with her indicates:

> "I was very struck by your portrait.... And at the very moment when I opened the door, I was also thinking about you, and suddenly there you were."
> "But how did you recognize me?"
> "From the portrait and..."
> "And?"
> "And also because that was precisely how I imagined you... It's as if I've also seen you somewhere."
> "Where? Where?"
> "As if I've seen your eyes somewhere...but that can't be! I'm just... I've never even been here before. Maybe in a dream..."[57]

Nastasya has indeed suffered much, both in her childhood and in being sexually exploited as a young woman. She responds to the prince's acceptance of and fixation upon her by handing over to him her power of decision. She has made it known when she will announce whether she is going to accept marriage to Ganya, an arrangement planned by her exploiter, Totsky. When the time comes, she asks the prince, "Tell me what you think: should I get married or not? I'll do as you say."[58] Myshkin says not to, and when Totsky impugns the seriousness of the procedure, she retorts:

> "You heard me say to the prince: 'It will be as you say.' If he had said 'yes,' I would have consented at once; but he said 'no,' and I refused. My whole life was hanging by a hair—what could be more serious?"[59]

---

54 Ibid., p. 70   55 Ibid.
56 Fyodor Dostoevsky, *The Idiot*, translated by Richard Pevear and Larissa Volokhonsky (Everyman's Library, 2002), p. 36
57 Ibid., p. 105   58 Ibid., p. 153
59 Ibid., p. 154

Relationships & Reality

Her explanation for choosing the prince is, "He believed in me from the first glance, and I trust him."[60] Myshkin, for his part, vows, "I...love you...Nastasya Filippovna. I will die for you, Nastasya Filippovna. I won't let anyone say a bad word about you, Nastasya Filippovna."[61] It is as though they have abandoned their identities to each other. Rogozhin later observes to the prince, "The two of you agree in everything now."[62] Yet they do not have a real identity between them. Nastasya gives Rogozhin hope that she could be his bride, and, obsessed with her and ever watching the prince, he enters their emptiness. Myshkin and Rogozhin exchange crosses in sign of brotherhood and Rogozhin tells him, "She's yours! I give her up to you!"[63]

There is a glimmer of light for the prince amidst the darkness that the three of them share in the person of Aglaya, whose name etymologically (from the Greek) denotes shining and so light.[64] She is the other person he could marry. In a climactic scene, she, Nastasya, Myshkin and Rogozhin are alone in a house. The two women quarrel terribly. Myshkin is forced to choose between them. At this critical moment:

> He only saw before him the desperate, insane face, because of which, as he had once let slip to Aglaya, "his heart was forever pierced." He could no longer bear it and with entreaty and reproach turned to Aglaya, pointing to Nastasya Filippovna:
> "It's not possible! She's ... so unhappy!"[65]

Aglaya cannot endure his hesitation and runs out. The prince runs too, but:

> Arms seized him on the threshold. Nastasya Filippovna's stricken, distorted face looked at him point-blank, and her blue lips moved, saying:
> "After her? After her?..."
> She fell unconscious in his arms.[66]

---

60 Ibid.
61 Ibid., p. 164
62 Ibid., p. 214
63 Ibid., p. 223
64 Yuri Corrigan, *Dostoevsky and the Riddle of the Self* (Northwestern University Press, 2017), p. 77
65 Fyodor Dostoevsky, *The Idiot*, translated by Richard Pevear and Larissa Volokhonsky (Everyman's Library, 2002), p. 571
66 Ibid., p. 572

THE MYSTERY OF IDENTITY

When she comes round, she sends Rogozhin away. Myshkin is lost to Aglaya and he is Nastasya's. Light has failed to break into the darkness of their compulsion. There are just the two of them. They proceed to get married, but as the bride approaches the church she catches sight of Rogozhin's eyes and sees a chance to escape from her compulsion. She rushes up to him, "like a madwoman," seizes him by both hands exclaiming, "Save me! Take me away! Wherever you like, now!"[67] They speed away to the station.

The next day the prince follows them to St. Petersburg. Eventually he finds Rogozhin or, rather, is found by Rogozhin. Rogozhin has killed Nastasya and invites Myshkin to lie with him next to her body, with the intention, "not to confess or let them take her out."[68] When dawn comes, his heart oppressed "with infinite anguish," Myshkin presses his face to "the pale and motionless face of Rogozhin," tears flowing from his eyes onto Rogozhin's cheeks. Their identity is merged. And:

> When, after many hours, the door was opened and people came in, they found the murderer totally unconscious and delirious. The prince was sitting motionless on the bed beside him, and each time the sick man had a burst of shouting or raving, he quietly hastened to pass his trembling hand over his hair and cheeks, as if caressing and soothing him. But he no longer understood anything of what they asked him about, and did not recognize the people who came in and surrounded him.[69]

All three, their selves collapsed into each others', have lost their identity: Nastasya dead, Rogozhin rambling, and Myshkin again what he was before his treatment abroad: an idiot.

A weak sense of identity coming from a flight from interiority due to an unwillingness to face what is within, especially difficult memories, drives such destructively compulsive relationships. Essentially, the dynamic is the same as that which drives unreasonably identifying others as enemies. That can be a projection of what is dark within onto others. The psyche in the first case says as it were, "I cannot cope with this: I'll give it to you, you can take it because you are my friend." In the second case it says, "I cannot

---

67 Ibid., p. 593   68 Ibid., p. 608
69 Ibid., p. 611

bear to acknowledge this: I'll blame it on you because you are my enemy." In both cases there is a weak sense of personal identity. The healthy way to repair it is by facing what is within, which becomes possible through the conviction that we are (while yet sinners)[70] infinitely loved by God and ultimately through the presence of Christ, and so of His light, deep within the soul. That comes about through retreat from relationship, through prayerful solitude, but it also comes about through a positive relationship with others, which can indeed awaken the slumbering interior life. There is a powerful image of what needs to be done in Dostoevsky's description of Rogozhin's house in *The Idiot*. It is a shuttered, dark and gloomy habitation which "resembles a graveyard."[71] On one of the walls in it is a copy of Holbein's painting of the dead Christ.[72] The ultimate dark secret, not simply of the individual soul but of the race, is the killing of Christ: the murder of the divine life within. The only remedy is the resurrection, the inflowing of unlimited life. Relationships can either impede or facilitate (explicitly or implicitly) this abundant vitality.

The difference between the two kinds is implied in this verse of the Bible: "The thief comes only to steal and to kill and destroy. I came that they may have life and have it abundantly."[73] The "thief" is the devil, seeking to destroy; "I" is Christ with "the power of an indestructible life."[74] The former seeks to possess, the latter to set free. The relationship with the diabolic is confining, while the relationship with the divine is enabling. The individual who is possessed wants to control, while the Christian set free wants to be humble before the mystery of the person. Dostoevsky, the master psychologist, maps the dynamics of both the diabolic devouring of identity and the Christ-given flowering of identity. *Demons*, as its title suggests, focuses on the first—only hinting at the second, which receives a fuller treatment in his last and greatest novel, *The Brothers Karamazov*. Corrigan argues that Dostoevsky's study of demonology in *Demons* "emerges from his depiction of the flimsy, depthless, possessive and possessed personality of the tutor, who

---

70 Cf. Romans 5.8
71 Fyodor Dostoevsky, *The Idiot*, translated by Richard Pevear and Larissa Volokhonsky (Everyman's Library, 2002), p. 407
72 Ibid., pp. 217–18   73 John 10.10
74 Hebrews 7.16

THE MYSTERY OF IDENTITY

in his hunger to dissolve himself in others, develops a pedagogical practice with destructive consequences for the wounded, ravenous, and 'unfinished' selves that grow up in his care."[75] The tutor is Stepan Trofimovich, who is in the habit of waking up his ten- or eleven-year-old charge, Nikolai Stavrogin, in the middle of the night to pour his own emotional distress into his heart so that it becomes his also. Stepan's failure to integrate his own interior life into a boundaried personal identity impedes the development of Nikolai's own consciousness and identity and teaches the latter a diabolic way of relating so that he ends up encircled by a "host of seemingly mesmerized interlocutors" who function "as extensions or echoes of his being."[76] Stepan himself has been taken over by Nikolai's mother, Vavara Petrovna, with whom he has a long-term platonic and financially dependent relationship. He is in practice a sort of extension of her identity—she even decides how he is to dress. He has a son, Pyotr Verkhovensky, with whom he has had very little contact before the latter turns up in the town.

When he does arrive there, Pyotr manipulates its whole society, bringing about mayhem, conflagration and murder. While not manifesting any personal emotional engagement with them, he manipulates the weakness of both revolutionaries and those in governance to produce massive destruction. Their absence of strong identity enables him to use them as extensions to himself. He binds a small revolutionary group to himself by involving them, against their better judgment, in a political murder and (literally) dictates the acceptance of responsibility for this to a man who has decided to, and finally does, commit suicide. The truth comes to light, but he has escaped by train leaving behind a very young follower who tells him, "I know you only do what's necessary for the common cause" and "you must preserve your person, because you're—everything, and we're—nothing"[77] and pathetically regrets that Pyotr does not press his hand more warmly.

Pyotr Verkhovensky treats those over whom he exerts power with insouciance, as evidenced in his cutting of his nails while a vital

---

[75] Yuri Corrigan, *Dostoevsky and the Riddle of the Self* (Northwestern University Press, 2017), p. 87
[76] Ibid., p. 86
[77] Fyodor Dostoevsky, *Demons*, translated by Richard Pevear and Larissa Volokhonsky (Vintage, 2006), p. 627

conference of conspirators is taking place.[78] There is one person, however, with whom he is intensely bonded: Nikolai Stavrogin. Nikolai learnt in his childhood from Pyotr's father to export his emptiness and is the son of his father's friend, Varvara Petrovna. Their relationship is diabolically unhealthy. As Rowan Williams puts it, "The face of the demonic in the novel is finally the two figures bound together, active and passive, devilish will incarnate in a body that is empty of the capacity for real willing."[79] Pyotr needs Nikolai to be the "Tsarevich," the one who will be the figurehead for his dominance of Russia, the identity of the movement he is master-minding. Nikolai sees someone very different from the insouciant person the conspirators see:

> This was not the same look, not the same voice as always, or as in the room just now; he saw almost a different face. The intonation of the voice was not the same: Verkhovensky was imploring, beseeching.[80]

Pyotr tells Nikolai later in the novel, "You are the light, the sun."[81] He even calls him, "my main half."[82] The distinction between Nikolai and the people Pyotr uses is brought home to him, to his fury, as he walks with one of the latter: himself occupying the pavement while the other has to walk in the muddy road. With his "main half" he himself walks in the mud, while Nikolai occupies "the entire sidewalk."[83] After all, Nikolai is the nearest thing he has to an identity. But Nikolai has no abundance of life to share; his self is not fully formed. In his final testimony he writes, "My desires are far too weak; they cannot guide."[84] He hangs himself. The narrator comments, "Everything indicated premeditation and consciousness to the last minute."[85] The sum of his deliberateness has opposed life. He has been bound up in a network of mutual possession that locks together the characters of the novel in the absence of, and flight from, personal identity.

---

78 Ibid., p. 402
79 Rowan Williams, *Dostoevsky: Language, Faith and Fiction* (Continuum, 2008), p. 106
80 Fyodor Dostoevsky, *Demons*, translated by Richard Pevear and Larissa Volokhonsky (Vintage, 2006), p. 416
81 Ibid., p. 528
82 Ibid., p. 533
83 Ibid., p. 552
84 Ibid., p. 675
85 Ibid., p. 678

They are possessive and possessed; they kill and destroy. This is the Devil's work and, as Rowan Williams aptly comments: "The Devil is out to stop history; he is the enemy of narrative and so of the freedom of persons to shape their identity over time."[86]

There is a glimmer of resistance in Stepan Trofimovich walking away from Vavara Petrovna at the end of his life to become a wandering pilgrim. His compulsive telling of "everything, from the very beginning"[87] to a woman gospel-seller with regard to whom he is perhaps "greatly exaggerating"[88] and his falling at her feet and kissing "the hem of her dress"[89] indicate that he has not won through to full personal autonomy. However, his dying conviction that the "whole law of human existence consists in nothing other than a man's always being able to bow before the immeasurably great" and his talk of the "immeasurable and infinite"[90] suggest that he has at least glimpsed its source. The novel as first written makes reference to the possibility of reaching personal autonomy through a relationship of guidance. In it, Nikolai goes to the spiritual elder Tikhon to make his confession. The latter was too shocking for publication and Dostoevsky revised the novel, but in the original draft Nikolai refuses guidance and, not being able to cope with Tikhon's spiritual insight, walks away from him. It is more difficult, though not impossible, to accept regenerative guidance when one is no longer a child. When one is, the guidance of a saint may not be necessary.

TRUE FATHERHOOD

Dostoevsky's view, expressed in his *Diary of a Writer*, was that even "the most fallen of fathers" could "transplant the seed of this great idea and great feeling into the impressionable souls of his pitiable children." Joseph Frank, who cites this in his biography of the author, glosses "great idea" as meaning "the idea of the Christian morality of love and the Christian promise of eternity" and speculates that Dostoevsky's "far from blameless father had nevertheless succeeded in planting these seeds in the hearts of his

---

[86] Rowan Williams, *Dostoevsky: Language, Faith and Fiction* (Continuum, 2008), p. 93
[87] Fyodor Dostoevsky, *Demons*, translated by Richard Pevear and Larissa Volokhonsky (Vintage, 2006), p. 647
[88] Ibid., p. 649   [89] Ibid., p. 651
[90] Ibid., p. 664

children."[91] The aforesaid idea makes the growth into a real personal identity possible for two reasons. It opens up the possibility of a loving relationship with others which does not use them by projecting what is dark and burdensome in one's interior life onto them, whether as friends who are bound by it or as enemies who are blamed for it, and concomitantly receiving a reciprocal recognition that is free of illusion and truthfully identifying. At the same time it gives the strength to take the risk of such truthful living through enabling a rooting in the infinite and eternal. So rooted, the individual enjoys an identity which is different from that of the other which neither needs to be co-opted or fought because it is essentially the same because springing from the same infinite source. The abundance of divine love is there for both and that very abundance gives an infinite quality to the individual identity which therefore does not need to make quantitative inroads into other identities. It is a fullness of identity: joyfully different, joyfully the same. It is a father's particular task to foster such. That does not need to be a biological father. Arkady, the eponymous adolescent in the Dostoevsky novel referred to above, longs for such from his father Versilov, but finds it in his adoptive father, Makar Ivanovich. He knows the quality of the man from his laughter, "the surest test of a soul," which he finds "childlike and incredibly attractive."[92] This is an indication of purity of heart, of being one who will see God,[93] and so of being one who can mediate the divine fathering of identity, of sameness and difference.

The Brothers Karamazov is the supreme meditation on fatherhood in Dostoevsky's work and, arguably, in all of modern fiction. While it was being written there was an assassination attempt on the life of the Tsar, the father of the Russian people, and multiple killings of officials of the regime. The book's context is parricidal rage. The man who killed the head of the secret service became a Russian teacher for Constance Garnett, the first translator of Dostoevsky's works into English. Dostoevsky died shortly after completing the novel and it was discovered that he and his family had been living

---

91 Joseph Frank, *Dostoevsky, A Writer in His Time* (Princeton University Press, 2010), p. 734
92 Fyodor Dostoevsky, *The Adolescent*, translated by Richard Pevear and Larissa Volokhonsky (Everyman's Library, 2003), p. 353
93 Cf. Matthew 5.8

next to an executive member of a terrorist organization, *Narodnaya Volya* (the People's Will). Its narrative circles around the killing of an ignoble, sensualist, and cynical father and at the trial of the person accused of it—Dmitri, one of his sons—the defense lawyer raises the question of whether such a father is even entitled to filial love, echoing the sense of the nation that the paternalist rule under which it labors is questionable. The novel can illustrate for us issues relating to the nurturing and growth of identity because it faces head-on questions about fathering. What hope is there of true fathering? Who will bring light to the sons and daughters of Mother Russia? Can people who have been wounded in childhood find a father who will repair the damage? Yuri Corrigan illuminates what the novel has to say about these questions and the account that follows is much indebted to him, though it is a presentation of my thought rather than his. He argues that all the offspring of the murdered father, Fyodor Karamazov, are carrying wounds from their earlier life and all of them are trying to escape their wounded self in compulsive relationships.[94] Dmitri is engaged to Katerina who is proud and controlling. Ivan, the intellectual among the brothers, is co-dependent with Smerdyakov, Fyodor's bastard son (as is thought). He has introduced Smerdyakov to atheist thinking and the idea that everything is permissible. The latter, in his capacity as lackey, takes his identity from Ivan, but Ivan becomes dependent on him, trying to find, futilely and furiously, his own thoughts and feelings by interrogating him. These desperate bondings are no more capable of fathering identity than those in the earlier novels. Dmitri breaks free of Katerina, whose manipulation is based on seizing the moral high ground at any cost, for another desperate—but more equal and honest—relationship with Grushenka. Katerina finally takes revenge when her testimony against him at his trial collapses from an extremely noble endorsement of his character to the hysterical presentation of circumstantial evidence that is fatal to his case. Huge suffering surrounds any quest that he can then make to find his true self. Ivan is bound into Smerdyakov's murder of their father at least by failing to stop Smerdyakov making the assumption that his own leaving of town was a positive response to Smerdyakov's implicit

[94] Yuri Corrigan, *Dostoevsky and the Riddle of the Self* (Northwestern University Press, 2017), Chapter Seven

Relationships & Reality

request for approval of the deed. When Smerdyakov (like Nikolai Stavrogin) hangs himself, Ivan—initially apparently the most independent of the brothers—suffers a total mental breakdown.

Alyosha, the youngest brother, and the one obviously favored by the persona of the story's narrator, is in an important respect different from his brothers and the characters in compulsive relationships in earlier Dostoevsky novels. Like them, he is looking to another to find himself, but that other does not want to take him over but rather to free him to live his own life in the world. He is under the direction of the monk and elder, Zosima. His choice of the monastic way of life is "only because it alone struck him at the time and presented him, so to speak, with an ideal way out for his soul struggling from the darkness of worldly wickedness towards the light of love."[95] Zosima is the elder to whom he is attached "with all the ardent first love of his unquenchable heart."[96] His soul is, in his own words, "bound" and "welded ... to this man."[97] The narrator explains the tradition in which this happens:

> An elder is one who takes your soul, your will into his soul, and into his will. Having chosen an elder, you renounce your will and give it to him under total obedience and with total self-renunciation. A man who dooms himself to this trial, this terrible school of life, does so voluntarily, in the hope that after the long trial he will achieve self-conquest, self-mastery to such a degree that he will, finally, through a whole life's obedience, attain to perfect freedom—that is, freedom from himself—and avoid the lot of those who live their whole life without finding themselves in themselves.[98]

This indicates both that Alyosha is trying to find himself through another and that he has a hope of indeed finding his true self in this way. Yet the compulsive dependency that is in his brothers' relationships is not altogether absent from this one. This is manifest in his hysterical reaction when Zosima dies and his body, contrary to the expectation of Alyosha and others, begins to decay. What is absent, however, is selfish manipulation by the

---

95 Fydor Dostoevsky, *The Brothers Karamazov* (Oxford University Press, 1994), Richard Pevear and Larissa Volokhonsky (Everyman's Library, 1997), p. 18
96 Ibid.   97 Ibid., p. 221
98 Ibid., pp. 27-28

object of his love. Zosima, discerning Alyosha's true path, has told him he is to leave the monastery and go out into the world. Even as he approaches death, he tells Alyosha to go and see his family as he has promised.

Zosima might have made his own his Lord's words, "It is for your advantage that I go away,"[99] for it is in the context of his death that Alyosha finds within himself the source of light and life which gives him an autonomous identity. This finding begins with prayer by the beloved elder's coffin. Somewhat distracted, Alyosha listens to the reading of the gospel over the body. It is the account of Jesus's first miracle, the turning of water into wine at the wedding at Cana. This is a symbol of the abundance of life that He brings and of the transformation of passing and mortal existence into eternal bliss. It speaks of course of what Zosima is entering into, but also of the unboundedness of what will spring up in Alyosha's soul. Significantly, Smerdyakov, the parricide, cannot stand poetry: the mere rationalism that he has learnt from Ivan cannot tolerate the enigmatic and unbounded. Alyosha, by contrast, finds that as he falls asleep to the words of the gospel he is in a room that is expanding: the mystery of infinity is coming to birth in his soul. Zosima is in his dream, "joyful and quietly laughing."[100] He invites Alyosha to join in merrymaking, saying, "We are drinking new wine, the wine of a new and great joy. See how many guests there are?" He enjoins Alyosha to take up his place in the world and points to the One who will make that possible:

> "Begin, my dear, begin my meek one, to do your work! And do you see our Sun, do you see him?"
>
> "I'm afraid ... I don't dare to look," whispered Alyosha.
>
> "Do not be afraid of Him. Awful is his greatness before us, terrible is his loftiness, yet he is boundlessly merciful, he became like us out of love, and he is rejoicing with us, transforming water into wine, that the joy of the guests may not end. He is waiting for new guests, he is ceaselessly calling new guests, now and unto ages of ages."[101]

---

99 John 16.7
100 Fydor Dostoevsky, *The Brothers Karamazov*, translated by Richard Pevear and Larissa Volokhonsky (Everyman's Library, 1997), p. 361
101 Ibid., pp. 361-62

In one sense Alyosha's dream is an expression of who he is: "spirit and soul and body,"[102] in the words of Saint Paul and in traditional anthropology. Spirit is indicated by the presence of Christ, his soul by Zosima who is its master, and body by his own physical presence. Yet there is an important difference between his dream and Ivan's nightmare (later in the story) in which the devil appears in an everyday, worldly form so that Ivan can plausibly call him, "my fantasy."[103] Christ in Alyosha's dream is the Other through whom and in relation to whom identity is found. Unlike Ivan, Alyosha is not bounded within a solipsistic self and when he awakes from the dream he is open to the infinite and the mysterious. He goes outside. "Filled with rapture, his soul yearned for freedom, space, vastness. Over him the heavenly dome, full of quiet, shining stars, hung boundlessly.... The silence of the earth seemed to merge with the silence of the heavens, the mystery of the earth touched the mystery of the stars."[104] True identity is openness to the infinite (an identification with all that is) and to mystery (difference from all that is): it is the image of God, infinite and mysterious, immanent and transcendent. Alyosha falls to the ground and kisses the earth, weeping and sobbing, following Zosima's injunction, "Water the earth with the tears of your joy." It is an experience of universal reconciliation:

> It was as if threads from all those innumerable worlds of God all came together in his soul, and it was trembling all over, "touching other worlds." He wanted to forgive everyone and for everything, and to ask forgiveness, oh, not for himself! but for all and for everything, "as others are asking for me," rang again in his soul.[105]

It is the moment when he reaches what Arkady, in *The Adolescent*, only stretches out towards: a mature identity. "He fell to the ground a weak youth and rose up a fighter, steadfast for the rest of his life, and he knew it and felt it suddenly, in that very moment of his ecstasy." This is made possible by the presence he knew in his dreams: "'Someone visited my soul in that hour,' he

---

102   1 Thessalonians 5.23
103   Fydor Dostoevsky, *The Brothers Karamazov*, translated by Richard Pevear and Larissa Volokhonsky (Everyman's Library, 1997), p. 642
104   Ibid., p. 362   105   Ibid.

would say afterwards, with firm belief in his words."[106] Christ has touched him.

Alyosha becomes in his turn one who can engender communion. The novel ends with him exhorting boys who have gathered after the funeral of one of them: "Well, let's go! And we go like this now, hand in hand," and receiving the response, "And eternally so, all our lives hand in hand!"[107] Alyosha is already in a sense a spiritual father. He can, like Zosima, echo the words of Saint Paul, "I became your father in Christ,"[108] echo the words of countless spiritual fathers and mothers through the ages who have passed on from generation to generation the way to winning a true identity.

FRIENDS IN CHRIST

It is not just parents, or those who take a parental role, who are involved in bringing about the visit of Christ to the soul: it is also friends. This is eloquently explained by St. Aelred of Rievaulx in his treatise, *Spiritual Friendship*. Although this is set in a monastic context, he is explicit that such friendship can also be between spouses.[109] Aelred sees human friendship as a way to friendship with Christ, beginning with the virtue He inspires and ending with His presence:

> In friendship, then, we join honesty with kindness, truth with joy, sweetness with good will, and affection with kind action. All this begins with Christ, is advanced through Christ, and is perfected in Christ. The ascent does not seem too steep or too unnatural, then, from Christ inspiring the love with which we love a friend to Christ's offering himself to us as the friend we may love, so that tenderness may yield to tenderness, sweetness to sweetness, and affection to affection. Hence a friend clinging to a friend in the spirit of Christ becomes *one heart and soul* with him. Thus mounting the steps of love to the friendship of Christ, a friend becomes one with him in the one kiss of the spirit.[110]

---

[106] Ibid., p. 363   [107] Ibid., p. 776
[108] 1 Corinthians 4.15
[109] Aelred of Rievaulx, *Spiritual Friendship*, translated by Lawrence C. Braceland (Liturgical Press, 2010), p. 66
[110] Ibid., p. 75

This is an opposite dynamic to that of the destructive relationships described in *The Idiot* and *Demons*. The reason destructive relationships do not form identity and good ones do is given clear expression by the philosopher, Robert Bolton:

> The illusory sense of the self which gives rise to evil can …be said to arise when the will's choices harden into unthinking compulsions. When this condition is dominant, it gives rise to what could deservedly be called 'the cosmic illusion.' The idea of an illusory identification of the self applies to the self in relation to things peripheral to itself or not personal at all, while the self-identifications involved in personal relationships, on the other hand, may or may not fall into this category. The more the relationship is based on shared values, the more free it must be from being a part of the cosmic illusion, because there would then be no question of self-identification with anything of a lower nature than that of the real self.[111]

Compulsions, such as those driving Dostoevsky's most wounded characters, make for an unreal sense of identity because in their narrowness and exclusion they fail to accord with the eternal law of open-hearted love written in the fabric of creation, but shared values, such as those spoken of by Aelred, take us towards being who we truly are because they open us to reality, nothing less than the whole of which is integral to our identity.

Christ offers a relationship based on ultimate shared values, absolutely free of cosmic illusion, promising, "You will know the truth and the truth will set you free."[112] He is both friend and father. He is our friend if we share His values, telling us, "You are my friends if you do what I command you"[113] and ready to make known to us all He has heard from His Father.[114] He is our Father since "whatever the Father does, that the Son does likewise"[115] and He can say, "Whoever has seen me has seen the Father."[116] He is, in the words of Origen, "the Father of every soul."[117] He gives us our identity.

What, then, is His identity?

---

[111] Robert Bolton, *Self and Spirit* (Sophia Perennis, 2005), pp. 41-42
[112] John 8.32   [113] John 15.14
[114] John 15.15   [115] John 5.19
[116] John 14.9
[117] Origen, *Prin.* 4.3.7, cited in *RB 1980* (Liturgical Press, 1981), p. 360

4
Christ & Conquering

INCARNATION

The recognition of identity, I said in Chapter Two, is sought for the sake of lives being meaningful. Money cannot truly buy meaning; politics in our day has become fraught with competing demands for meaningful recognition; sometimes personal relationships offer a recognition of identity that gives meaning to lives, sometimes they do not. If Christ is in the former category, what meaning does a relationship with Him offer? What does He mean?

Saint John's gospel answers by identifying Him as "The Word."[1] That is to say, He contains meaning as such. This is not simply a denotation of meaning such as a word gives, it is a giving of meaning to all that is. This is more than giving meaning to one's life in the way that, for example, Desdemona gives meaning to Othello's life. Though it certainly includes that, it is giving meaning as a concomitant of existence itself. He articulates life in the double sense of speaking its significance and joining its parts so that they work together. In God, the two are one: it is only fallen Man who speaks empty words. God, who speaks His eternal Word can say, "It shall not return to me empty, but it shall accomplish that which I purpose."[2] God's Word is "in the beginning," the primal source. God's Word is with God and is God.[3] God's Word is wholly creative. "All things were made through him, and without him was not any thing made that was made."[4] In Him is life and that life is "the light of men."[5] Life is light: it shows us what we mean, it shows us who we are. The articulation of the body is the articulation of meaning. As the French phenomenologist philosopher Merleau-Ponty has argued, metaphors from bodily existence establish meaning. Primordially, dance is sheer meaning. Meaninglessness is death (as with Othello), but death is not meaninglessness: "The light shines in the

---

[1] John 1.1 [2] Isaiah 55.11
[3] John 1.1 [4] John 1.3
[5] John 1.4

THE MYSTERY OF IDENTITY

darkness, and the darkness has not overcome it."[6] Christ has risen bodily from the dead; the Morning Star has shone upon us; the life that gives light is stronger than death.

If the body gives meaning and life gives light, why should there be any meaninglessness and death? Why should we need a Friend to enlighten us as to who we truly are, to enable us to realize our identity? The answer to both questions is: because of the mistaking of what shows for what is shown, of the sign for the reality, of the creation for the Creator. This is given Biblical expression in the story of the tower of Babel. When "the whole earth had one language and the same words"[7] everything on earth simply spoke of its Creator by virtue of being what it was, but people wanted to make a name for themselves,[8] to be themselves the source of meaning, to speak identity for themselves. This led to a fissiparous identity: the language that clothed it was no longer one and they began, as it were, to live on separate planets, in a state of mutual incomprehension. If "the LORD confused the language of all earth"[9] it was only because its inhabitants had withdrawn the attention of their hearts from the true source of meaning and sought significance in the mere signifier.

So meaning came among us: walked with us; ate with us; suffered with us. "The Word became flesh and dwelt among us."[10] The distinguished theologian Rowan Williams draws out the implications of this for our identity:

> The incarnation manifests the essential quality of the world itself as 'sign' or trace of its maker. It instructs us once and for all that we have our identity within the shifting, mobile realm of representation, non-finality, growing and learning, because it reveals what the spiritual eye ought to perceive generally—that the whole creation is uttered and 'meant' by God, and therefore has no meaning in itself.[11]

The incarnation, in other words, reminds us of and re-establishes for us our identity as given by God and saves us from the error of supposing that it is defined by the world (or its tokens, such

---

6 John 1.5
7 Genesis 11.1
8 Genesis 11.4
9 Genesis 11.9
10 John 1.14
11 Rowan Williams, *On Augustine* (Bloomsbury, 2016), p. 45

as cash) in itself. Rather, the world is the language through which we speak who we are, the words that point to what is beyond them, the envelope in which the card that announces the honors bestowed on us is concealed. The world—because it is defined by the parameters of time and space—is that which (under God) gives identity in its aspect of distinctness, reflecting but not replicating the absolute distinctness or uniqueness of the divine; God is the One who gives identity in its aspect of sameness, imaged in the being which each shares with all.

The incarnation does more than speak about what the world means: it shows us the fullness of meaning in the human body. Of course, these are intimately related: traditionally (and relatedly in modern physics in the form of the anthropic principle) the human body is a microcosm of the entire cosmos. God shows (in a veiled way) who He is through the world; God speaks or articulates who He is in the human body, above all in "this Jesus."[12] Incorporated in Christ, our bodies participate in both the distinctness of Jesus of Nazareth and the absolute self-identity of the eternal God. They cannot, however, show fully in this life who we are. They are like seeds. Each is "sown a natural body" and "raised a spiritual body."[13] Our body is a promise that we shall "bear the image of the man of heaven."[14] It is therefore worth considering in greater particularity how it expresses our identity.

A SOMATIC TERNARY

To know someone (other than in the Biblical, carnal) sense, one looks into her or his eyes. If we want to verify whether someone is telling the truth, we say, "Look me in the eyes and say that." The eye is as it were a window into the soul, the true life of a person. It is also the way a person receives what is true. Robert Bolton explains the relationship between eye and identity like this:

> The pupil of the eye performs a function on the physical level which aptly symbolizes that of the self, inasmuch as the latter is the nexus through which all experience and all kinds of knowledge must pass.[15]

---

12 Acts 2.23 13 1 Corinthians 15.44
14 1 Corinthians 15.49
15 Robert Bolton, *Self and Spirit* (Sophia Perennis, 2005), p. 2

THE MYSTERY OF IDENTITY

The eye, we can say, is I. It is no accident that the iris is used as a means of identification. "There's no art/ To find the mind's construction in the face,"[16] but the eye is a window into what is beyond outward appearance. Eyes express what is in the heart, as in Donne's love poem *The Extasie*: "Our eye-beams twisted, and did thred/ Our eyes upon one double string."[17] Through eyes, hearts become one. They express love through the dilation of the pupils. Looking and loving are linked, as when Jesus speaks with the rich young man and "looking at him, loved him."[18] His love-filled eyes show us who we are, as when:

> The Lord turned and looked at Peter. And Peter remembered the saying of the Lord, how he had said to him, "Before the rooster crows today, you will deny me three times." And he went out and wept bitterly.[19]

His eyes show us love and truth. They show us who He is. The incarnation shows us God and in doing so gives us our identity.

Yet the blind do not lack identity, only one way of mutually communicating it. The messenger is not the message. The message is in the heart. Even from an exterior, physical perspective, the heart can show who a person is. *The Economist* reported a system which is:

> able to measure, from up to 200 metres away, the minute vibrations induced in clothing by someone's heartbeat. Since hearts differ in both shape and contraction pattern, the details of heartbeats differ, too. The effect of this on the fabric of garments produces...a "heartprint"—a pattern reckoned sufficiently distinctive to confirm someone's identity.[20]

The heart embodies a person's essential identity. When Jesus says, "Learn from me, for I am gentle and lowly in heart,"[21] He is saying who He is: One who is so gentle and lowly in His heart that He does not pridefully oppose Himself to anything that is

---

16 *Macbeth*, Act 1, scene iv, ll.11-12
17 *The Metaphysical Poets*, introduced and edited by Helen Gardner (Penguin Books, 1971), p. 75
18 Mark 10.21   19 Luke 22.61-62
20 *The Economist*, January 25th-31st 2020, p. 72
21 Matthew 11.29

real or true. He is saying that He is truth itself. He is inviting us to learn from Him; He is showing us what our true identity is. True identity, because it has no false pride, resists no known truth. It is open to all that is, and therefore contains (spiritually) all that is. There is, metaphorically, an even deeper indication of identity than the heart. This is the eye of the heart. This is the will accepting all that the consciousness declares to be true. This is the marriage of truth and love, the final goal of the spiritual life, both identity of mind and heart, identity of eye and heart, and identity as such. This is the seeing heart. This is the openness of Man's inmost being to his Creator and to all that He has created. This is devotion welcoming all that God does. This is the kernel of prayer: "Thy will be done."

And this is the identity of the One who said, "My food is to do the will of him who sent me, and accomplish his work."[22] That work is the establishing of human identity. That identity is embodied above all—or, better, within all—in the Sacred Heart of Jesus, whose beat includes all in its love and which is the coincidence of love and truth. This is the ultimate intersectionality, the center where the vastness of creation is focused in a single heart, a single-hearted love, a love stronger than death. This is the identity that truly contains all, focuses all insight, encompasses all truth. The I that loves in this heart, the truth-seeing eye of this heart, is ultimate authenticity, absolute sincerity, perfect integrity. This I, the eye of this heart, is universal identity. Here subjectivity and objectivity are one, here the all-loving heart is in exquisite harmony with the all-seeing eye, here the longing of all humanity kisses the reality of all that is manifest. The whole is in the whole-heartedness of this heart. The essence of all creation is enshrined here, the meaning of every word is revealed here, the joy that beckons through every desire is given here. And from this heart come forth "blood and water,"[23] comes forth love, which my God feels as blood but I as wine,[24] comes forth living water whoever drinks which will never thirst again.[25] United to this heart our hearts are a source of "rivers of living water"[26] since

---

22 John 4.34   23 John 19.34
24 George Herbert in *The Metaphysical Poets*, introduced and edited by Helen Gardner (Penguin Books, 1971), p. 120
25 John 4.14   26 John 7.38

THE MYSTERY OF IDENTITY

"God's love has been poured in our hearts through the Holy Spirit who has been given to us."[27]

The heart, the essence of a person's life, includes others through a loving gaze, whether of the eyes or—more intuitively—of the eye of the heart. It identifies with them, as Christ identifies with the suffering, saying:

> I was hungry and you gave me food, I was thirsty and you gave me drink, I was a stranger and you welcomed me, I was naked and you clothed me, I was sick and you visited me, I was in prison and you came to me.[28]

In doing this the heart shares in the universal identification, the universal identity, of the Sacred Heart. It shares in the life of God which is the source of universal identity since all alike are kept in being by His life. It shares the blessing God gives, which is His unique identity since no gaze is like His, since the manner of each heart's looking is in its way unique. And that blessing is given not by gaze only, but also by voice: the gaze receives and includes the other's identity in the heart; the voice expresses and sends the identity of the heart. This is more primary than the look, for it reaches the child in the womb which the look cannot. It conveys faith in love—the love that is God—since "faith comes from hearing."[29] It is no accident that the reading of sacred texts in worship—for example, in the monastic office of Vigils and in the Mass—is not replaced by an overhead projection of words that worshippers can take in with a sweep of their eyes. God incarnate teaches through His voice. The Good Shepherd goes before His flock "and the sheep follow him, for they know his voice."[30] The voice expresses identity, and like the iris and the heartprint it can be a technical means of identification. It can also be a personal means of identification. That is common enough with phone calls, but I remember also recognizing at an airport a friend whom I had not seen for something like thirty years through his voice: his appearance had so changed over time that he did not stand out from the welcoming party, but his voice did. Another friend, who sings, wrote this:

---

27 Romans 5.5
29 Romans 10.17
28 Matthew 25.35–36
30 John 10.4

> My teacher has been working with me to help identify my own sound instead of the generic 'singing voice' that I had been aiming for—which feels both liberating and scary at the same time. In terms of singing the voice is a really unique instrument, in the sense that it's so personal, so tied to everything that's going on inside mentally and physically. And our hearing is so tuned to pick up every emotional nuance of the human voice that singing makes you feel very vulnerable on some level. It's interesting how almost everyone hates to hear recordings of their own voice, and I'm sure it's in part because it makes us feel exposed in ways we would rather we could hide.

In other words, our voice shows who we are. It gives shape to our identity, or at least to our own and other people's sense of our identity.

So we have a ternary: eye, voice, heart—these three. The body is who we are in the sense of being unique and different, and in the sense of being limited, for uniqueness and difference in this world of space and time entails that limitation, and these three show our identification with all that is, our identity in the sense of sameness, for the eye, which sees all, images the omniscience of God the Father; the voice, which speaks to everyone, images God the Son who speaks all the Father has to say; the heart, which cherishes all, images the Holy Spirit who is love and the Spirit of all truth. The body in its frailty gives us our particular and personal life; the Spirit in its transcendence enables us to share in universal and divine life; our loving and our knowing (in persons of integrity they are integrated) is where the body and the spirit touch each other and so, somatically, they embrace in the heart. The eye, looking lovingly, shows the heart and receives the truth into it; the voice "speaking the truth in love"[31] expresses what is in the heart. Together they participate in the identity of God which is always different, always the same.

THE STORY OF IDENTITY

This showing of identity takes place in time: as Rowan Williams observes, "the shaping of a sense of self is a narrative business" and "the passage of time is inscribed in our knowing (of ourselves

---

31 Ephesians 4.15

THE MYSTERY OF IDENTITY

and of our world)."[32] And so identity is a story. It is the story of the Son of Man. He is humanity as such and His story is Man's story. His birth in time is the source of difference, gives His life its particularity; His eternal birth makes Him "the same yesterday and today and forever."[33] The Lord of all, come into time, does battle—in time and over time—for the identity of all of humanity: the identity that makes us "children of God,"[34] sharers in the immutable and eternal, and, yet, in no way exempt from "the heart-ache and thousand natural shocks/ That flesh is heir to,"[35] except that He shares them with us. This human identity is given in the incarnation, but it is not simply delivered with the baby; it is claimed and conquered through the changes and challenges of time. Although it is intrinsic, it is won in the sense that it is triumphantly defended from the forces that would warp it.

Any true identity comes from God. It is the special work of the young to renew the absolute and eternal basis of identity. That is why they are characteristically idealistic, whether in a wholesome or extremist way. The mere form, inherited from their folk, will not satisfy. It needs to be transcendentally verified. So it is that Jesus does not simply go along with His family. He stays behind in Jerusalem when they go back from attending the Feast of the Passover there, so they go back to look for Him.

> After three days they found him in the temple, sitting among the teachers, listening to them and asking them questions. And all who heard him were amazed at his understanding and his answers. And when his parents saw him, they were astonished. And his mother said to him, "Son, why have you treated us so? Behold, your father and I have been searching for you in great distress." And he said to them, "Why were you looking for me? Did you not know that I must be in my Father's house?" And they did not understand the saying that he spoke to them.[36]

This is the beginning of the work of winning identity. His primary relation is with God His Father. He works out the truth about this in listening and questioning the learned in divine law. It is

---

32 Rowan Williams, *On Augustine* (Bloomsbury, 2016), p. ix
33 Hebrews 13.8   34 1 John 3.1
35 *Hamlet*, Act 3, scene i, ll.61-62   36 Luke 2.46-49

necessary for the maturity of His identity. Its establishment takes priority over avoiding the discomfiture of His people. The same priority is enjoined on His followers, when He makes loving Him more than father or mother a condition of being such. This is so because He is the way to the Father.[37] His relationship to the Father is a mystery to His parents: they do not understand it. It is the mystery of identity, which necessarily opens to the infinite and the eternal and so to what is beyond comprehension in the double sense of being clear and being included. It is the mystery of human identity, whose enemies He here begins to conquer, starting with human respect, even that of His own nurturing family. He is to face a far more formidable enemy, "the dread and intelligent spirit, the spirit of self-destruction and non-being" (in Dostoevsky's words),[38] but before that His identity receives affirmation—from a man of God and then directly from God. That affirmation is first of all of His particular identity; but it is concomitantly an affirmation of human identity as such, for He identifies with all and invites all to participate in His life. It shows that human identity comes from God. This identity is gifted, though that gifting does not absolve from struggle any more than being appointed a general dispenses from fighting. It does, however, show what the struggle is about.

John the Baptist, man of God, identifies Jesus as "the Lamb of God."[39] This evokes the prophecy of Isaiah, "He was oppressed, and he was afflicted, yet he opened not his mouth; like a lamb that is led to the slaughter."[40] The identity has a double aspect: that of frailty, of being subject to contingency, of vulnerability and that of divine immutability, of being in the beginning, of living eternally. Such is human identity: limited in time and space yet open to the infinite and to mystery. The struggle of Christ, undertaken for us His adopted siblings, is to accept the frailty of limitation without transposing immutability where it does not belong by making an idol of what passes, an absolute of what can only point beyond itself to the true absolute. This work, the work of Christ and so of His followers, is only possible

---

37 Cf. Matthew 10.37; John 14.6
38 Fydor Dostoevsky, *The Brothers Karamazov*, translated by Richard Pevear and Larissa Volokhonsky (Everyman's Library, 1997), p. 251
39 John 1.29   40 Isaiah 53.7

THE MYSTERY OF IDENTITY

in the knowledge of being beloved of God: the conviction that if payment is not made in the coin of this world eternal riches will follow, the faith that "for those who love God all things work together for good."[41] Without this love, frailty provokes panic and a sense of futility. This love is manifest when John has baptized Him and He is praying and:

> The heavens were opened, and the Holy Spirit descended on him in bodily form, like a dove; and a voice came from heaven, "You are my beloved Son; with you I am well pleased."[42]

The prayer is Jesus in loving communion with His heavenly Father; the opening of the heavens is the showing of infinite mystery; the Holy Spirit is the love that gives every human trial untold meaning and value. The declaration of this love, the identification of Jesus as "beloved," is for humanity as such: those formally incorporated in His life and those whom He identifies with simply by sharing their humanity alike. The boy's seeking in the temple has become the man's finding of the mystery of God's absolute love.

This Man's work is now to bring humanity to that love by believing in and reciprocating it without reserve, acting in the person of humanity to trust and be entrusted to it. The love itself begins this work, for it is nothing other than the Spirit which "immediately drove him out into the wilderness."[43] At stake is His relationship to the Father. That is given in the sense that the Father's love is always and eternally there, but it is not yet accomplished in the sense that His whole life has not yet been lived with an unswerving adhesion to the principle, "whatever the Father does, that the Son does likewise,"[44] and He has not yet been able to say of His life's work and mission, "It is finished."[45]

TEMPTATION IN THE DESERT

John Milton in *Paradise Regained*, his sequel to *Paradise Lost*, locates its accomplishment in the resisting of Satan's temptations in the desert. His song is of:

---

41 Romans 8.28
43 Mark 1.12
45 John 19.30

42 Luke 3.21-22
44 John 5.19

> Recovered Paradise to all mankind,
> By one man's firm obedience fully tried
> Through all temptation, and the tempter foiled
> In all his wiles, defeated and repulsed,
> And Eden raised in the waste wilderness.[46]

Angelic choirs celebrate this as a remaining true to His identity:

> True image of the Father, whether throned
> In the bosom of bliss, and light of light
> Conceiving, or remote from heaven, enshrined
> In fleshly tabernacle, and human form,
> Wandering the wilderness, whatever place,
> Habit, or state, or motion, still expressing
> The Son of God.[47]

In Milton's account, He receives this identity first from His mother, who tells him:

> Thy father is the eternal King, who rules
> All heaven and earth, angels and sons of men.[48]

He confirms it by searching the scriptures for "what was writ/ Concerning the Messiah"[49] so when his Father's voice pronounces Him "his beloved Son, in whom alone/ He was well pleased"[50] it is not a revelation of what is unknown to Him but rather an indication that He should no longer be unknown. To prepare for His public exercise of divine authority, His sense of identity is made strong by combat with the devil who would sow "distrust"[51] of His Father's providential and affirming love. He gains this identity not from "the people's praise"[52] but from God, who:

> Looking on the earth, with approbation marks
> The just man, and divulges him through heaven
> To all his angels, who with true applause
> Recount his praises; thus he did to Job.[53]

---

46 John Milton, *Paradise Regained*, Book One, ll.3-7 in *Milton: Complete Shorter Poems*, edited by John Carey (Longman, 1971)
47 Ibid., Book Four, ll.596–602   48 Ibid., Book One, ll.236-37
49 Ibid., Book One, ll.260–61   50 Ibid., Book One, ll.285-86
51 Ibid., Book One, l.355   52 Ibid., Book Three, l.48
53 Ibid., Book Three, ll.61-64

Job gave glory to God by refusing to curse Him even in the midst of great afflictions. By being faithful to His bond with the Father even in agony, the Savior does likewise. Giving glory to God is constitutive of His declaration of identity. He does not seek it for himself, asking and answering a rhetorical question:

> Shall I seek glory then, as vain men seek
> Oft not deserved? I seek not mine, but his
> Who sent me, and thereby witness whence I am.[54]

He is proof against the devil's questioning of "in what degree or meaning" He is the Son of God in order to introduce ambiguity into His identity. The good angels can tell him that "by vanquishing temptation" He has "regained lost Paradise."[55]

Milton is of course giving an incomplete account of the regaining of Paradise: his version of the story locates it in the firming up of Christ's steadfastness in preparation for His mission. This may be the seed of His soteriological triumph, but there is far more struggle to come. Yet the temptations in the desert do contain a struggle on behalf of true identity, not only for Him but for all humanity in the ages that are to follow. The point is made forcibly by Dostoevsky. "The Grand Inquisitor" in the parable of that name in *The Brothers Karamazov* tells Christ that "in these three questions all of subsequent human history is as if brought together into a single whole and foretold; three images are revealed that will take in all the insoluble historical contradictions of human nature over all the earth."[56] Dostoevsky sees the rejection of the temptations as a defense of the freedom of humanity. A key theme in his writing is the central importance to humankind of free will: his characters often act even against their own interests to assert this. The psychology of this is articulated by the narrator of *Notes from Underground*:

> Man may purposely, consciously wish for himself even the harmful, the stupid, even what is stupidest of all... so as *to have the right* to wish for himself even what is stupidest of all and not be bound by an obligation to wish for himself only what is intelligent... because in any event

---

54   Ibid., Book Three, ll.105-7   55   Ibid., Book Four, ll.607-8
56   Fydor Dostoevsky, *The Brothers Karamazov* (Oxford University Press, 1994), translated by Richard Pevear and Larissa Volokhonsky (Everyman's Library, 1997), p. 252

it preserves for us the chiefest and dearest thing, that is, our personality and individuality.[57]

The Inquisitor argues the opposite case, telling Christ that He rejected the forces of "miracle, mystery, and authority" and "gave [Himself] as an example of that."[58] The former sees these as the forces which alone are "capable of conquering and holding captive forever the conscience"[59] and so take away human freedom for the sake (as he sees it) of human welfare. His discourse is a prophetic anticipation of the claim of communism: that feeding people justifies controlling them. The Inquisitor, who is on the devil's side, would limit human good to this world. As Rowan Williams points out in his book on Dostoevsky: "A central element in the diabolical strategy is always going to be the undermining of belief in immortality, as a way of forcing people toward the conviction that all value depends on the choice of the will and no more." This enthroning of what the will chooses leads to "an essentially *abstract* view of what counts as human happiness, since it has no ground for affirming the unique value of each person; the result of this is the mentality that can contemplate with equanimity the mass slaughter of human beings in the name of the general good." The point is that "the demonic always 'de-realizes' or 'disincarnates.'"[60] The incarnation of Christ stands against this and Christ's rejection of the devil's temptations wins freedom for humanity, an establishment of the truth of human identity, a declaration to those who believe in Him that "you will know the truth, and the truth will set you free."[61]

This truth, denied by the devil and his acolytes, is that human identity is essentially open. A human person is limited by space and time because living bodily in this world—that is to say, from a sublunary perspective uniquely different; but is also capable of identifying with all that is—that is to say, from an eternal perspective the same as all reality, infinite in its scope, sharing in the divine. Hamlet acknowledges this latter aspect of identity

---

57 Fyodor Dostoevsky, *Notes from Underground*, translated by Richard Pevear and Larissa Volokhonsky (Everyman's Library, 2004), pp. 27-28
58 Fydor Dostoevsky, *The Brothers Karamazov* (Oxford University Press, 1994), translated by Richard Pevear and Larissa Volokhonsky (Everyman's Library, 1997), p. 255   59 Ibid.
60 Rowan Williams, *Dostoevsky: Language, Faith and Fiction* (Continuum, 2008), p. 82   61 John 8.32

THE MYSTERY OF IDENTITY

even as he struggles with loss of joy in it, saying:

> What a piece of work is a man, how noble in reason, how infinite in faculties, in form and moving, how express and admirable in action, how like an angel in apprehension, how like a god![62]

It is the truth underpinning the traditional Jewish saying that he who saves a life saves the world. A human person is never *only* part of the world; he or she is *also* the whole of the world, of creation and even—by participation—the whole life of God. Christ's resistance of each temptation in the wilderness defends and asserts this openness to all that the devil would foreclose. We may waver or be in error about our true identity, but "if we are faithless, he remains faithful—for he cannot deny himself."[63] He knows that He is the beloved Son of the Father and that His mission is to direct all things to Him, so that God—Infinite Possibility—may be "all in all,"[64] so that everything speaks of what is beyond it: the smallest flower of uncreated beauty; the cosmos of its Creator and the human person of both these.

The first temptation of Christ comes to Him when He is hungry and the devil says to Him, "If you are the Son of God, command these stones to become loaves of bread."[65] The strong and necessary urge to eat is proposed as a master and not a servant, as a goal and not a means, as the final end for His divine power. To accept this proposal would be to see human aspiration as finite and so human value as ultimately nugatory; it would be to foreclose the mystery in human identity; it would reduce human life to mere quantity of provision. Christ has no difficulty with multiplying loaves, but to those who think that is what He is there for—in other words that feeding is the fulfillment of human identity, the identifying mark of our destiny—He says:

> Truly, truly, I say to you, you are seeking me, not because you saw signs, but because you ate your fill of the loaves. Do not work for the food that perishes, but for the food that endures to eternal life, which the Son of Man will give you.[66]

---

[62] Act 2, scene ii, ll.303-7
[63] 2 Timothy 2.13
[64] 1 Corinthians 15.28
[65] Matthew 4.2-3
[66] John 6.26-27

He has another food: "to do the will of him who sent me and to accomplish his work."[67] This is "the food that endures to eternal life"; this is being open to the infinite; this is being in a relationship with the Father which signals who we truly are. And so Christ responds to the devil with words of Scripture: "Man shall not live by bread alone, but by every word that comes from the mouth of God."[68] Man lives not by his stomach only, for that cannot be his god, but by God's word of love spoken to His people of whom He said, "I will allure her, and bring her into the wilderness, and speak tenderly to her."[69] It is an eternal word, "for his steadfast love endures forever!"[70] It is this word, speaking more loudly than his hunger, which Christ hears in the desert on behalf of all humanity so that we may know that we are children of God destined to a life unbounded by constraints of time and place.

The next temptation (in Matthew's account) also tries to constrain Christ within the bounded life of this world. It is a temptation not to be the person who can say, "I do not receive glory from people,"[71] the temptation to make an impression in this world, to cash in or monetize His divinity in dividends of fame. As is characteristic of the devil's temptations of those who are committed to God, it claims a divine inspiration:

> The devil took him to the holy city and set him on the pinnacle of the temple and said to him, "If you are the Son of God, throw yourself down, for it is written, 'He will command his angels concerning you,' and 'On their hands they will bear you up, lest you strike your foot against a stone.'"[72]

The devil interprets the psalm as promising protection in this-worldly terms. It is twisted towards triumph in time and space, passing over the fact that it also says, "You have made the LORD your dwelling place."[73] It tries to obscure the truth that Christ belongs to "the Jerusalem above,"[74] not that below. The Grand Inquisitor, who is in a sense the devil's spokesman, sees clearly the implication of his interpretation of the psalm. He says to Christ:

67	John 4.34	68	Matthew 4.4
69	Hosea 2.14	70	Psalm 118.29
71	John 5.41	72	Matthew 4.5-6
73	Psalm 91.9	74	Galatians 4.26

"You did not come down from the cross when they shouted to you, mocking and reviling you: 'Come down from the cross and we will believe that it is you.' You did not come down because, again, you did not want to enslave man by a miracle and thirsted for faith that is free, not miraculous. You thirsted for love that is free, and not for the servile raptures of a slave before a power that has left him permanently terrified."[75]

Christ's rejecting the devil's temptation of seeking special protection in this world makes His heart steadfast for the baptism with which He is to be baptized, the cup He is to drink, the sacrifice He is to offer. The desert anticipates Gethsemane. And when His hour is come He quotes a psalm like the devil, but His quotation has a very different import. He prays, "My God, my God, why have you forsaken me?"[76] His comfort, His solace, His divine bliss is not in the limitations of this world, where He has "no lasting city."[77] He has set his mind on "the things that are above."[78] In this, He is "the founder and perfecter of our faith"[79]—the faith that we have no need to lock our aspirations into what passes or to estimate ourselves according to the territory we can dominate for, although our identity is grown in time and space, this vale of soul-making, its fruition is in the abundance that knows no end or limit: the great and glorious day of His resurrection, the eternal Sabbath, the heavenly Jerusalem.

His rejection of the temptation to disbelieve that "for those who love God all things work together for good, for those who are called to his purpose"[80]—that is, His resolution to accept obscurity and, ultimately, shameful death—takes the form of letting God be God, unmanipulated, uninstrumentalized. In the desert, where it is first presented to Him, He gives the devil His own scriptural citation, "Again it is written, 'You shall not put the Lord your God to the test.'"[81] God is an end, not a means: our joy, not our way of making ourselves look good by such feats as being

---

[75] Fydor Dostoevsky, *The Brothers Karamazov* (Oxford University Press, 1994), translated by Richard Pevear and Larissa Volokhonsky (Everyman's Library, 1997), p. 256
[76] Matthew 27.46
[77] Hebrews 13.14
[78] Colossians 3.1
[79] Hebrews 12.2
[80] Romans 8.28
[81] Matthew 4.7

miraculously rescued. Christ "endured the cross, despising the shame" because of "the joy that was set before him."[82] A purehearted joy in His heavenly Father enabled Him to turn aside from any show of privilege, either in the desert or at Calvary. His Father's will is the only nourisher of Christ's soul: He will not try to bend it to a different purpose. The devil fails to divert Him from the source of His identity.

The final temptation is to settle for dominance in this world, ignoring the spiritual source of this:

> Again, the devil took him to a very high mountain and showed him all the kingdoms of the world and their glory. And he said to him, "All these I will give you, if you will fall down and worship me."[83]

Again, it is a temptation to receive glory from people. More fundamentally, it is a temptation to live in the finite. The kingdoms of the world do not exceed the boundaries of the world and in time no more will remain of their glory than shattered fragments in "the lone and level sands."[84] To give way to this temptation would be to accept a limited identity, an identity limited to space and time and to allow the evil one to frustrate true and eternal identity which opens not only to all that is but to its very source. Ultimately, it includes this source, for it involves becoming one out of whose heart "will flow rivers of living water."[85] Christ points the way to it with His words of dismissal:

> Be gone, Satan! For it is written, "You shall worship the Lord your God and him only shall you serve."[86]

True identity involves worship because it reaches out to all that is and to its source. This identity is both living in the limitation of the flesh and being illuminated by the light that is the beginning and making manifest of all creation.[87] More than that, it is trusting openness to the darkness that is before and beyond all creation: the very mystery of God. That is why it cannot be satisfied with the trappings of power belonging to this world, why it sometimes

---

82 Hebrews 12.2   83 Matthew 4.8-9
84 Percy Bysshe Shelley, "Ozymandias" in *The Norton Anthology of Poetry* (Norton, 1970), p. 619
85 John 7.38   86 Matthew 4.10
87 Genesis 1.3

THE MYSTERY OF IDENTITY

presents itself in the guise of "one from whom men hide their faces,"[88] why Jesus says to Pilate, "My kingdom is not of this world."[89] In the context of this assertion of identity, Satan has no place, so "the devil left him, and behold, angels came and were ministering to him."[90] These "angels and ministers of grace"[91] are a sign of where His true identity is: "seated at the right hand of God."[92] In rejecting temptations against it, He has (in the words of a scholar's description of Dostoevsky's understanding of the narrative) begun His mission "to safeguard the liberty of human conscience and preserve humankind from enslavement to external and material forces";[93] He has begun to win the identity of the New Adam, the One who obeys the Father; He is ready to show who Man can be, a child of God.

WHO DO YOU SAY THAT I AM?

That does not mean that Man knows who He is. The people of "Nazareth, where he had been brought up"[94] do not believe Him when He says, "The Spirit of the Lord is upon me."[95] They say confidently, "Is not this Joseph's son?"[96] not knowing that He was conceived in His mother as a child "from the Holy Spirit."[97] This same Spirit leads Him into the desert, leads Him to the defense and establishment of His identity. This same Spirit communicates His identity, for He and the Father are one (as He says)[98] and the Spirit is the love between Him and the Father, the knowledge that He and the Father have of each other, their bonding. The Spirit makes them one, expresses their identity with each other. That is reciprocal, for Jesus can say, "Whoever has seen me has seen the Father."[99]

If "God is light"[100] then He is knowledge and understanding (for that is what light gives and, symbolically, shows); if "God is love"[101] then love is, at its deepest, knowledge, for God cannot

---

[88] Isaiah 53.3
[89] John 18.36
[90] Matthew 4.11
[91] *Hamlet*, Act 1, scene iv, l. 39
[92] Colossians 3.1
[93] Joseph Frank, *Dostoevsky, A Writer in His Time* (Princeton University Press, 2010), p. 772
[94] Luke 4.16
[95] Luke 4.18
[96] Luke 4.22
[97] Matthew 1.20
[98] John 10.30
[99] John 14.9
[100] 1 John 1.5
[101] 1 John 4.8

be divided. Truly to know, therefore, is to love and to love truly is to understand, which is precisely what the father of lies cannot do. To know everything, as the French say, is to forgive everything; the Omniscient is the All-Merciful, the perfectly just is the One who forgives. His identity extends to identifying with sinners, for Christ was made sin for our sake.[102] When God, "the Father of mercies,"[103] pours forth the Spirit into the world through the death and resurrection of His Son, He gives identity to those who have lost or tarnished it: the Spirit gives meaning to our lives by identifying them with the life of His Beloved Son, making them like adopted children being given the family name. The Spirit expresses the Father's love for us, identifying us as His children. "See what kind of love the Father has given to us," exclaims Saint John, "that we should be called children of God; and so we are."[104] Having the "right to become children of God" we are "born, not of blood nor of the will of the flesh nor of the will of man, but of God."[105] This birth from above identifies us with the Father through the Spirit. This Spirit, identifying the Son and those incorporated in His life, with the Father, is in a sense identity as such: the Spirit "hovering over the face of the waters" gives primordial identity to that which "was without form and void";[106] the Spirit makes us "a new creation" in Christ.[107] The quest for identity is the quest for the Holy Spirit, the treasure of these earthen vessels, the bond of the life of this fragile and circumscribed clay with the infinite glory of the Eternal One, the anointing of our impotence by the Omnipotent.

This being co-opted into Christ's identity, this becoming adopted sons and daughters of the Father, this gifting of the Spirit is possible because of Christ's winning of His identity. He wins it in the sense of living it: although given from conception, it is not a static object but realized in the flux of time and the society of people. Because that identity is from above, it is not recognized by the people of Nazareth, for "no prophet is acceptable in his hometown."[108] His task includes getting it recognized. In winning it, and winning recognition for it, He acts for all who share in

---

[102] 2 Corinthians 5.21
[103] 2 Corinthians 1.3
[104] 1 John 3.1
[105] John 1.12-13
[106] Genesis 1.2
[107] 2 Corinthians 5.17
[108] Luke 4.24

THE MYSTERY OF IDENTITY

His life as priest, prophet and king. His mission effectively extends to identity as such, since:

> He is the image of the invisible God, the firstborn of all creation. For by him all things were created, in heaven and on earth, visible and invisible, whether thrones or dominions or rulers or authorities—all things were created through him and for him. And he is before all things, and in him all things hold together.[109]

In being the One by whom "all things were created" He gives them their identity and is Himself identified with the Spirit "hovering over the face of the waters"[110] at the creation of the world and is therefore identified with identity as such. As Rowan Williams observes, "the eternity of God involves absolute self-identity."[111] God sources identity and has no need of it from beyond Himself. Christ, therefore, not only shows the Father to humanity, but also speaks the Spirit. His words are "spirit and life."[112] Williams, presenting Saint Augustine's teaching, observes, "We may say that the answer to 'Who is speaking?' where Christ is concerned is always *sapientia*."[113] He is Wisdom, "the Spirit of truth,"[114] the love through which all is made.

Christ's great work of living, showing, and speaking human identity can only bear fruit in the renewal of humanity if His own identity is recognized. If He is not known, He cannot be made known; if He is not made known, He cannot communicate His identity. The question of who He is therefore becomes *critical* in the strongest sense of the word. To those arguing with Him about His paternity, He says, "You are from below; I am from above. You are of this world; I am not of this world."[115] The essential is to recognize Him as the One sent from heaven; He tells them, "Unless you believe that I am he you will die in your sins."[116] That is to say, they will frustrate their true being by limiting themselves to the things of this earth as though these could satisfy the infinite yearning of their hearts, unless they

---

109 Colossians 1.15-17   110 Genesis 1.2
111 Rowan Williams, *On Augustine* (Bloomsbury, 2016), p. 180
112 John 6.63
113 Williams, *On Augustine*, pp. 148-49
114 John 16.13   115 John 8.23
116 John 8.24

recognize that they are being offered an identity that opens up to eternity through the person of Jesus. A seeming familiarity with Jesus blinds "some of the people of Jerusalem"[117] to this identity oriented to eternity, so He makes it explicit:

> "You know me, and you know where I come from. But I have not come of my own accord. He who sent me is true, and him you do not know. I know him, for I come from him, and he sent me."[118]

This meets with a divided response, with some "seeking to arrest him"[119] but "many of the people"[120] believing in Him, and so being open to heaven-sent identity. The essence of this is that it is from another: Jesus does not come of His "own accord," He is "sent." For both Jesus and His followers, the struggle for true identity will be in the giving up of ownership, the readiness to receive, the acceptance of gift. The mystery of identity eludes those who want to be in control of it, as Jesus slips away from His enemies until His hour is come.

Those who do not cling to the attempt to be in control, who truly follow Jesus, are represented by Peter, who is told, "Another will dress you and carry you where you do not want to go."[121] He learns and grows into this identity which is suffered rather than acted, received rather than grasped, given from the super-abundance of eternity rather than the constraints of time. Its essence is that it is from above. It is the connection with what is above which makes possible its recognition. When Jesus asks, "Who do you say that I am?" Peter replies, "You are the Christ, the son of the living God." And he is told, "Blessed are you... For flesh and blood has not revealed this to you, but my Father who is in heaven."[122] Unlike those who see Jesus simply as a prophet—or, like Herod, as John the Baptist[123]—Peter is open to what is beyond this world, to God who is the source of identity. However, at this point he has yet to learn that a concomitant of a life given identity by heaven is that it is not necessarily what the world identifies as a good life. That is to say that it is not a life of worldly comfort and safety.

---

117 John 7.25
119 John 7.30
121 John 21.18
123 Mark 6.14-16

118 John 7.28-29
120 John 7.31
122 Matthew 16.15-17

THE MYSTERY OF IDENTITY

So when Jesus explains that He is to "suffer many things" and be killed, Peter rebukes Him saying, "This shall never happen to you, Lord!" He needs to be taught what Jesus defended in the desert: an identity that does not seek dominion in this world. He needs to know that Satan, the enemy of God and man, wants to divert human aspiration from heaven, to make it infernally inspired so that the heart made for the infinite is locked in the limited. Hence Jesus—for the sake of teaching—identifies Peter with the one whose project he has adopted, telling him, "Get behind me, Satan!"[124] He makes this acceptance of what is contrary to mere worldly satisfaction a general instruction, saying, "If anyone would come after me, let him deny himself and take up his cross and follow me."[125] To learn from Him who we are, we need to follow it.

TRANSFIGURATION

Immediately after the development of this teaching in Matthew's gospel there follows a direct presentation of Jesus's heavenly identity, as if to highlight that the cross—for Him and His followers—is an opening to glory rather than a final ignominy:

> Jesus took with him Peter and James, and John his brother, and led them up a high mountain by themselves. And he was transfigured before them, and his face shone like the sun, and his clothes became as white as light.[126]

Peter, James, and John are key witnesses to the identity of Jesus. Letters in the New Testament are attributed to all three. Peter, as leader, has already been given a divine inspiration about who He is, and the second letter of Peter explicitly refers to being "eyewitnesses to his majesty" and being "with him on the holy mountain."[127] The letter of James reiterates the teaching about the value of taking up one's cross that immediately precedes the account of the transfiguration in Matthew's gospel: "Count it all joy, my brothers, when you meet trials of various kinds."[128] The first letter of John teaches that "God is light,"[129] which links the transfiguration of Jesus (His face shining like the sun, His clothes as white as light) to His divinity. Light is significant, for it is through

---

124 Matthew 16.21-23
125 Matthew 16.24
126 Matthew 17.1-2
127 2 Peter 1.16, 18
128 James 1.2
129 1 John 1.5

light that everything is seen. Light symbolizes the universal aspect of identity, the capacity to identify with all that is, which comes from God and, in its fullness, simply is God. This is identity in the sense of being the same as the other, its open or heavenly aspect. It is only truly identity when it is linked to identity in the sense of being different or unique, its limited or earthly aspect. As applied to God, this aspect is not only earthly: there is also the supreme and absolutely unique identity of the only true God, which—transcending being—is totally other. This—and here is the miracle of the Incarnation—is identical with the unique because limited and earthly aspect of the identity of Jesus Christ, true God and true Man. The distortion of human identity (otherwise known as evil) comes about when we confuse these two aspects of identity (the uniquely universal and the uniquely different). When this happens, we mistake limited and earthly identity for supreme and absolutely unique identity. This is a sort of spiritual cancer where a part (one sort of cell, as it were) replicates throughout the organism, instead of playing its part of serving the whole. Its name is pride. Its cure is the honoring or worship of the true supreme and absolutely unique (and so divine) identity. This is humility. Unlike pride, it acknowledges that this supreme uniqueness is not private property: like the sun, it shines on all; like the rain, it waters all; like the air, it is breathed by all. Jesus Christ, exemplar and teacher of true human identity, showed the way to being "gentle and lowly of heart."[130] He turned no stones into bread when He was hungry; He claimed no permanent residence in which to lay His head; He invoked no legion of angels when He was arrested. Further, He:

> Though he was in the form of God, did not count equality a thing to be grasped, but emptied himself, by taking the form of a servant, being born in the likeness of men. And being found in human form, he humbled himself by becoming obedient to the point of death, even death on a cross.[131]

It is *this* that is the triumphant living out of the supreme identity, *this* on account of which He is given "the name that is above every name."[132] He, uniquely embodying the supreme identity, never

---

[130] Matthew 11.29   [131] Philippians 2.6-8
[132] Philippians 2.9

turned it to selfish advantage, but lived it for all, allowed it to be for all, gave it in the service of all. That which is highest in heaven is lowliest on earth, and vice versa.

So the ascent to the "high mountain" where Jesus is transfigured is both a climbing to heaven and also a move towards the lowliest places of the earth. That is why they cannot "make three tents" there as Peter would have liked.[133] It is an ascent to identity both in its universal, or celestial, aspect and in its particular, or earthly, aspect. The latter involves a particular cultural and spiritual context. That is why, when Jesus is transfigured, "there appeared to him Moses and Elijah, talking with him."[134] Moses personifies the law and Elijah the prophets: this is the tradition into which Jesus is born and in which His identity is expressed. There is no such thing as an abstract human identity, any more than there is a view from nowhere. Peter, James and John bear witness to a particular human identity, revealed at a particular place at a particular time. On behalf of them, and—by anticipation, all believers—Peter declares:

> When he received honor and glory from God the Father,
> and the voice was borne to him by the Majestic Glory,
> "This is my beloved Son, with whom I am well pleased,"
> we ourselves heard this very voice borne from heaven, for
> we were with him on the holy mountain.[135]

This is an affirmation of the identity of Jesus, full, majestic, and divine; but it is not for Jesus alone. It is for every human person, for Jesus wants to share His life with all. He identifies with all and wants all to identify with Him. The affirmation is a reprise of God's seeing "everything that he had made, and behold it was very good."[136] It is a saying to His creatures that He made them, He loves them in their particularity, and invites them to be open to His universal life which neglects nothing and contains everything.

SHARING IDENTITY

Jesus's mission is to draw people into this love. He identifies with people for this, He loves them that they may know this, He gives His life to accomplish this. He identifies with people in their

---

133 Matthew 17.4
135 2 Peter 1.17-18
134 Matthew 17.3
136 Genesis 1.31

fragile particularity: that is, in the earthly, limited aspect of their identity. In His parable about the final accounting, or making clear what has happened in people's lives, He indicates that what has been done for the most vulnerable people has been done for Him, "the Son of man" and "the King" who makes the last judgment:

> Then the King will say to those on his right, "Come, you who are blessed by my Father, inherit the kingdom prepared for you from the foundation of the world. For I was hungry and you gave me food, I was thirsty and you gave me drink, I was a stranger and you welcomed me, I was naked and you clothed me, I was sick and you visited me, I was in prison and you came to me."[137]

His identity includes all those who are suffering, everyone who is lacking something, and indeed—for these simply describe the human condition—every person. This is reflected in there being no historical record of any particular physical characteristics of His. He, manifest to humankind in His particularity, identifies with the particular circumstances of each person. In doing that, He proposes a personal identity which is relative to other particular identities: that is to say, one which does not attempt to dominate others by making a particular identity an absolute, but rather unites with them in spirit and fellow feeling. Concomitantly, He invites a sharing in His absolute identity which is not on an earthly but a heavenly plane and through which we can participate in His identification with all people. The assurance of this absolute identity makes possible a life that does not cling to the particular as if that defined and denoted its all, and so a life generous in giving to others. Christ gives this assurance through His resurrection and shows that the acceptance of particular and limited life—from swaddling bands to cross—works with and for an eternal identity. The unique identity on this earth, limited by time and place, is the seed for the participation in the unique identity which is above and beyond all that passes and which Christ came to make known.

Yet even in this life, there is participation in it in a veiled way. Christ shared His identity, physically encapsulated, when He said, "This is my body, which is for you."[138] Through this, He offers Holy Communion. This is three-fold: it is communion with His

---

[137] Matthew 25.31-40   [138] 1 Corinthians 11.24

Spirit; it is communion with other people, accepting them in their particularity because bonded with them through Christ's heavenly, absolute identity; it is communion with His Body, miraculously present in the Eucharist. Christ as it were gives away His identity in giving His Body in communion, for He disappears in the bread, identifying with those who receive Him. And this creates the community of those receiving communion, the Church. Christ identifies with His Church: when Saul persecutes it, He says to him, "Saul, Saul, why are you persecuting me?" And when asked by Saul who He is, He replies, "I am Jesus, whom you are persecuting."[139] Christ is identified both with all of humanity and with His Church in particular, just as He is identified both with all of humanity and as Jesus of Nazareth in particular. It follows that His Church is identified both with all of humanity and with Him in particular. His Church is His identification with all of humanity, hence her imperative to reach out in love and care for all. She is His love and care.

ACCEPTING ALIENATION

That love and care, that identification is possible because there is one God and Father of us all, making us all siblings, and because Jesus has lived that reality. He has realized it in His identification with us: Sibling to sinners and Son of the Most High. The distance between the two identifications tears His body, breaks open His identity, makes us His own. The fidelity to His Father requires that He accept the alienation of those outside the city, beyond the bond of civility, bereft of brotherhood. That acceptance means estrangement from His Father. God is torn apart, yet God is One. Distance and closeness coincide. An atom releasing energy as it is broken apart is merely an echo of what is unleashed when God is broken open: a light that cannot be swallowed up, a love that cannot be conquered, the Spirit which first ordered the universe and made it whole renewing all things, restoring lost integrity, making humanity holy once more. The fidelity, the acceptance, the obedience which realizes this, makes it possible, makes it happen, is no light undertaking. It involves bitter struggle. As the voice from heaven at His baptism saying, "You are my beloved Son"[140] strengthened Him for the fight with the devil in the desert, so

---

[139] Acts 9.4-5   [140] Luke 3.22

the voice at the transfiguration saying, "This is my beloved Son"[141] strengthens Him for the contest with His own nature in the Garden of Gethsemane.

Here He struggles to find His true identity in His Father's will, to grow into who He is by being nourished by His true food, which is "to do the will" of the One who sent Him and "to accomplish his work."[142] Here He finds the identity of the new Adam, becomes the One who obeyed in the Garden and so undoes the damage of the one who disobeyed in the garden. His identity is His mission and He wins it by obedience. He receives His mission: He does not make it Himself. His identity is, objectively, what His Father wants Him to do. His task, His bread, His life is to do His Father's will; it is to pray with His entire being, "Thy will be done, on earth as it is in heaven." This prayer is in the same spirit as the prayer to be saved from temptation, for the primordial and ever-present temptation is not to do the Father's will. This is simply not being the person one truly is, failing to realize one's identity. Jesus tells the disciples with him, "Pray that you may not enter into temptation"—twice in Luke's account: at the beginning and the end of His own prayer.[143] It is significant that He brings companions with Him, since the building of identity is a corporate affair for recognition and affirmation give it social realization: Peter's recognition of the identity of Jesus establishes it in human society. The more lonely the winning of identity is, the more crucifying it is. And, of course, Jesus is lonely; for His fellows sleep while He struggles against what would take Him away from the will of the Father and so from giving true life to humanity. His prayer is constitutive of human identity; and prayer in His name restores personal identity or, rather, participates in His restoration of it. As He prays, He carries the full weight of all the distortions and diseases of human identity and so is "in agony" which prompts Him to pray "more earnestly" so that His sweat becomes "like great drops of blood falling down to the ground."[144]

Matthew reports Him as being "sorrowful and troubled"[145] even before He begins His prayer. The source of the trouble is clear from the words of His prayer:

---

141 2 Peter 1.17
143 Luke 22.40 & 46
145 Matthew 26.37

142 John 4.34
144 Luke 22.44

THE MYSTERY OF IDENTITY

"My Father, if it be possible, let this cup pass from me; nevertheless, not as I will, but as you will."[146]

His natural instincts are struggling against what is asked of Him. Saint Thomas Aquinas says that prayer is in a sense interpretative of human will. What we want according to our sensual nature we only want somewhat; what we want according to deliberate reason we want absolutely. God hears prayer when this truest will is fulfilled.[147] Prayer is finding what we want at the deepest level, and this is always what God wants. He wants better for us than we want for ourselves. He wants our true life. Our true life is our identity. Prayer realizes our identity. It is a process. That is clear from the fact that the second time Jesus prays in the Garden He uses different words: "My Father, if this cannot pass unless I drink it, your will be done."[148] The primary request is no longer that the cup passes, it is that the Father's will be done. The first prayer made its request conditional—"if it be possible"—but it was for the satisfaction of nature, the passing of the cup; the second prayer subordinates this to the Father's will—the cup will be drunk if that is necessary. True will, true life, true identity emerges from prayer. Jesus prays "the same words again"[149] in His third time of prayer, sealing this identity. His commitment to the will of the Father is absolute. When He is arrested, he stops a violent response from one of those with Him, saying, "Do you think that I cannot appeal to my Father, and he will at once send me more than twelve legions of angels?"[150] He is not going to ask: He refuses to do anything that would seek to manipulate the Father. He accepts His destiny, His Father's will, His true identity, "that the Scriptures of the prophets might be fulfilled."[151]

This identity is not one that is to be won by force of arms. Jesus's explanation to Pilate, "My kingdom is not of this world. If my kingdom were of this world, my servants would have been fighting," makes it clear that it in no way depends on respect given to superior force. His kingdom is not "from the world."[152] It belongs to His mission, the task of His life, the reason for His birth:

---

146 Matthew 26.39
147 Thomas Aquinas, *Summa Theologiae*, 3a.21.4
148 Matthew 26.42   149 Matthew 26.44
150 Matthew 26.53   151 Matthew 26.56
152 John 18.36

> For this purpose I was born and for this purpose I have come into the world—to bear witness to the truth. Everyone who is of the truth listens to my voice.[153]

The truth is in opposition to the lies that characteristically are linked to violence, agent of sway in this world; it is opposed to the temptation of the devil, the Father of lies, to claim such sway; it is the gift of "the Spirit of truth"[154] who led Jesus into the desert to confront this lie. It is personified in Jesus who self-identifies as "the way, and the truth, and the life."[155] He, like the truth, is "from above."[156] His mission is to reorient people to the transcendent truth, the truth of God in order that they, like Him, may find their true identity in that enduring relation of love rather than in the falsity dependent on the fragility of force. Those who are "of the truth" hear Him; those who are open to what is above them pay attention to Him; those who have not taken it upon themselves to define by their own edict what is true listen to Him. The difficulty in this, and the difficulty of our age, is accepting the mystery: the mystery of truth beyond what our minds can contain and delimit, the mystery of truth in whose light we are ignorant, the mystery that gives us identity. There is always the temptation to dismiss it, saying with Pilate, "What is truth?";[157] refusing to grant it reality because we cannot master it, rejecting it because we want to nail it down. All this latter can lead to is the crucifixion of Truth Incarnate, its demise—and then a resurrection which breaks all boundaries, a life beyond all that the mind can conceive, the ultimate mystery.

SILENCE

Mystery is the heart of truth because truth is ultimately divine. Nothing is so like God as silence. God is the all-possible, the One with whom nothing is impossible, the silence in which the eternal Word through whom all things are made speaks. God is the ground of being and so the silence out of which comes all music, all harmony. God is absolute stillness relative to which all movement happens. God is absolute identity in whom the

---

[153] John 18.37
[154] John 15.26
[155] John 14.6
[156] John 8.23
[157] John 18.38

THE MYSTERY OF IDENTITY

unique and the universal are one. So Christ's silence speaks more eloquently than any words in this exchange:

> When he was accused by the chief priests and elders, he gave no answer. Then Pilate said to him, "Do you hear how many things they testify against you?" But he gave him no answer, not even to a single charge, so that the governor was greatly amazed.[158]

To give an answer would be to situate His identity within the matrix of accusation and counter-accusation, to say that this world could define Him, to concede that His glory came from people. The refusal to plead speaks of the coincidence of complete degradation and the highest exaltation, the all but impossible identity of sinful humanity and divine glory. His silence is not guilty but innocent. This is the innocence not of the freshly fashioned world and its first inhabitants but the innocence of the hands from which that world came. The silence is the mystery of the name that cannot be spoken, the Tetragrammaton. The silence is the mystery of the identity of God.

That silence is incarnate in the weakness of the Crucified; it is visible in "darkness over all the land";[159] it is present in the absence of response to the taunt, "Let him come down now from the cross, and we will believe in him";[160] it is a silence that Jesus hears, crying out "with a loud voice, saying, 'Eli, Eli, lema sabachthani?' that is, 'My God, my God, why have you forsaken me?'"[161] It is in the absence of condemnation when He prays for those killing Him, "Father, forgive them, for they know what they do";[162] it is in the not speaking of the thief's wrongdoing when He says, "Truly, I say to you, today you will be with me in paradise";[163] it is in the cessation of all speech when He breathes His last. It is the fulfillment of the prophecy:

> He was oppressed, and he was afflicted, yet he opened not his mouth; like a lamb that is led to the slaughter, and like a sheep that before its shearers is silent, so he opened not his mouth.[164]

---

[158] Matthew 27.12-14
[159] Matthew 27.45
[160] Matthew 27.42
[161] Matthew 27.46
[162] Luke 23.34
[163] Luke 23.43
[164] Isaiah 53.7

The watching centurion recognizes this silence as the opposite of guilty, exclaiming, "Certainly this man was innocent!"[165] It is the final realization of His mission, of which He can say with His last breath, "It is finished."[166] It is the silence of infinite identity.

His resurrection overcomes the constraints of a merely earthly identity. He can appear to Mary Magdalene weeping by His tomb;[167] He can come to His followers behind locked doors;[168] He can walk unrecognized with those who are journeying.[169] In His resurrection body He manifests a new human identity. That is His victory. By making that victory his own, He can promise to "the one who conquers":

> I will write on him the name of my God, and the name of
> the city of my God, the new Jerusalem, which comes down
> from my God out of heaven, and my own new name.[170]

He offers to share His unbounded and eternal life, to make us participators in His divinity, to give us an identity that is not limited by the finite.

How do we make this our own?

---

165 Luke 23.47
167 John 20.11-18
169 Luke 24.13-16
166 John 19.30
168 John 20.19
170 Revelation 3.12

5
Desert & Devils

BEING A CACTUS

Plants such as cacti often flower in response to harsh conditions, such as lack of water. The same seems to be true of people. They can flourish in adversity. In times of difficulty they turn to the light, like the cacti on my window sill. So it is not surprising that people seek out challenges, that they build up their strength with weight training, that they enhance their resilience and resistance to infection by taking cold showers or swimming in cold lakes. But why would someone want to share the natural habitat of a cactus and go into the desert? Consider the lilies lazing in a lake and by contrast the cacti enduring the dry desert. The difference is that water is all around the lilies, but within the cacti. These latter are adept at keeping water within them. I can go away for weeks, or simply forget to water my cacti, and they will keep growing all the same—or perhaps better than if they had been subject to my over-solicitude. So it is with people who share a cactus life. They adapt in the desert so that the Spirit—which is what water means—is within them. The Holy Spirit is the source of identity, so cacti people have their sense of who they are within them; unlike the languid lilies they do not depend on outside recognition to know who they are. So people go into the desert to find themselves. Or, more accurately, people are led into the desert by the Spirit so that they may be told who they are. In this of course they are following Christ who was led into the desert by the Spirit.[1]

There is a long Christian tradition of this. The very practice of observing the restrictions of the season of Lent is a conscious following of Christ into the desert. It is a time of withdrawal from outward distractions, not just of the palate but also of society: a pause from partying. Then there are monks, whose whole life according to Saint Benedict should be a Lent, though he recognizes that this isn't quite so in practice. Monks are in any case linked

---

1   Mark 1.12

THE MYSTERY OF IDENTITY

to the desert: Christian monasticism began in the desert. There is a large body of wisdom in the sayings culled from this epoch. One such saying is Abbot Poemen's, "He who knows himself is a man."[2] To know oneself, of course, is to have realized one's identity. The desert is the place for this. Immediately the absence of visual and auditory stimuli makes it easier to be aware of what is in one's heart. It is also a place of isolation, an escape from the network of relationships that distort, designated in the Bible as "the world" which is obviously not the world which God saw "and behold, it was very good."[3] In the desert there is no one who can give flattery, no associates who can anesthetize the conscience, no one on whom to project the darkness within. It is not possible to have the sort of compulsive relationship described in Dostoevsky's novels, in which one person latches onto another as embodying the woundedness carried within, preventing it from being faced and so ultimately preventing the finding of Christ within the soul. The desert obliges a person to face what is within.

FACING UP

This has been described as the "martyrdom of the conscience." A religious sister who spent many years as a solitary gave me this account of it:

> In extended solitude, the solitary suffers a withdrawal of identity from the normal spheres of identity 'reception.' It is relentless and feels like the fragmentation of the self. Your life is played back before your inner eye repeatedly and all your faults, failures, human awfulness is seen and felt. This brings the solitary into the depths of the abyss, the crisis, and if there is a surrender to this journey the solitary finds God in the abyss, the Lamb at the heart of the Abyss. Then there is a new identity and sense of self in relation to the 'Thou' who is God. This can happen repeatedly.[4]

She referred to Brian Keenan's book *An Evil Cradling*, which describes an experience of extended captivity, to indicate the nature of

---

2 *The Desert Fathers: Sayings of Early Christian Monks*, translated by Benedicta Ward (Penguin, 2003), p. 101
3 Genesis 1.31   4 Slightly edited

the abyss. However, she noted, this account does not include a surrender. It is this surrender—the acceptance of powerlessness to define oneself, the giving in to the mystery, the letting God be God—which births the new and essential identity. The ascetic endeavor of the desert, the reclusion of the hermit, the silence and solitude of the cloister are all oriented to this: the dawning of Christ in the soul, a participation in His divinity, an identity that is not limited by the finite.

Essentially, this is an encounter with mercy. It is no accident that traditional spiritual writing indicates that it comes at a time of darkness. "The endurance of darkness leads to great light"[5] wrote Saint John of the Cross and adumbrated this truth in his teaching about the dark nights of sense and of the soul. It is precisely in knowing the limitations of the world and of one's self that one becomes open to the unlimited. A sense of personal identity that is mediated by surroundings and society and self is necessarily occluded in solitude until finally there is only a self that has to be lost for life to be found. *The Cloud of Unknowing*, the classic English mystical treatise of the Middle Ages, describes this awareness of the burdensomeness of the self. It is this awareness that leads to light and life for finally, if there is faith in mercy, the self is simply allowed to be, no longer expected to supply meaning. The limited is left for the unlimited, darkness for light, self for God. And God, who is wholly other, is received as the giver and sustainer of true identity. The light of His truth was already there in the awareness of the shortcoming and narrowness of the self; the surrender to it is the move from resentment about not looking good to looking at the good. To do that is to be lit up.

BEING COLD OR HOT

How does this identity differ from that ordinarily received from society? The Book of Revelation answers the question:

> I know your works: you are neither cold nor hot. Would that you were either cold or hot! So, because you are lukewarm, and neither hot nor cold, I will spit you out

---

5 *Letters*, p. 685 in *The Collected Works of St. John of the Cross*, translated by Kieran Kavanaugh, O. C. D. and Otilo Rodriguez, O. C. D. (Institute of Carmelite Studies, 1979)

> of my mouth. For you say, I am rich, I have prospered, and I need nothing, not realizing that you are wretched, pitiable, poor, blind and naked.[6]

This is about folk who take their temperature from the ambient surroundings. They have neither the coolness of clear vision nor the hot ardor of Spirit-led activity. In other words, they have no connection with transcendental truth, which would show them how what surrounded them was lacking and/or fire them up to change what needed to be changed. Their identity is simply conformism, but it does not conform to the truth, in the light of which they are indeed "wretched, pitiable, poor, blind and naked." There is a way to move on from this. Christ says to them:

> I counsel you to buy from me gold refined by fire, so that you may be rich, and white garments so that you may clothe yourself and the shame of your nakedness may not be seen, and salve to anoint your eyes, so that you may see.[7]

The gold suggests "faith—more precious than gold that perishes though it is tested by fire."[8] This is the trust that will surrender the "wretched, pitiable, poor, blind and naked" self to the Savior with confidence in His mercy. That mercy clothes nakedness with the innocence that divine forgiveness restores. Then sight can be healed so that the eyes may be directed to God who is light, as the eyes of the blind man were healed in the miracle recounted in Saint John's gospel when the Savior applied salve made with His spittle to them.[9] This begins a relationship with Him who is "the light of the world."[10] It begins with training, passes through companionship and ends in sharing victory and kingship with Him:

> Those whom I love, I reprove and discipline, so be zealous and repent. Behold, I stand at the door and knock. If anyone hears my voice and opens the door, I will come in to him and eat with him, and he with me. The one who conquers, I will grant him to sit with me on my throne, as I also conquered and sat down with my Father on his throne.[11]

---

6 Revelation 3.15-17   7 Revelation 3.18
8 1 Peter 1.7   9 John 9.6-7
10 John 8.12   11 Revelation 3.19-21

Desert & Devils

To journey into the desert is to enter the training ground. The training involves depending less on the environment and more on the Spirit within, like the cactus storing water. Its discipline is a reduction of affirmation from without, so as to facilitate inner life. In this way the ascetic is able to drink the Spirit through belief in the Savior and so become such as Scripture testifies to in the words, "Out of his heart will flow rivers of living water."[12] To do this is to "never be thirsty again"[13] for superficial, worldly recognition of identity. This living water becomes "a spring of water welling up to eternal life"[14]—a life that opens to the infinite and so is not insecure about possible threats to what it is, to its identity. Water is a symbol of the Spirit giving us such life, but it is not the only one. Breath, too, is Spirit: indeed, in former times when metaphorical and literal meaning were as one (as explained by Owen Barfield in his book *Poetic Diction*) there was virtually no distinction. Jesus breathing His last on the cross is thus also His final gift of the Spirit. Breath as a symbol of the Spirit is powerfully apparent in the way in which sustained breathing exercises can enable a person to adapt to cold conditions, for example swimming in the cold sea. This parallels the cactus in the desert having enough water: the oxygen in the person's system facilitates an autonomous warmth less dependent on surroundings. In both cases what is within gives freedom from slavish dependence on what is without. There is either heat of the metabolism within, resisting the cold without, or cold of the water within resisting the heat without. In neither case is there the lukewarmness of accommodation to mediocre values engendered by a compulsive need for the scraps of recognition that the world can throw in one's direction. What is within symbolizes the Spirit, but what is without also has a positive symbolic significance. Both the cold and the heat are a sort of silence and, as Meister Eckhart said, nothing is more like God than silence. Cold is silence because there is no stimulation of the body from outside warmth; the only stirrings come from within. Heat is silence because in the desert nothing grows for lack of water; the only irrigated life is within. In silence we hear who we really are; we know what God sees when He looks at us.

---

12 John 7.38
13 John 4.14
14 John 4.14

Moving into this silence requires great confidence. To leave behind an ordinary self-complacency (or lukewarmness) can feel like death as well as darkness: those little recognitions that we receive from people, acknowledgments that we are somebody, those little achievements that mark us out, those little things that adorn our persons or living spaces, those little responsibilities that give us a sort of authority—all of them feed a sense of self and all somewhat deaden the conscience. To be alone with what we have done in our lives, whether the aloneness comes from moving into a new and unknown social milieu or moving into the solitude of the desert, is to become—in the words of *The Cloud of Unknowing*—"a stinking lump,"[15] congealed complacency beginning to rot, something we thought we were not. Faith in God's mercy here in practice means staying in this place where we would rather not be and believing that there is light we cannot see, a comfort we cannot feel, a goodness that is not ours. To journey deliberately to this place is an act of great faith; to stay there is transformative.

The journey can be made in many ways: the traditional monastic wisdom that if you stay in your cell, your cell will teach you everything is one; accepting a prison sentence is another—though prison cells are not so instructive now that they have televisions; being true to one's vows of marriage to a spouse and being open to the sharp-eyed offspring of the union, who relentlessly reflect back who you really are rather than the person you would like to think you are, is a third. One way or another, the journey confronts the one who makes it with this truth: "If we say we have no sin, we deceive ourselves, and the truth is not in us."[16] It can only be faced through confidence in the merciful words that follow: "If we confess our sins, he is faithful and just to forgive us our sins and to cleanse us from all unrighteousness."[17]

DISIDENTIFICATION

This cleansing is not a once-off happening. It is a whole program of life which is summed up in the beatitude, "Blessed are the pure in heart, for they shall see God."[18] What, then, is the way to that blessed vision? How do we look towards God, how can we be open

---

15 Chapter 44, quoted in Luke Bell, *The Meaning of Blue* (Angelico Press, 2014), p. 223
16 1 John 1.8
17 1 John 1.9
18 Matthew 5.8

to the infinite, how can we realize the mystery of our identity by setting no limits on what is included in what we are through our ideas of what that might be? In practice, more is involved than simply making a fresh start, for habits of being satisfied (not deep down, of course) with the limited, of preferring gratification to bliss, are hard to break. A start, however, is needed and in the traditional teaching—as in *The Cloud of Unknowing*—this involves confession, saying what has been wrong to date. Such a declaration is in effect saying, "This is not really who I am." In ordinary speech we use expressions that say similar things: when someone is uncharacteristically ill-humored, we say, "He is not himself today" or when there has been some mistaken policy for a nation or a company, we say "That is not who we really are." We tend to want to identify with our values, which is, ultimately, to say that we get our identity from God. The instinct is to follow the injunction of the Sermon on the Mount, "Be perfect, as your heavenly Father is perfect."[19] The obvious difficulty with this counsel of perfection is that failure can lead us to identity ourselves as rubbish and, becoming despondent, we give up on the glorious project of being open to all in love even as God cherishes all He has made.

That, however, is not identifying with our true selves. Every wrong choice is in some sense superficial: it takes us away from our deepest self, from Christ present in our souls. Identifying with it is self-alienation. It gives limitation the last say, granting power to whatever wrong is involved to continue to determine our action, making us prisoners of the passing. We can escape by disidentifying from whatever is wrong. This is not the same as refusing to accept responsibility: it is not saying, "This has nothing to do with me." Rather, it is a matter of how we relate to what has happened: we acknowledge it, allow it its full weight, but at the same time know that our true life is not there. We remain open to a future without it: if the impulse recurs, we disidentify with it. For example, if consumed with rage we can say, "I am angry, but I am not my anger." The red mist may be all-encompassing, but the very fact that we are aware of the red mist shows that we are not the red mist. It couldn't be aware of itself. We let it be, let it tell us what it has to tell us (maybe something needs to be corrected), but do not let it decide what we should do. It is

---

19 Matthew 5.47

THE MYSTERY OF IDENTITY

like a child—part of the family, but not the one in charge. This technique of disidentification is expounded in the psychologist Piero Ferrucci's book *What We May Be*, which develops the idea of sub-personalities to describe tendencies that can take over our personality, making it appear that they are who we are. He observes, "Sub-personalities become harmful only when they control us."[20] If, as the French say, everyone has the defects of his qualities, it is also true that tendencies that can seem negative have also a positive aspect: the tendency for the red mist to rise, for example, can also be the ability to take decisive and energetic action when it is needed. And so:

> The knack to be learned is flexibility, so as not to be dominated by our sub-personalities nor to suffocate their expression and ignore their needs—in other words, to have a sense of compassionate, playful mastery.[21]

If to all appearances we are the angry (or over-passive) sub-personality, we may yet be who we really are: the one who is master. As such, we can decide what to give attention to, what to feed and encourage—and what to let be, not ignoring its right to exist but refusing it the right to take over. This is an ascetical work whose difficulty is that of disidentification. If we are used to being recognized as a certain sort of person, if we believe that without certain characteristics we shall cease to have a real existence, then it will be difficult to let them be and let them go. The overcoming of that difficulty is in finding our true identity in God: if He validates and vivifies our true self, freeing it from needing recognition from without, we can have the independence of mastery. Dependence on Him is independence of influences.

That dependence of course becomes easier in the relative isolation of the desert or the cloister, yet even in the course of the world's busyness it is possible to take quiet time out to be alone with God, whether for an hour or for a week. That is more or less necessary to becoming aware of who we really are. That time apart (or life apart, for those living in the desert or in monasteries) is a time of disidentification with what we might casually assume is

---

20 Piero Ferrucci, *What We May Be: The Vision and Techniques of Psychosynthesis* (HarperCollins, 1990), p. 52
21 Ibid., p. 53

Desert & Devils

our identity. This, as Ferrucci explains, is "a state of psychological nudity." He distinguishes this from "the way things usually work" when our consciousness "takes the form of whatever it comes in contact with"—whether that be gladness, toothache, or ice cream.[22] There is of course a sense in which we are whatever we come in contact with: each soul, as Aristotle said, is in a sense all things and our life is our awareness of everything. Yet that is only identity in the sense of being the same as: there is also, necessarily, identity in the sense of being uniquely different. If that were not so, we wouldn't really have a personal life at all: determinism or monism (two sides of one coin) would argue against this, but they are not compatible with a Christian belief in God as Creator. If everything is simply one Supreme Being, then, as Robert Bolton argues, "simply by being the sole possessor of reality, such a being, if believed in, could serve only to drain meaning and reality from everything else, which is the opposite of what is involved in the idea of a creator."[23] It follows that we are other than what we are aware of. Even if our awareness does give a sense of who we are, it can never be absolutely what we are: that is as much the case for our awareness of our most inward thoughts and feelings as for our perceptions of what is around us. Indeed, not understanding that the former does not give us any absolute identity can blind us to the latter. As Ferrucci says:

> As long as we are identified with sensations, feelings, desires, thoughts, it is as if our sense of being were sewed onto them, and therefore they can submerge us, control us, limit our perception of the world.[24]

Far from denying ourselves, disidentification with particulars (whether inner or outer) frees us to include more in who we are, allows us to identify with what might otherwise have been blotted out by, for example, a passionate resentment that tends to exclude perception of anything but injury. It says, "This is not who I am: I may have a resentment, but I am not resentment." Ferrucci tells us how to do it:

---

22 Ibid., p. 62
23 Robert Bolton, *The One and the Many* (Sophia Perennis, 2008), p. 113
24 Piero Ferrucci, *What We May Be: The Vision and Techniques of Psychosynthesis* (HarperCollins, 1990), p. 62

> We dis-identify by observing. Instead of being absorbed by sensations, feelings, desires, thoughts, we observe them objectively without judging them, without wanting to change them, without interfering with them in any way. We see them as distinct from us, as if we were looking at a landscape.[25]

Disidentification is essentially contemplative: it is living not in what we see but in our seeing, not in what we have but in what we are, not in our empires but in our essence. Roberto Assagioli, who taught Ferrucci what he expounds in the book I am citing, sums it up:

> I have a body, but I am not my body. I have feelings, but I am not my feelings. I have desires, but I am not my desires. I have a mind, but I am not my mind.[26]

THE BODY AND IDENTITY

This is, really, the work of the desert ascetic: to avoid absolutizing any of these identifications. None of them tells us absolutely what we are: only God can do that. If we are in the desert seeking to know God, and so receive entirety of being from Him, we need to know that our mind cannot know Him: identity is not found there. If we are pilgrim souls who would be at Jerusalem, we need to struggle against the desires that want to be all that we are: we cannot be as little as that. If we are praying, we need to realize that wholeness or holiness is not in feelings: our sacred identity is deeper than that of which they can speak. Above all—and this is the core of the ascetic tradition—the body is not our confining and absolute identity. That is to say our body is not our final, immortal, eternal identity; yet it is integral to our identity in this world and who we are in this world determines what we shall be in the next. So there are many ambiguities and complexities about the relation between our body and our identity. The body is the instantiation of the self-identity of God: identity in this world in the sense of being the same. Just as, eternally, God is always the same, so there is a continuity in the body. It is, in one sense, who we are. When it is said in a legal context *"habeas corpus"* the point is being made that the body of a living person is in custody and there is an

---

25 Ibid., p. 65   26 Ibid., p. 67

obligation to make a case to justify this on the grounds of what this person—understood as the one acting in this body—has done or failed to do. The body integrates a person's life: it is what makes what is done by or to this person at different times done by or to the same, identifiable, person. And indeed the body stores memory: that of unresolved trauma, in various psychosomatic illnesses, but also that of being loved, in a sort of existential rosiness. As well as assuring identity in the sense of sameness, it assures identity in the sense of difference. By the very fact that its position in time and space is different from that of all other bodies, of whatever sort, it has identity in the sense of a unique difference, which is an instantiation of the unique difference of God its creator. That difference is the necessary foundation of any sort of knowing, including of ourselves. These predicates of sameness and difference belong to the body in the way they do not belong to the feelings, the desires, and the mind. I have already considered, in Chapter One, the implications for identity of the truth that we can fall out of love and of the truth that we can desire a lamb cutlet, but when it arrives in the restaurant actually prefer a cheese salad. The mind, too, can be changed. We can work against this, as in Shakespeare's "Let me not to the marriage of true minds/ Admit impediments"[27] or in marriage promises or religious vows; yet such pitches for a stable identity are made by people who were something else before: not yet friends, spouses or consecrated religious. It does not offer a lifelong identity as the body does.

Yet the body cannot offer an absolute identity such as belongs to God. Cells in it are dying and replicating all the time. At any particular moment, it is not constituted of the same matter as when it began: much has been lost and much has been replaced by means of potatoes, peas, sausages and so on. The body changes in size—it is bigger for adults and for people in general just after Christmas—and it is sometimes healthy and sometimes not. Finally, the body dies. In the Christian understanding, "There are heavenly bodies and earthly bodies."[28] As I said in the last chapter, in the context of the incarnation, our body is like a seed.

> It is sown in dishonor; it is raised in glory. It is sown in weakness; it is raised in power. It is sown a natural

---

27 Sonnet 116   28 1 Corinthians 15.40

> body; it is raised a spiritual body. If there is a natural body, there is also a spiritual body.[29]

In this, eternal, context it makes more sense to say that the spiritual body, not the earthly one, is who we truly are. If that were not so, it would be difficult to make sense of people giving their lives for causes: whether fighting in battle or bearing witness to the truth of faith. The earthly body as be-all and end-all makes a very sorry lodestar. If it is King—or Queen—and all is done according to its commands, then even its very self will be degraded, never mind the life of the one who lives in it: it will become bloated through its commandeering of cheese, stressed by its pursuit of sex, somnolent through its prioritizing of sleep. Hence the ascetic—or anyone really who wants to live a healthy life—needs to say, "I am not my body." The body cannot be the pilot steering the ship of life.

For all that, the body nonetheless has a certain authority. It is what God gives us to be who we are; it has in a sense a divine authority: through it God's Word says who we are. So there is ambiguity: we are this; we are not this. That of course reflects the ambiguity of any statement about God: whatever we say about Him (as in cataphatic theology) we also have to unsay (as in apophatic theology). Everything that shows us who God is also veils Him. Analogously, everything the body says about who we are also conceals the mystery of our identity. That ambiguity, and the body's natural frailty, leads to complexities in determining how far, and in what circumstances, the God-given authority of identity communicated through the body holds legitimate sway. Take hair. I was told of a little boy who absolutely refused to be taken to the barber's for a haircut. For him, it was losing (at least some of) who he was and he was very upset (not just being awkward) about this happening. And in the nineteen-sixties, when I was growing up, the great bone of contention with school authorities was how long our hair could be. Once we left school we let it grow very long. We wanted to be who we were. If this seems whimsical, then consider the sense of belonging to God, giver of hair, given by hair in the Old Testament prescriptions for becoming a Nazirite, vowed to God:

---

29 1 Corinthians 15.43-44

> All the days of his vow of separation, no razor shall touch his head. Until the time is completed for which he separates himself to the LORD, he shall be holy. He shall let the locks of hair of his head grow long.[30]

Consider Samson. He acts with God-given power because he is such a Nazirite, as he fatally explains to Delilah:

> A razor has never come upon my head, for I have been a Nazirite to God from my mother's womb. If my head is shaved, then my strength will leave me, and I shall become weak and be like any other man.[31]

Once his hair is shaved, he is easily seized by the Philistines who gouge out his eyes and bind him with bronze shackles.[32] And consider Saint Paul: the Acts of the Apostles implies that he took a vow like that of the Nazirites, if only for a limited time.[33] Yet on the other side of the question, there is the practice of nuns shaving off their hair to put on their headdress: marking their willingness to leave behind vanities belonging to the world for the sake of God. And there is the religious practice of circumcision, albeit superseded in the Christian tradition. Body modifications may or may not be seen as honoring the Creator. Some, like trimming nails, may be little more than personal hygiene; others, like suppressing through powerful drugs what we are told through natural pain about a spiritually damaging lifestyle, can be an attempt to escape the truth about who God means us to be. The body is who we are, and yet it is not: at least not indefinitely or eternally. I remember discussing a funeral liturgy with mourners who insisted on calling the ashes of the deceased by her name. That was perhaps more sad than funny, but its inappropriateness pointed to the limits of somatic identity. Even after her death, she was more than her ashes. Yet we cannot simply impose an identity on our somatic selves, as if a man (or woman) were author of him (or her) self. The physical is an ineluctable aspect of who we are, a speaking of God that cannot be ignored in favor of some sort of technological paradigm that reduces actors to wired brains like the Daleks, the enemies of humanity in the long-running science fiction series *Dr Who*. Our nature, received from God, commands respect.

---

[30] Numbers 6.5
[31] Judges 16.17
[32] Judges 16.21
[33] Acts 18.18

THE MYSTERY OF IDENTITY

TO EAT OR NOT TO EAT

All of these ambiguities can be gathered in a single existential question: to eat or not to eat. To eat is to prioritize the body at the risk of mistaking it for an absolute statement of who we are, so traditional ascetical practice includes fasting to maintain the opposite truth. To refuse to eat is to refuse totally to be who we are, and so the struggle to eat can also be a quest for true identity. Many are the accounts of the former and its value in finding an identity that does not ignore the spiritual; I want rather to focus on the latter for it shows the quest has to include the corporal. In her book, *The Silent Struggle*, a Carmelite nun, Sister Marie Thérèse of the Cross, describes what she calls "a search to find my real self."[34] The main work of this search was eating, for she suffered from anorexia, a condition brought about by being sexually abused at a very early age. The abuse made her feel guilty and unclean, so that her body seemed to her to have no right to exist and deserved to be starved into non-existence. That meant that the ordinary sense of being comfortable in one's own skin was denied to her:

> To understand, for example, how anyone could feel happy in a woman's body or find pleasure in going out for a meal was quite inconceivable to me because of the feelings associated with them for me.[35]

Following a childhood vision of Saint Thérèse, she became convinced that she had a calling to be a Carmelite nun. That necessitated a body, which was problematic for her:

> I wanted to belong totally to God, but I did not want a woman's body and what I now think of as my "anorexia voice" was very strong. These two voices were contradicting each other all the time, making it impossible for me to be consistent.[36]

Identity, in the sense of remaining the same, eluded her. Her anorexia became what Ferrucci refers to as a "sub-personality," one which stood in the way of what she was meant to become:

---

34 Sister Marie Thérèse of the Cross, *The Silent Struggle* (Redemptorist Publications, 2008), p. 6   35   Ibid.
36 Ibid., p. 35

she writes, "Without my knowing it, anorexia had gained control of my life; food was a constant preoccupation."[37] It stood in the way of her becoming well and becoming a Carmelite:

> The good part of me that wanted to get well was being overpowered by the anorexia. Again, it subtly told me that I was not good enough to be a Carmelite and if I wanted God the surest way was to get rid of the body and go to heaven. I was so ill I believed this.[38]

It could use religious thoughts, for example of "the saints who fasted," to prevent her escaping from her hatred of "the whole idea of having a woman's body."[39] This "inner rejection" she felt for her body expressed itself in a compulsion to avoid eating, or keeping down, food. It kept her "far away" from her "real self."[40] The quest to find this involved what appeared to be losing this self: she was admitted to a program in a hospital ward in which she was known not by her religious name, but the name she had before she entered religious life. When the newcomers to the program were welcomed, she reported:

> I was too nervous to look up. I could feel every eye on me and I felt suddenly sad. I had lost my identity. Here, I would be known as Sheila, but who was she? No one there knew Sr Marie Thérèse. Looking round the room full of people I did not know, I wanted to cry; I realised the step I had taken. Were Carmel and Sr Marie Thérèse just a dream? I wanted them back.[41]

During her stay in hospital she "began to develop a real identity crisis." She was very grateful when she received a tape from her religious community "with personal messages of love from each one" but reflected "they were all to Sr Marie Thérèse. Here, I was known as Sheila, someone suffering from anorexia." She was "heartbroken" asking herself, "Would I ever find Marie Thérèse again? I did not want Sheila."[42]

She did find Marie Thérèse again, through a heroic struggle to accept her suffering body, to accept her suffering; struggle to

---

37 Ibid., p. 53
38 Ibid., p. 56
39 Ibid., p. 73
40 Ibid., p. 155
41 Ibid., p. 199
42 Ibid., p. 215

accept Sheila's suffering body, to accept Sheila's suffering. She came to the realization that eating as well as fasting can give glory to God, and on a visit home resolved on the eve of Good Friday, "Tomorrow, while the sisters fasted for God, I was going to eat for him."[43] Her acceptance of somatic identity, acceptance of Sheila, became a proper basis for her identity as a person given to God and, no longer hating her womanliness, she learnt that:

> Sexuality is very close to the core of our being and, in many ways, shapes our human identity. It is what gives energy to our lives—we give our lives to God as sexual people.[44]

She came to a point where she no longer felt she needed to apologize for being who she was and found an identity through which she was able to relate to others and to live:

> Once I stopped saying sorry all the time I learned to be assertive and even to express my opinion, sometimes contrary to that of others. Gradually, I came to feel a real person, no longer needing the acceptance of others to survive. To my surprise, it was only then, when I could stand without their support, that I was free to make real relationships. Certainly, it was for me the beginning of life.[45]

She found a balance in her bodily life, like Saint Antony of the Desert who, after his nearly twenty years "pursuing the ascetic life by himself" in the desert, was "neither fat from lack of exercise, nor emaciated from fasting and combat with demons."[46]

CLOTHING

Sister Marie Thérèse found her identity through her body. The human body irreplaceably articulates who we are. As with the Son of Man Himself, the eye is the window into the soul, the heart embodies the essence of identity, the voice speaks what is in the heart. It is significant that, of all the tasks undertaken by artificial intelligence, replicating bodily actions is the most difficult to achieve. Simply mental computations, dealing with data and solving equations and so on, can be performed mechanically in a

---

43 Ibid., p. 230
44 Ibid., p. 266
45 Ibid., p. 271
46 Athanasius, *The Life of Antony and the Letter to Marcellinus*, translated by Robert C. Gregg (Paulist Press, 1980), p. 42

way that far outstrips human capacity, but manipulating things in three dimensions comes naturally to people and only with complication or clumsiness to machines. And while computers can transmit what people look and sound like, people need to be present in the flesh to communicate by touch. Furthermore, the body communicates in a special way when it is naked. There is a sense in which nudity is sacred: naked as we came from our mother's womb, in our birthday suit, we show who we are more fully than we do in the accretions of clothing. Nudity is the expression of a privileged intimacy: we reserve it for those from whom we do not wish to hide anything and refuse it to those from whom we wish to remain hidden. Clothing does not express us as well as its absence, yet it is a homage to the centrality of the body for communicating identity. It says who we are, in a partial way, through the body: displaying clothes on a table, for example in one's office or shop, would be a ridiculous failure in saying who we are. On the body, they say something, though not everything: a man can be a policeman in the day and an uncle in the evening. Professional, religious, or sacerdotal aspects of identity are formalized in clothing and informal modes of dress also habitually express something of who people are. Clothes can even speak without design of those who wear them: what is put on can show a failure to connect with reality, even if the clothes are warm enough and so on. Though it is difficult to give it a clear aesthetic definition, there is an insane way of dressing, just as troubles in the mind can lead to illnesses in the body.

    The body is not God, however, not the source and giver of all identity. It does not contradict this to say that God became incarnate: God, as Scripture says, is light, is love, but that is no reason for never turning out the lights or for caving in to every crazed passion. The body does not have unlimited rights. Extensions of the body may or may not truly express who we are, or they may express it in a limited way only. The bus driver whom I heard say, "I am full," was saying something different about herself than she would be if she used the same words at the end of her evening meal: she meant she had reached the limit of the number of people she could serve by taking them on the bus she was driving, a metric very distinct from the amount of food she could be served. The bus was an extension of her bodily identity, the face she might feed later more closely an expression of who she was. Vehicular extensions of identity may be true or they may be false in the sense that vehicles can be stolen, can be driven without the due care or attention that we give when we are true to ourselves, can be agents of harm and so not validated by a blessing from the divine source of true being. All operations in the physical domain can be either ultimately merciful and so blessed, or illegitimate assertions of identity, either epiphanies of love or egotistical statements. To see the whole world as an expression of the ego or as an aspect of our bodily identity is delusional, satanic pride. Yet the world is an expression of who we are: it is an expression of our soul, which contains it through perception rather than assertion. To find who we truly are, we need to train the body to keep its place, to put in under the pedagogy of the soul.

FASTING

Hence people fast. That may be simply to liberate the (true) slim personal identity lurking within the rolls of fat, but traditionally it has a religious and spiritual meaning. It identifies the one who fasts with Christ in the desert, whose fasting was integral to His resistance of the devil's attempts to subvert His identity, to make of Him someone who belonged to this world alone, by, for example, seeing Himself as having come into it merely to bring bread. It opens the soul to Christ as master, to the light that Alyosha Karamazov sees in his dream, so that the Spirit might direct the soul and the soul the body, to attain the goal Saint Paul set before the Thessalonians when he wrote:

> Now may the God of peace himself sanctify you completely, and may your whole spirit and soul and body be kept blameless.[47]

Sanctity is receiving one's identity from God; primarily in the spirit, the summit of the human person, and allowing the spirit to govern the soul, the life of the person, so that the life of the body becomes a true expression of that identity, "a temple of the Holy Spirit within."[48] It is true that the body is our God-given identity in this world, but it needs to be animated—a static identity in this world is the same thing as death—and that animation,

---

[47] 1 Thessalonians 5.23 [48] 1 Corinthians 6.19

Desert & Devils

or work of the soul, needs to be directed by God if it is to speak authoritatively of who we are.

The desert monks of old struggled to allow this identity to emerge. Without this knowledge of identity, the human person is in some sense deformed, and fasting is a weapon in the struggle to gain it. Traditionally, as in the *Conferences* of Cassian, fasting enables the control of lust. We could say that this is the control of the proper boundaries of bodily life: the definition of it, as it were. Lust tends to appropriate improperly, mistakes what is the other's as its own. Bodily life lived in merciful love eschews such transgression. It eschews lust in the broader sense, the *libido dominandi* (lust for domination) of which Saint Augustine wrote. This latter would lay claim to control what is not properly to be controlled, to act as God in a domain which is not one's own, as though it were all a God-given extension of one's body, which it is not. The opposite is knowing the limits of one's corporal or earthly identity and so knowing who one truly is. Of course, on the plane of the spirit there can be identity with God insofar as His will and purposes with regard to one's life are totally shared. That is true, light-filled, divinely-given identity: the error, against which the struggle in the desert (whether literally there or in a relative seclusion) takes place, is the attempt to transpose this godliness to the earthly level by replacing this divine (and so universal) center with a private, quasi-divine, dominion over things in this world, where identity is, necessarily, parcelled out.

Saint Luke records Christ's teaching relating to these two possibilities. He says to those who fast, "Blessed are you who are hungry now, for you shall be satisfied."[49] Only God can truly satisfy us, and so it is a blessing to be unsatisfied on the earthly plane so that we may know our deeper, spiritual, lack of satisfaction and turn to God and be satisfied. It is preferring love to food, saying to the Divine lover, "Let him kiss me with kisses of his mouth!" and "Draw me after you,"[50] instead of feeding the face. It is finding a spiritual identity in relationship with God rather than allowing oneself to be denoted by mere bulk of flesh brought on by allowing the teeth to range where they will. To the one who does the latter Christ says, "Woe to you who are

---

49 Luke 6.21   50 The Song of Solomon 1.2 & 4

full now, for you shall be hungry."[51] Hunger for the word of God, for the meaning which makes sense of life, which tells us who we are, cannot be satisfied by bread alone. This struggle of the desert with the demon who would tell us that bread is the be-all and end-all tends in practice to be lifelong. Saint John of the Cross, master of the spiritual art, tells us:

> The world is the enemy least difficult to conquer; the devil is the hardest to understand; the flesh is the most tenacious, and its attacks continue as long as the old man lasts.[52]

The old man is the old Adam who has forgotten who he really is, who thinks he belongs to this world only, who imagines that by extension in it (corporal or other) he can make himself truly great. He only fades out of the picture we make of ourselves when our deepest self, Christ present in our souls, is truly Master. The world is the easiest enemy of our true self to conquer because it offers relatively superficial versions of who we are, identifying us with merchandise and so on, as I explained in Chapter Two. The devil is another matter, because his cunning presents false options to us in the guise of good, disguising himself as "an angel of light."[53]

ASCENDING MOUNT CARMEL

The way to defeat him is to disidentify even from what is good. It is not enough to say that being involved in a particular shoddy practice is not who we really are (though it certainly helps): we need to say, too, that our good qualities are not who we really are. This is true in the sense that all the good we have is a gift of God, coming from Him and not ourselves. To say that it is from ourselves is a spiritual version of the ego extension manifest in overeating and lust of controlling people and things in the world. Traditionally, it is the most serious deformation of who we are: pride. It is possible to be given to lust (making pleasure a priority) or avarice (making the acquisition of worldly goods a priority) and still to think that this is not who we really are, not identifying with

---

51 Luke 6.25
52 *The Collected Works of St. John of the Cross*, translated by Kieran Kavanaugh, O. C. D. and Otilo Rodriguez, O. C. D. (Institute of Carmelite Studies, 1979), p. 656   53 2 Corinthians 11.14

Desert & Devils

these drives and aspiring to be truer to who we really are; but the possibility of illusion is much greater when we identify with that which is good. Just as anorexia can present itself as a good control of the appetite, so a cold aloofness can present itself as a mastery of lust. Any good can become an idol: spending time in church can be an idol to which the well-being of a family needing to eat can be sacrificed; esteem for another can be an idol to which the truth, at variance with what that other holds to be the case, can be sacrificed; devotion to work can be an idol to which health and family life can be sacrificed. The one who prays, the one who esteems, the one who works—none of these are the real self: in Ferrucci's terms, they are sub-personalities that need to have their place but should not be allowed to dominate: only the true self can be master. It may seem that it is doing oneself down to say, "I am not someone who controls appetite, prays, esteems the other, works and so on," but the reality is that this is an underestimate of who we are. It ignores the truth animadverted to in the previous chapter, that the human person is essentially open, in Hamlet's words "infinite in faculties."[54] If we are not any particular virtue, we can identify with all virtue: with the true Master, Christ in the depth of the soul. It is just that we do not and cannot own Him. Our deepest identity is not our own.

Yet we need to win through to it, to attain the glorious liberty of the children of God, the peace of not having to manage our image, the life that does not depend on this world. In this, Saint John of the Cross is a sure guide. He shows us how to avoid getting stuck with any lesser identity. In his sketch map at the beginning of *The Ascent of Mount Carmel*, the way is marked out. On it, he writes:

> To reach satisfaction in all, desire its possession in nothing; to come to the knowledge of all, desire the knowledge of nothing; to come to possess all, desire the possession of nothing; to arrive at being all, desire to be nothing.[55]

We are truly who we are when we are not living in anything, whether satisfaction, knowledge or possession: then we are truly

---

54 *Hamlet*, Act 2, scene ii, l.304
55 *The Collected Works of St. John of the Cross*, translated by Kieran Kavanaugh, O. C. D. and Otilo Rodriguez, O. C. D. (Institute of Carmelite Studies, 1979), p. 67. My punctuation.

THE MYSTERY OF IDENTITY

alive in ourselves, not in what we think we are. We tread the path to this abundance of life by desiring to be nothing because that way nothing will occlude our reception of all that is. The path leads to being all, identifying with everything and everybody, because all selfish partiality has been left behind. We win this universal identity by avoiding settling for less. The saint explains:

> When you turn toward something, you cease to cast yourself upon the all, for to go from the all to the all you must leave yourself in all. And when you come to the possession of all, you must possess it without wanting anything.[56]

Turning toward something, making something some sort of absolute requirement, identifying with something is reductive of who we are. It limits us to this only; it kills the mystery. Not to want anything, even when we possess everything, is to lack nothing, to be fully and completely who we are. Identifying ourselves with all that our lives have brought us awareness of, or even all that is, fails to say properly who we are: as with statements about God, we have to unsay it also, for it would suppress the enigma of our identity to reduce it to what we have known or indeed to all that is. There is a transcendence about our identity: it is not simply the same as what we identify with, it is also that which identifies. The latter is utterly, mysteriously, different. We ignore this truth to our own frustration when we identify with any particular thing as an absolute: our hearts are made for more than this, made for that wide and lonely knowing that we can only find in God, for only God has it. If we go into the desert (of whatever kind) to find it, devils will try to stop us, saying: you could be successful, that would be who you are; you could be admired, that would be who you are; you could be powerful, that would be who you are. Yet truly we are none of these; nothing can denote us truly—no diamonds, no hat, no honey.[57] "Blessed are the poor in spirit, for theirs is the kingdom of heaven."[58] Not owning anything in this world, not dressed in its riches, not identifying with what passes, they are citizens of above where identity is not parceled out in time and space, not exclusive

---

56 Ibid., my punctuation
57 Andrew Harvey, title of a book of poetry (Houghton Mifflin, 1985)
58 Matthew 5.3

Desert & Devils

of other possibilities, not ever a source of conflict, for all belongs to all. They can treat those two impostors, triumph and disaster,[59] with equal insouciance for, in the words of Saint John of the Cross:

> In this nakedness the spirit finds its rest, for when it covets nothing, nothing raises it up, and nothing weights it down, because it is in the center of its humility.[60]

On the saint's map showing the way up Mount Carmel, the word "nothing" is repeated six times:[61] the way to the summit is refusing to settle for any good, whether earthly or heavenly, in place of the Giver of every good; this is refusing to limit oneself to any identity as a substitute for identifying with, for being one with the Giver of all identity. That union is both summit and center, for He is transcendent and immanent; the summit of Mount Carmel is the vantage point from which all can be seen in perspective, the center of the spirit's humility is the perfect littleness where there is nothing to block the view of all that is. There is nothing of our own in the center of the onion.

THE DAYS THAT WERE FORMED FOR ME

Yet we cannot simply detach ourselves from earthly life. When I first learned and enthusiastically embraced the teaching of Saint John of the Cross, a wise old monk told me I needed to be detached from detachment. Sister Marie Thérèse had to accept her embodiment before she could follow the teaching of Saint John of the Cross in her Carmelite monastery. We have to accept that our story is to be written in time and space and that that is our contact with the transcendent God who, after all, wrote His story in time and space so that we might know Him. We belong to Him, and His life which He lovingly shares with us in Christ is the life of knowing. "In him was life and the life was the light of men"[62] wrote Saint John, indicating that the Word through which we understand illuminates creation so that we may know what is. Sharing His life, we in a sense know as God knows. Yet we are not

---

59 Rudyard Kipling, "If—" https://www.poetryfoundation.org/poems/46473/if—
60 *The Collected Works of St. John of the Cross*, translated by Kieran Kavanaugh, O. C. D. and Otilo Rodriguez, O. C. D. (Institute of Carmelite Studies, 1979), p. 67
61 Ibid.
62 John 1.4

THE MYSTERY OF IDENTITY

God: for Him to know something is for that thing to be whereas we are participators in being—procreators rather than originators. Our identity is not mere knowing: we are also creatures who are known through the Word through whom we are articulated. Being known gives us the life through which we know. And that life is always a narrative, to use the fashionably neutral word, though it could also be a story or a myth (in the older sense of a tale of great expressive power, rather than one that is not true). Certainly it is not a tale told by an idiot,[63] as Macbeth thought when he had given his eternal jewel to the common enemy of mankind. Rather, it is a tale of God's telling, as the godly or god-fearing through history have recognized, seeing His loving providence or justice in it all.

The divine source and knowledge of the story of our identity is given inspired expression in Psalm 139:

> O LORD, you have searched me and known me! You know when I sit down and when I rise up; you discern my thoughts from afar. You search out my path and my lying down and are acquainted with all my ways. Even before a word is on my tongue, behold, O LORD, you know it altogether. You hem me in behind and before, and lay your hand upon me. Such knowledge is too wonderful for me; it is high; I cannot attain it.[64]

God is more intimate with us than we are with ourselves, for all that we are comes from Him: He knows what we are up to; He is aware of our thoughts before they are formulated; He discerns what we will say before it is heard. Our identity is hidden in the mind of God. It belongs to "God's mystery, which is Christ in whom are hidden all the treasures of wisdom and knowledge."[65] It comes from the life in our soul of Christ, the Universal Man, God's creating Word. God Our Father knows us in Christ His Son. The Holy Spirit of love and truth which unites them encompasses us also. God surrounds us. As Saint Paul told the men of Athens, "In him we live and move and have our being."[66]

His knowledge of who we are is beyond our reach: that is why our identity is a mystery. We cannot escape this mystery because we cannot be where God is not:

---

63 *Macbeth* Act 5, scene v, ll.26–27   64 Psalm 139.1–6
65 Colossians 2.2–3   66 Acts 17.28

> Where shall I go from your Spirit? Or where shall I flee from your presence? If I ascend to heaven, you are there! If I make my bed in Sheol, you are there! If I take the wings of the morning and dwell in the uttermost parts of the sea, even there your hand shall lead me, and your right hand shall hold me. If I say, "Surely the darkness shall cover me, and the light about me be night," even the darkness is not dark to you; the night is as bright as the day, for darkness is as light with you.[67]

It is a mystery that can be dark for us, and indeed we can bring darkness upon ourselves, but it is never dark for God: if we are ignorant, He is omniscient; if we are perplexed, He is at peace; if we exile ourselves, He is holding our hand. Discovery, peace, homecoming are simply a matter of turning from ourselves to Him, praising Him as our Creator in words such as these:

> You formed my inward parts, you knitted me together in my mother's womb. I praise you, for I am fearfully and wonderfully made. Wonderful are your works; my soul knows it very well. My frame was not hidden from you, when I was being made in secret, intricately woven in the depths of the earth. Your eyes saw my unformed substance; in your book were written, every one of them, the days that were formed for me, when as yet there was none of them.[68]

The mystery and wonder of our entire life is known by God. This knowledge is who we are. God tells our days; we are His story, belonging in His book. So it is to the mind of God that we look in any quest for our true identity, and we can only marvel at its infinite riches:

> How precious to me are your thoughts, O God! How vast is the sum of them! If I would count them, they are more than the sand. I awake, and I am still with you.[69]

FINDING OURSELVES IN GOD

If God is so interior to us, then we need to look to Him to find who we are. The philosopher Robert Bolton observes that for the

---

67 Psalm 139.7-12   68 Psalm 139.13-16
69 Psalm 139.17-18

THE MYSTERY OF IDENTITY

soul "to contemplate God and to contemplate its own essence have much the same effect";[70] and the theologian Rowan Williams comments on the fact that Augustine's autobiography, *Confessions*, takes the form of a prayer: "to work out who I am, I need to be speaking to and listening to God."[71] We know who we are through a life lived in dialogue with God. That is because God is Infinite Possibility: whatever we are, He can make it happen. It is the opposite extreme from, for example, filling out an online form where you can only check boxes for a predetermined and strictly limited number of possibilities. As Williams puts it, "Only in relation to the infinity of God can we get any purchase on the sort of beings we are—moving through time and 'growing into' ourselves in encounter with an inexhaustible other."[72] The implication of this is that we can neither tell each other nor be told by each other who we are: "Each man and woman is defined by relation to God, finally; I can't lay down for you your everlasting destiny, nor you lay down mine—that is the sense in which no human being can be an 'end' for another human being."[73] Any definitive statement about another is reductive, for he or she finds true identity only in relation to the infinite possibility of God. The implication of this is two-fold. Firstly, being truthful entails respect for others who can find new life in God up to the very moment of death, who are (at least potentially) temples of the Holy Spirit and whom we insult when we say that anything at all, however distinguished, is all they are. Secondly, what other people say about our character has only a provisional value. We do need input from others when as children we are guided into adulthood, when as seekers we are given spiritual accompaniment, when as professionals we learn our craft, but this counsel and direction (even at its best) is simply scaffolding enabling the building to be put up or a stake in the ground to help the tree grow upright. Its purpose is to allow us to find our identity in God, not to give us our identity. If it is wholesome, it will always look to disappear as the fullness of its purpose is realized. Others do not write the book of our life and nor do we: God alone knows the twists and turns in the plot that unfolds. In the contemplation of Him, we can see what it is, who we are.

---

70 Robert Bolton, *Person, Soul and Identity* (Minerva Press, 1994), p. 38
71 Rowan Williams, *On Augustine* (Bloomsbury, 2016), p. 3
72 Ibid., p. 4   73 Ibid., pp. 210-11

Desert & Devils

And Christ shows us God. "No one has ever seen God; the only God, who is at the Father's side, he has made him known."[74] He says to Philip, "Whoever has seen me has seen the Father."[75] He says to Thomas, "I am the way, and the truth, and the life."[76] He is the path we tread as we find the way to who we truly are; He is the truth of God in whom is contained all reality, including our own; He is the abundance of life from which the tapestry of our personal story is spun. When He says to those who believe in Him, "If you abide in my word, you are truly my disciples, and you will know the truth, and the truth will set you free,"[77] He offers freedom from limitation, freedom from false and flimsy identities, freedom from the father of lies through resting in His presence, His life, and His teaching. His story is the essence of our story. That story is told through all those who accept that to which God has called them, through all His saints. It is told, too, in the Bible, in which His most personal words are not only those directly attributed to Him (printed in red in some editions), but also the words of the psalms as is implied by His words, "Everything written about me in...the Psalms must be fulfilled."[78] Rowan Williams, expounding Augustine's teaching, says this about how we find identity through praying them:

> As we truly assimilate the identity of the psalmist as paradigmatic human sufferer and struggler, we assimilate the identity of Christ who chooses those same words as his own; and thus we are given to speak the words that Christ speaks to the Father, because the humility and love that grounds his acceptance of our condition is the expression of the eternal love that unites him with the Father. What is distinctive about any hermeneutic of the Psalms is that singing them is quite simply and literally an appropriation of Christ's life, in history and eternity.[79]

Hence seekers of God, seekers of their true identity, have always recited the psalms, whether in the desert or the cloister. To recite them is like looking at a crucifix: they are a means of identifying our sufferings with those of Christ and so finding meaning in

---

[74] John 1.18
[75] John 14.9
[76] John 14.6
[77] John 8.31-32
[78] Luke 24.44
[79] Rowan Williams, *On Augustine* (Bloomsbury, 2016), p. 30

what seems to lack it, form in what looks fragmented, identity in "one from whom men hide their faces"[80] yet who has "life in himself."[81] In Him, what seems bad in our lives becomes good because it becomes, like His sufferings, a gift of love to the Father, so that we can say with the Apostle:

> We know that for those who love God all things work together for good, for those who are called according to his purpose. For those whom he foreknew he also predestined to be conformed to the image of his Son, in order that he might be the firstborn among many brothers. And those whom he predestined he also called, and those whom he called he also justified, and those whom he justified he also glorified.[82]

Conformed to that image, we have a true identity, a fulfillment of our destiny, a life journeying to justice and glory, for "to all who did receive him, who believed in his name, he gave the right to become children of God, who were born, not of blood nor of the will of the flesh nor of the will of man, but of God."[83] We enter on that life's journey by (in Williams's words) "identifying our individual narratives with that of Jesus." We do this by sharing in "Christ's acceptance of the fallen and struggling condition to which we are without exception destined." We thus become "a sign of God," our true identity.[84]

IDENTITY IN CHRIST

To accept fully who we are, realizing (in the double sense) the presence of Christ the Pancreator in the depths of our soul, is to drink "the new wine, the wine of new happiness, of great happiness" of which Zosima speaks to Alyosha in his dream. This joining in the merry-making prefigured by the wedding at Cana is the goal of the traditional monastic struggle with demons in the desert. It is a matter of not being superficial: of not thinking we are merely who people say we are, or even that we can put any limits to who we are by our own thoughts. We can only be who God knows we are and we can only hear His speaking this to us in our hearts

---

80 Isaiah 53.3   81 John 5.26
82 Romans 8.28-30   83 John 1.12-13
84 Rowan Williams, *On Augustine* (Bloomsbury, 2016), p. 37

Desert & Devils

when our hearts are as devoid of distraction as they are, or would be, in the desert. And then, when distance stills the distractions of the world and simplification of diet and style of life diminishes the demands of the flesh, we are ready to confront the spiritual enemy who would try to persuade us that we can know ourselves other than as known and loved by God, who would lie to us, for (again in Williams's words) "knowing ourselves as loved creatures is the only way of knowing ourselves truthfully."[85] In the desert, in the heart, in the crucible of our life, we "fight the good fight of the faith"[86]—faith that we are loved by God, that our life has meaning, that God will tell us who we are. We put on "the whole armor of God," we fasten on "the belt of truth," we protect ourselves with "the breastplate of righteousness"[87] which is loving God and our neighbor as our self. We identify with God's will as manifest through the tradition and the promptings of His spirit, with His ways, not with any desire of our own other than that hidden in the depth of our heart: the desire for Love to call us by our name, for Christ to tell us who we are, for Him to give us "a new name" written on "a white stone" which "no one knows except the one who receives it."[88] This new name which Christ gives to "the one who conquers" is also His own "new name," the name of His God, the name of the city of His God, "the new Jerusalem"[89] for "Christ plays in ten thousand places … through the features of men's faces"[90] and in His father's house are "many rooms."[91] He lives in many and various persons since "all things were made through him, and without him was not any thing made that was made"[92] and so all share the same life. Each is identified with all: this life gives them identity in the sense of sameness. Yet each also has identity in the sense of distinctness: God shares with them His own absolute, transcendent uniqueness. This is a mystery, for in themselves all God's creatures are nothing, no more apparent to any view than a landscape in the dead of a moonless and clouded night. Yet somehow they distinctively color the life that He gives them,

---

85 Ibid., p. 175
86 1 Timothy 6.12
87 Ephesians 6.11, 14
88 Revelation 2.17
89 Revelation 3.12
90 Gerard Manley Hopkins, "As kingfishers catch fire," ll. 12 & 14, p. 90 in *The Poems of Gerard Manley Hopkins* (Oxford University Press, 1970)
91 John 14.2
92 John 1.3

THE MYSTERY OF IDENTITY

the life that is "the light of men."[93] This mystery of particular and distinct identity is embodied in Christ Himself, Jesus of Nazareth.

And "this Jesus"[94] not only bestows identity: He models identity and calls to identity. His modeling of identity is in His acceptance of the limitations of being born into a particular time and culture with the concomitant adversities. He accepts what is given, as gift. And He calls persons to be who they most deeply are. Peter is paradigmatic. There is a scene of mutual recognition in which Peter knows who Jesus is and He identifies Peter:

> He said to them, "But who do you say that I am?" Simon Peter replied, "You are the Christ, the Son of the living God." And Jesus answered him, "Blessed are you, Simon Bar-Jonah! For flesh and blood has not revealed this to you, but my Father who is in heaven. And I tell you, you are Peter, and on this rock I will build my church, and the gates of hell shall not prevail against it."[95]

In believing in Jesus as "the Son of the living God," Simon Peter enters into a relationship with the Christ in which he finds his deepest identity: Peter, which means rock. That is his eternal identity, for the rock in its solidity and stability symbolizes the eternal. Of course, Peter in himself is impulsive and unfaithful, but he learns through his failures to rely not on himself but on God and in this reliance he finds his true self: he is one on whom others can rely as he guides them in the life of faith. He recognizes the truth of what his fellow apostle, Paul, says: "We have this treasure in jars of clay, to show that the surpassing power belongs to God and not to us."[96]

In perhaps the most touching recognition scene in the gospels, the dynamic is the other way around from that in Peter's: Jesus is recognized for who He is only when he has named the one who is talking to Him.

> [Mary Magdalene] turned around and saw Jesus standing, but she did not know that it was Jesus. Jesus said to her, "Woman, why are you weeping? Whom are you seeking?" Supposing him to be the gardener, she said to him, "Sir, if you have carried him away, tell me where you have laid

---

93 John 1.4
95 Matthew 16.15-18
94 Acts 2.32
96 2 Corinthians 4.7

him, and I will take him away." Jesus said to her, "Mary." She turned and said to him in Aramaic, "Rabboni!" (which means Teacher).[97]

There is no change of name for her: she is simply Mary, as she always has been. Yet she is a new person. She came to the tomb of Jesus by moonlight and she leaves in the light of dawn, the light of resurrection from the dead. She becomes one whose soul is taught by Jesus, becomes the apostle to the apostles, the one who announces the resurrection. His naming of her in the light of the resurrection gives Mary her true identity. His call is who she is.

In a sense every Christian finds identity in the call of Jesus. "The sheep follow him, for they know his voice."[98] Christ gives them true identity, and abundance of life, so that they can say with Saint Paul, "It is no longer I who live, but Christ who lives in me."[99] "Paul" is the new name of Saul, of whom it is said by his Lord, "He is a chosen instrument of mine to carry my name before the Gentiles and kings and the children of Israel."[100] This name is in effect the identity of Christ, exported from His own people to all the nations of the earth. He lives in all who receive Him and in some sense in all of humanity as such. He says, "I, when I am lifted up from the earth, will draw all people to myself."[101] In a poet's words, "To hero of Calvary, Christ,'s feet—/ Never ask if meaning it, wanting it, warned of it—men go."[102] Called by the Holy Spirit, they say, "Jesus is Lord."[103] Following Him, they learn to make their own His words, "I do not receive my glory from people."[104] They know from God who they are. They are "imitators of God, as beloved children,"[105] united to the Son who says, "Whatever the Father does, that the Son does likewise"[106] and so "called children of God."[107]

---

[97] John 20.14-16   [98] John 10.4
[99] Galatians 2.20   [100] Acts 9.15
[101] John 12.32
[102] Gerard Manley Hopkins, "The Wreck of the Deutschland," stanza 8 in *The Poems of Gerard Manley Hopkins* (Oxford University Press, 1970), p. 54
[103] 1 Corinthians 12.3   [104] John 5.41
[105] Ephesians 5.1   [106] John 5.19
[107] 1 John 3.1

6
Universe & Universality

THE CHRISTIAN RELIGION IS NOT A FOOTBALL TEAM
"Snakes and Ladders" is a board game in which you move along according to the throw of the dice, except that if you land on a square with a ladder you progress rapidly upward and if you land on a square with a snake you plunge swiftly down. In the quest for identity, finding Christ—to understate the case—is like landing on a ladder square: as I have explained in the last couple of chapters, in Christ we have an identity which is not dependent on people's opinions and which opens us to the whole of creation. It is analogous to the divine identity which is completely distinct from and totally other than everything in creation and also includes everything in creation as something that expresses but does not limit it. This human identity is distinct from what it knows, never reducible to what is perceived, and at the same time finding form in all that plays out before it. Each human life is, ultimately, what the person concerned is to be for all eternity and also the adventures of that person in a body in time and place, just as Jesus Christ is the King of heavenly glory and the poor man who walked in Nazareth. It encompasses both the abundance of the divine presence which knows no impossibility and the constraints and limitations of a particular earthly journey. For Christ's followers it is, as He promised, an abundant life, for it is a participation in the life of Him through whom "all things were made"[1] so that Saint Paul can say to those who have it, "all things are yours,"[2] adding the vital context, "and you are Christ's, and Christ is God's."[3]

This abundant and happy life is that of innocence, like that of the child we are told to become to enter the kingdom of heaven. Thomas Traherne had an intuition of it from his recollections of childhood:

> Eternity was manifest in the Light of the Day, and something infinite behind everything appeared: which talked

---
[1] John 1.3 [2] 1 Corinthians 3.21
[3] 1 Corinthians 3.23

> with my expectation and moved my desire. The city seemed to stand in Eden, or to be built in Heaven. The streets were mine, the temple was mine, the people were mine, their clothes and gold and silver were mine, as much as their sparkling eyes, fair skins and ruddy faces. The skies were mine, and so were the sun and moon and stars, and all the World was mine; and I the only spectator and I enjoyer of it.[4]

This is the life of Paradise, before Eve and Adam divided it up by choosing to eat the fruit of the tree of the knowledge of good and evil, so deciding to include some things but not others in their lives and thus diminishing who they were. It is all-encompassing, including the whole cosmos: it is the original identity of the human race.

That is where the snake comes in.

It comes in not just for Eve and Adam, but also for those who have reached the top of this ladder or at least are the inheritors of those who have done so. They know, or have heard tell, that those belonging to Christ will inherit all things, that here they have found the truth, that the reach of their apprehension is universal. So, with an identity apparently in place, they happily roll the die to go forward from their high position on the board toward the finish. But they do not reckon on landing on a snake square. If they do, they risk their last state being worse than their first. The snake's temptation is to understand their Christian identity as being over and against the identity of others. They feel themselves urged, in the current of the identity politics that I considered in Chapter Two, to fight against others for recognition of who they are in a zero-sum contest to big themselves by belittling others. This is not the way to find a true identity. The dynamic at work here is discerningly described by H. A. Williams in his book, *Chastity, Poverty and Obedience*:

> For, instead of worshipping the true God who gives and establishes my personal identity, it is easy enough for me to worship an idol which robs me of identity and puts its own ugly self in my place. Then, in the name of religion, I want to reduce everybody else to

---

4 Thomas Traherne, *Centuries of Meditation* (Faith Press, 1969), 3.2, p. 110

my own non-entity so that my idol's empire may be further extended.[5]

Even the Christian call to compassion can be enlisted in this battle to belittle and its call to a universal love for humanity made into a cudgel to beat down those who do not identify themselves in the same way. But the Christian religion is not a football team to be supported as it endeavors to defeat other football teams with which we do not identify. It teaches the way to universal love; it shows us how to see every human person from the perspective of the all-loving Creator who sustains all that is; it guides us into the heart of that love, so that as the sun rises on all so its followers can gladden, and share gladness in, all and as the rain falls on all so their tears can respond to all human sorrow.[6] To try to replace that empathy with empire and that tenderness with a tendency to partiality is to lose Christ-given identity and go all the way down a long and slippery snake back to a crude, contemptuous identity that is socially fueled rather than spirit-led. A campaign to have one's identity paid for out of the reserves of social capital replaces the struggle of the desert to allow God to reign in the heart.

UNIVERSALITY IS UNIVERSAL

A sense of human universality, a sense that who one is includes all who are and all that is, is by no means the private property of those who identify themselves as Christian. It is natural. The teaching of Christianity enables us to recover the natural ability to identify with all in love and compassion and to reverence the whole of creation. But that sort of teaching is not exclusive to Christian teachers. There are parallels in other religions which also teach that humanity is one, including even that that oneness is personified. And then there are those specially gifted individuals in whom the sense of identity has not hardened into a carapace of conventional hand-me-down signifiers but who are sensitive after the manner of primordial people to every expression that God has given through the creation to His (and therefore to ultimate) identity: there are poets. D. H. Lawrence describes the way of knowing that religion and poetry have in common as "a process of association, linking

---

5 Cited as the frontispiece to Robert Bolton, *The One and the Many* (Sophia Perennis, 2008)   6 Cf. Matthew 5.45

THE MYSTERY OF IDENTITY

up, binding back (*religio*) or referring back towards a centre and a wholeness." It is, he says, "the way of poetic and religious consciousness, the instinctive act of synthesis."[7] Human nature, the religions of the world and poets are all telling us: don't go down this snake, don't mistake your ghetto for the reality of the universe, don't think that your folk alone know that all folk are one. In the remainder of this chapter I shall unfold the sayings of human nature, the religions and poets against the snake.

There is a natural way of knowing that each person contains the whole universe. You don't need the teaching of religion for this and you don't need to be a poet, though poets have written much about it. You simply need to fall in love. Then the other person will mean the world to you and, if you are of a disposition to contemplate higher things, the sun, the moon and the stars also. To love another person is to know the world (and so on) as that person does. It is in a sense to be given all things afresh; it is to know everyone anew; it is to see the complete cosmos rather with the loved one's eyes than one's own. That is enough to teach us that the complete picture is not our private property, but it goes further than that. However reciprocated the giving of cosmic significance to the dearly beloved is, there are going to be other significant others in that person's life who will expand the universe of the one who loves to include not only the beloved in person but also these significant others and their drinking in of the creation. They, too, will have significant others who will in turn have their perception of the whole cosmos. Consequently, human identity, in its aspect of similarity or identification with what is perceived as opposed to its aspect of utter distinctness of perspective and apprehension, is not only universal in the sense of including all that is in awareness: it also includes an ever-expanding circle of other persons with universal awareness. This can start with loving somebody, go on to include those who matter to that person and end with being wholly aware, or—simply—holy. So we could reverse the old joke about Adam being in Paradise because he had no mother-in-law and say that Adam fell from grace because he had no in-laws to stop him thinking that the significance of the universe ended with him and his own. So nature—it is natural to love—teaches us that (in the felicitous phrase of a contemporary

---

7   D. H. Lawrence, *Apocalypse* (Penguin Books, London, 1995), p. 190

theologian) "A person is first and foremost a limitless capacity, a place where the all shows itself with a special inflection."[8] The being without limit comes first from the individual's identification with the universe and then multiplies indefinitely through others' identification with it and those others' identification with others and so on, making of identity a kaleidoscope of gloriously variegated colors. It is natural to have an identity so boundless that nothing ever perceived is excluded from it.

However, it is a matter of common observation that people can find in-laws difficult and tiresome. Identity is in practice less than all-embracing. My point is not that everyone in the world loves everybody else, but that moving in this direction is proper to human nature and that we can tell that it is so from what happens when we fall in love. Exemplifying this, we could say that the heartless system of Soviet communism collapsed because Gorbachev loved his wife. A recent drama suggests as much. Its director said, "I am convinced that *perestroika* could not have happened had it not been for Raisa and his love for her" and a report about it observes that in the play "—and perhaps, in reality—it was his devotion to her that compelled Mr. Gorbachev, as Soviet leader, to value human life above ideology or geopolitics."[9] If nature teaches us the direction to go to realize our full identity through loving another and then others too, it follows that religion clarifies and enables the journey by healing rather than destroying and rebuilding. This is particularly clear if we think of Christ as being the loved one in the process I have been outlining, for loving Him not only entails love of His Mother but also, according to His explicit teaching, love of every human person. "This is my commandment," He says, "that you love one another as I have loved you";[10] and He identifies Himself with those in need, such as the thirsty and the hungry.[11] That identification is also with those who are in need of mercy, because alienated by their sin. So Saint Paul says that "for our sake" He was made "to be sin":[12] in other words, He is identified with the whole of humanity. He is the Universal

---

8   David Bentley Hart, *That All Shall be Saved: Heaven, Hell and Universal Salvation* (Yale University Press, 2019), p. 153
9   *The Economist*, January 16th-22nd, 2021, p. 76
10 John 15.12   11 Matthew 25.31-46
12 2 Corinthians 5.21

THE MYSTERY OF IDENTITY

Man and calls us to be as He is: open to all humanity even in its degradation. Father Zosima, in *The Brothers Karamazov*, singles out this identification with the sinfulness of all humanity as the purpose of monastic life. He teaches about a monk's life that:

> When he knows that he is not only worse than all those in the world, but is also guilty before all people, on behalf of all and for all, for all human sins, the world's and each person's, only then will the goal of our unity be achieved. For you must know, my dear ones, that each of us is undoubtedly guilty on behalf of all and for all on earth, not only because of the common guilt of the world, but personally, each one of us, for all people and for each person on this earth. This knowledge is the crown of the monk's path, and of every man's path on earth.[13]

That is to say that it is natural for identity to include everybody else, whatever they may have done, and monastic spiritual endeavor, or simply human realization, works towards this. The snake suggestion that our identity, even if it is a Christian one, becomes stronger when others are denigrated is a lie: the truth is our nature is inclusive of all.

That truth is recognized in the work of philosophers. Such was Leibniz who (in his words) "tried to uncover and unite the truth buried and scattered under the opinions of all the different philosophical sects" and developed the idea of monads, "the only true substances"[14] which "all strive after the infinite, the whole."[15] A monad in this sense is immaterial and has its own individual God-given identity. The human person is such *par excellence*. Leibniz regarded souls as "living mirrors or images of the universe of created things" and minds as "images of the Deity or Author of nature Himself, capable of knowing the system of the universe."[16] Robert Bolton, writing in this tradition, describes this reciprocal relationship between the identity of the universe and the individual:

---

13 Fydor Dostoevsky, *The Brothers Karamazov* (Oxford University Press, 1994), translated by Richard Pevear and Larissa Volokhonsky (Everyman's Library, London, 1997), p. 164
14 https://plato.stanford.edu/entries/leibniz/
15 Leibniz, *The Monadology and Other Philosophical Writings*, translated with introduction and notes by Robert Latta (Oxford University Press, 1898), p. 250
16 Ibid., p. 266

> In reality, science, culture, religion, the world itself as we know it, depend on the creative intentionality which is sustained by the energies of the soul of the individual. The essential building-blocks of the universe must in this case be not things, but centers of cognition and creative energy. Here is the central issue common to both spirituality and personal identity.[17]

He concludes that "the individual and the universal are not alternatives, since each is derived from the other" and that "the individual being is a world-containing entity."[18] If, as Proclus (a likely influence on Leibniz) says, "Every soul is all things,"[19] I am all that I observe—everything except my contemplating self. Yet, if I am my contemplating self then in being what I observe I am what I am not, for I am not what I see—even of myself—for it is I who see it. So there is an apparent paradox here: I am identified with my experience of all that I perceive (which is nothing other than my life) and also disidentified with it. This images God's relation with His creation, for as Saint Paul writes to the Romans, "His invisible attributes, namely, his eternal power and divine nature, have been clearly perceived, ever since the creation of the world, in the things that have been made"[20] and He also utterly transcends the world which manifests His immanent presence. For both the human person and for God there is the double aspect of identity that I began this book by observing: it means both being the same as and being uniquely different. We cannot have an identity without having a life with which we are identified in the sense of being constituted by these experiences, this awareness or this knowing, yet we are dead if there is not someone—whether this is called a monad, or a center of cognition and creative energy, or simply a human person—who has these experiences or awareness or knowing and that someone is uniquely different, in the image of God who is utterly other. Indeed, we need to find this identity as a uniquely different person in order to be able to identify with all that is. This gives us freedom from being dependent on what certain others think of us and freedom

---

17 Robert Bolton, *Self and Spirit* (Sophia Perennis, 2005), p. 43
18 Ibid.
19 Cited in Robert Bolton, *Person, Soul and Identity* (Minerva Press, 1994), p. 153   20 Romans 1.20

to be open to everyone. In Ferrucci's words, "From a discovery of self-reliance and individuality there can be a progressive transition to an all-embracing realization of universality."[21]

RELIGION TEACHES UNIVERSALITY

So both philosophy and psychology point to this capacity for universal identification. Religion is about realizing it, for it is about being friends with God through whom all was made and in whom all is sustained in being. Religion teaches us to be open to the universe and that each other person also in some sense contains the whole universe and is capable of realizing it. Religion also proclaims or echoes the idea of a Universal Man. Religion as such is in some way related to universality. Judaism, although an ethnic religion (one belonging to a particular people), aspires according to Biblical texts to embrace all of humanity. It looks forward to a time when, in the words of the prophet Zechariah, "Ten men from every nation shall take hold of the robe of a Jew, saying, 'Let us go with you, for we have heard that God is with you.'"[22] It has a special emphasis on welcoming the stranger: its people are instructed to love the stranger, for they were strangers in Egypt once.[23] It values every human life, as in the Talmudic saying, "Whoever saves a life, it is considered as if he saved an entire world."[24] It looks forward to a Messiah with a universal role, who is told by the Lord, "I will make you as a light for the nations, that my salvation may reach to the end of the earth."[25]

This latter is explicit in the Christian tradition. It might seem that this would, or even should, set its followers against people who do not fully accept Jesus as the Christ. Yet this is the view of an excessively low Christology, one that tends to see Jesus as a mere man and so to feel it has to say, "Our man is better than your man." If, on the other hand, Christ is the Universal Man, God Incarnate and the Embodiment of Humanity, then "your man" is also "our man," for "all things were created through him and for him."[26] Only a weak belief in Christ wants to try to diminish the universe of another tradition, for a firm belief recognizes Him

---

21 Piero Ferrucci, *What We May Be: The Vision and Techniques of Psychosynthesis* (HarperCollins, 1990), p. 69   22 Zechariah 8.23
23 Deuteronomy 10.19   24 Mishnah Sanhedrin 4:5
25 Isaiah 49.6   26 Colossians 1.16

in each other person, acknowledging that by taking human flesh God in some sense shares His universal sovereignty with every human being. Each person is the whole world, a microcosm who as vicegerent relates to the macrocosm as God relates to all peoples, places, and times. In the strength of their belief in Christ, Christians can be open to all the spiritual riches of the world. As Pope Francis observes in *Fratelli Tutti*, "A healthy openness never threatens one's own identity" and "authentic identity" is not "preserved by an impoverished isolation."[27] The Church is, therefore, "a home with open doors"[28] with "a heart open to the whole world."[29] Her very rootedness in the particular demands this, for

> It is impossible to be "local" in a healthy way without being sincerely open to the universal, without feeling challenged by what is happening in other places, without openness to enrichment by other cultures, and without solidarity and concern for tragedies affecting other peoples.[30]

The unhealthy alternative is a narcissism for which anything beyond certain boundaries is a threat. This comes from a weak identity. A strong identity has no difficulty in speaking out (as Pope Francis does) for "religious freedom for all believers."[31] It can allow others to be, to worship in their own way, and to have their own say. And it can be a gift and a blessing to those who have a different identity, for "the deeper, stronger and richer our identity is, the more we will be capable of enriching others with our proper contribution."[32]

CHRISTIAN IDENTITY

What, then, is Christian identity? In one sense, it is a characteristic of a civilization or culture and so of people who live in such a tradition. The historian Tom Holland, in his magisterial narrative of Christian history, *Dominion: The Making of the Western Mind*, argues convincingly that people inheriting the western intellectual tradition are Christian, since their values have been formed by Christian history. This, he claims, is so even if they disclaim any

---

27 Pope Francis, *Fratelli Tutti* (CTS, 2020), paragraph 148, p. 72
28 Ibid., paragraph 276, pp. 133-34   29 Ibid., title of Chapter Four, p. 63
30 Ibid., paragraph 146, p. 71   31 Ibid., paragraph 279, p. 135
32 Ibid., paragraph 282, p. 136

association with Christianity: simply a sense that people matter and that power is not the same as righteousness is something inherited from it. This identity does not depend on any belief in the supernatural. It is handed down from one generation to the next. Holland gives as an example knowing his loving godmother, Aunty Deb and her "unfailing kindness"[33] which left a mark on him even when he lost Christian belief. He came to realize that he was still a Christian through studying and writing about ancient Greece and Rome and becoming aware of his reaction to it: "The more years I spend immersed in the study of classical antiquity, so the more alien I increasingly found it." So he asked himself:

> Why did I find this disturbing? Because, in my morals and my ethics, I was not a Spartan or a Roman at all. That my Christian belief in God had faded over the course of my teenage years did not mean that I had ceased to be Christian. For a millennium and more, the civilisation into which I had been born was Christendom. Assumptions that I had grown up with—about how a society should properly be organised, and the principles that it should uphold—were not bred of classical antiquity, still less of 'human nature', but very distinctively of that civilisation's Christian past. So profound has been the impact of Christianity on the development of Western civilisation that it has come to be hidden from view. It is the incomplete revolutions which are remembered; the fate of those which triumph is to be taken for granted.[34]

That sort of identity is of course vulnerable: to history being forgotten, to a paucity of Aunty Deb figures, to systematic programs of extirpation. And, if its true values begin to fade from awareness, it can be exploited by political leaders who prioritize the assertion of ethnic dominance over the ethic of universal compassion.

It is rooted, as Holland traces in his book, in belief. Indeed, establishing that connection between identity and belief rather than, for example, identity and class or country, was itself born of the Christian tradition. He observes: "That an identity might be defined by belief was in itself a momentous innovation; but that the

---

33 Tom Holland, *Dominion: The Making of the Western Mind* (Little, Brown, 2019), p. 518   34 Ibid., pp. xxviii–xxix

learned and illiterate alike might be joined by it, 'becoming—despite their multitude—one single body', was no less startling a notion."[35] He gives an example of a prisoner arrested in Vienne replying to every question put to him by his interrogators, "I am a Christian."

> Rather than tell them his name, or where he had been born, or whether he were slave or free, he had instead repeatedly insisted that he had no status save that of a follower of Christ.[36]

That belief in one sense distinguishes the believer from others who do not believe and identifies him or her with those who do believe. In another, it identifies the believer with everyone, for it is a belief in God in whom all have their being and life.

"Catholic" has this double reference: to those holding Catholic belief and to everyone, for that is what "catholic" means. It is identity in the two senses of being different and being the same. In its particularity, the Catholic faith presents a path to becoming one with all in universal love, which is becoming a true human being, for each person is made in the image of God in whom are all possibilities. Spanning these two senses is a Church in which "There is no distinction between Jew and Greek,"[37] which is universal in the sense of including people of all nations and places, for "God is spirit, and those who worship him must worship in spirit and in truth,"[38] not restricting themselves to one place rather than another. The Catholic Church instantiates universal identity: it is the gathering of those who gather all into their hearts, especially the poor or those in need. It reiterates the paradox of the incarnation, of the universal present in the particular; it makes explicit that each person is identified with every person; it is present in a state—the Vatican—but is transnational. The tension between its distinctive and universal identity is in a sense resolved by the refusal of Jesus to fight when they come to arrest Him in the Garden of Gethsemane: being the body of Christ, it is not called to assert its identity against others, but rather to allow Him to fulfill His promise, "I, when I am lifted up from the earth, will draw all people to myself."[39] His way is the way of love and sacrifice.

---

35 Ibid., p. 106, citing Origen, *Commentary on John*, 10.237
36 Ibid., pp. 97–98
37 Romans 10.12
38 John 4.24
39 John 12.32

SUFI SAGACITY

Wisdom about the universal and the particular, about the double aspect of identity for God and the human person alike as being both the same and being uniquely different, is not found in the Catholic tradition alone. This apparent paradox, this ambiguity about how things are, this question of identity, informs the thinking of sages in other streams of thought. The mystery is universal. An outstandingly deep expositor of it is the Islamic Sufi Master, Ibn al-'Arabī (1165-1240). His theology envisages the double aspect of God's identity as being known through the human faculties of reason and imagination. Reason on its own can only know that God is unknowable: utterly different, yet the source of all reality in the universe. Imagination, however, can know (to put it in Saint Paul's words again) "His invisible attributes" through "the things that have been made,"[40] for they speak of Him who made them. Ignoring this latter speaking leads to separation from God and forgetting Him, as has in fact happened to a large extent in the western tradition with its primary emphasis on reason. Reason alone cannot receive revelation, because it relates to God's identity in its aspect of distinctness and distance; revelation, on the other hand, speaks through similarity, which is God's identity in its aspect of mercy and closeness, reaching out to humanity. God Himself is to be considered neither as merely transcendent, for then He would be unapproachable, or merely immanent, for that would just be pantheism. Revelation is known through both reason and imagination. In Ibn al-'Arabī's words, "Through reason one knows but does not see, while through unveiling one sees but does not know."[41] Theology needs both abstract thought and visionary language, which latter in contrast to the former uses the vocabulary of particular created things. These things themselves are "imagination" for Ibn al-'Arabī, for the term includes everything between the absolute reality of God and the nothingness of non-being. Creation is both real because God sustains it and unreal because without God it is nothing. So it is in the same category as poetry, prophecy, and dreams. All speak of God, none is God. Their images express God, but His mystery hides behind

---

40 Romans 1.20
41 William C. Chittick, *Imaginal Worlds: Ibn al-'Arabī and the Problem of Religious Diversity* (Suhail Academy, 2001), p. 165

their imaginal identity. That utter mystery is at the heart of the identity of every thing and person.

Yet human persons are distinct from things. In the words of William C. Chittick (to whose presentation of Ibn al-'Arabī's thought, here cited, my own is deeply indebted):

> All things other than human beings are defined by specific and delimited attributes. Human beings are defined by being the form of God.... The true meaning of existing as something other than a human being is to be defined by a specific limitation and to dwell in a "known station," but the true meaning of existing as a human being is to abandon all limitations and to enter the unknown station.... Once human beings are emptied of their own limitations, God discloses Himself fully within them, since they alone are made in His form.[42]

This is what Ibn al-'Arabī calls the "Station of No Station." Here the divine form is actualized and so there is no constraint by "any specific station," but rather a standing with the divine reality in every station.[43] It is a transcendence of limitation; it is being present with God in all His creation; it is the achievement of a universal identity.

I will say more in the final chapter about how this is achieved. My point here is that awareness of the possibility of a universal identity, such as Saint Paul intimated when he wrote "It is no longer I who live, but Christ who lives in me"[44] or claimed to be "all things to all people,"[45] is known in more than one tradition. Realizing, or becoming aware of, the mystery of God's presence in one's own person and so realizing, or becoming aware of, that mystery in all things is the calling of humanity as such: it is universal. Each of us has the potential to identify with the whole cosmos, as God does in His aspect of similarity or nearness.

UNIVERSAL MAN

'Abd al-Karîm al-Jîlî, another Sufi sage born about a century after Ibn al-'Arabī and writing in his tradition, puts it this way: "Each individual of human kind contains the others entirely, without

---

42 Ibid., p. 170
43 Ibid.
44 Galatians 2.20
45 1 Corinthians 9.22

THE MYSTERY OF IDENTITY

anything lacking." Jîlî means that he or she contains them, and indeed all existing things, through the presence of the divine reality which includes them. However, he makes this distinction: "some only contain things potentially, while others, that is the perfect among the prophets and saints, actually contain them." This containing is the realization of their identity with the essence of all existing things, of their sharing of the same essence. There are degrees to this. The highest is "the universal man" who is a "synthesis of all the essential realities of existence."[46] He "comprises in himself correspondences with all the realities of existence. He corresponds with the higher realities by his own subtle nature, and he corresponds with lower realities by his coarse nature."[47] He is to God "what a mirror is to a person who looks at himself in it."[48]

It follows that he participates in God's presence in the whole of creation. The essence of his life is also the essence of all creation. This essence identifies him with all that is. What then is the identity of this essence? It is necessarily beyond every form in creation, for "the things that have been made" are only partial expressions of it since they are mutually exclusive. So it cannot be denoted or defined. However, it can be pointed to by poetic language which does not identify it with anything particular but rather awakens an intuition of its presence by speaking through analogies of its elusiveness. Here are some lines from Jîlî which personify essence, whose articulated elusiveness is intensified by the lines being translated first into French (by Titus Burckhardt) and then (by me) into English:

> The Essence in you enjoys the purity of wine;
> All union outside of Her is only dispersion.
> She shows Herself transcending all description,
> Without analogy and without there being any relations within Her.
> As the rising sun effaces the gleam of the planets,
> Although they exist in principle through it,
> She is darkness without day and without dusk,
> But outside of Her dwelling, the troop wanders in the desert.

---

46 'Abd al-Karîm al-Jîlî, *De l'Homme Universel, extraits du livre Al-insân Al-kâmil*, traduit de l'arabe et commentés par Titus Burkhardt (Dervy-Livres, 1975), p. 27. My translation from the French.
47 Ibid., p. 28   48 Ibid., p. 29

Universe & Universality

What unsurpassable limits show themselves to the
  caravan that tends towards Her!
So that it remains perplexed by Her and cannot read
  the letters.
The paths towards Her are hidden, neither contours
  nor science betray Her.
She refuses intimacy; Her proud beauties defend Her.
A covered track, obliterated and narrow, leads towards Her;
The deluded traveler stops to one side.
She levels the sciences of the worlds as ignorance.
Never does the intellect master Her purity to mingle with it;
Never does thought smell Her intoxicating perfume.
The fire that guides remains ignorant of Her paths;
Sure light does not illuminate her roads.
The most perplexed of the perplexed shows Her most clearly;
For they neither live nor die in Her.
Her qualities are drowned in the Ocean of her glory,
Without dying, they perish in Her depth.
Nothing replies to the question: what is She?
Neither name nor attribute; the Essence is too sublime
  for that.[49]

Jîlî explains why she cannot be given a name or attribute: "when a quality or a name or any attribute whatever" is envisaged in the Unity of Essence "it is always in virtue of a particular point of view that such a quality exists and not in the Essence as Such." Essence, he says, is "absolute Being."[50] Any particular being is relative to it, not absolute, and so not universal.

KRISHNA

In the Hindu tradition, the universal is personified in the mythical figure of Krishna. In the sixth-century text, the *Bhāgavata-purāṇa*, he is addressed with these words: "O Soul of the Universe, thy birth and thy actions among the beasts, men, sages and sea monsters is ever a mystery, O thou who art non-born and non-acting." A Sanskrit scholar, Dominique Wohlschlag, gives this commentary:

> Krishna is here called Soul (or Self) of the universe (*viśvātman*), the root VIŚ signifying total penetration, from which

---

49 Ibid., pp. 81-82   50 Ibid., p. 82

THE MYSTERY OF IDENTITY

comes the meaning of the word 'all' for the adjective *viśva*. The translation of this by the word 'universe' is quite opportune since *universum* is 'the totality of things turned towards one (goal)', or perhaps better, 'that which is turned towards the one'.[51]

He is therefore "the supreme identity."[52] In such an identity it is possible to fulfill the commandment to love one's neighbor as oneself. To do this, it necessary to know the self one is loving. Wohlschlag explains:

> It is certainly not the petty ego which is to be loved, but the *ātman* which is in us and which is embodied by Krishna: 'I live in the heart of all beings' (*Bhagavad-gītā*, 15, 15). To identify this reality is to know oneself in the sense of the aphorism of Delphi. This is the supreme identity which makes God our only neighbour, intimate friend, and *alter ego*.[53]

He goes on to quote Ananda Coomaraswamy's words, "It is this Self that the man who really loves himself or others, loves in himself and in them."[54] Universality is universal: finding it in one religion does not entitle us to assume it is not present elsewhere. We should expect to find it elsewhere, for human nature is universal. The vital thing is to ask, "Who am I?" This is, writes Wohlschlag, "*vicāra-yoga*, the path of questioning" and gives the answer "that our true self is beyond the *nāmā-rūpa*," meaning beyond name and form. He continues:

> It is the cosmic illusion that makes us identify with our body, our ego, our thoughts, our desires, losing sight of the fact that our only true Self is none other than the Master of the senses, the only real agent. There is no true consciousness outside of this.[55]

---

51 Dominique Wohlschlag, *The Queen and the Avatar* (originally *La Reine et l'avatar: mythologie de Krishna*), translated by Deborah Bell (Matheson Trust, 2017), p. 74   52 Ibid., p. 76
53 Ibid., p. 90
54 Ibid., p. 91, citing Ananda K. Coomaraswamy, *Hinduism and Buddhism* (Greenwood Press, 1971), p. 13
55 Wohlschlag, *The Queen and the Avatar*, p. 109

Another way of saying this is that only right action, acting in accord with the divine will, is true to who we really are. The philosopher Robert Bolton observes:

> Moral evil typically results from a kind of forgetfulness and passional self-identification with something which is not of the same order as the true self. One can see a similar conception of the origin of moral evil in a story in the Hindu scriptures. At the beginning of the world, the gods and demons were being taught about the true self by a discussion. The first possibility considered was that this self was one and the same as the body. Once this was said, the king of the demons would hear no more, and went away telling everyone that this was indeed what the true self was.[56]

A limited sense of self leads to limited values in action. When there were riots in the United Kingdom some time back, one owner of a wrecked shop observed that the rioters just didn't see the big picture. That picture includes the universe and is universal. Identifying with something—or someone—less than the Lord of all blinkers you. The essence escapes you.

SILENCE, AGAIN

Yet, one way or another, the idea of a universal essence in which more partial and limited identities are subsumed is universal. The teaching of Buddhism presents it as a void, which is primary to all things. To enter the void is to gain the identity of the void, that is: to lose any particular identity. It is therefore to know all things through not knowing in the sense of closing oneself off from the mystery by assuming that one has apprehended reality. It is also to cease to suffer since loss is not possible if one is not identified with any particularity. This state is one in which division between entities—and, therefore, anything of an adversarial nature—ceases to be and so the one who exists in this space becomes one with the source of all compassion. This parallels Christian mystical teaching about union with God except that the void (since no characteristics are attributed to it) is not considered as a transcendent presence that contains all perfections. These latter—specifically generosity,

---

56 Robert Bolton, *Self and Spirit* (Sophia Perennis, 2005), p. 41

virtue, renunciation, wisdom, effort, forbearance, truthfulness, resolve, lovingkindness, and equanimity—are to be found rather in the person of the Buddha who is a universal man in the sense that he realizes and embodies all that is most true in humanity. According to the Jātakas, traditional Buddhist tales, he goes beyond particular identity in the sense that this perfection is the result of many lives. In the story of these tales, the one who is to become the Buddha says as he commits himself to this spiritual journey, "These ten perfections do not exist in the sky above; they do not exist in the earth below, or in any of the directions that start with the East. They are established right in the depths of my heart."[57] The big picture in this telling is no picture. Those who become enlightened no longer identify with this rather than that: universal compassion is born of lack of bias. In them privative passions are silent; they can hear; they can listen with their hearts.

Here I come back to the theme at the end of Chapter Four, where I first raised the question of a quest for unlimited identity: silence—the silence of mystery, the silence of meditation, the silence of innocence. It is a big mistake to think that true identity is about a dominating assertion that would drown out other voices; it is related rather to an active perception which, quietly and attentively, participates in all that is. It is a sort of universal receptivity. The Russian poet Osip Mandelstam captures the way silence includes everything in the first stanza of his poem, "Silentium":

> She has yet to be born:
> she is music and word,
> and she eternally bonds
> all life in this world.

Silence is as it were an embryo of creation, its essence and potentially its expression. It is a source from which he aspires to sing:

> May I too reach back
> to that ancient silence,
> like a note of crystal
> pure from its source.[58]

---

57   *The Jātakas: Birth Stories of the Bodhisatta*, translated by Sarah Shaw (Penguin Books, 2006), p. xxx
58   *The Penguin Book of Russian Poetry*, edited by Robert Chandler, Boris Dralyuk and Irina Mashinski (Penguin, 2015), p. 277

POETRY

The poet especially listens to this silence, receives inspiration from the Creating Spirit, is attentive to what Heidegger called "the Open which poetry lets happen."[59] The poet is the apostle of the mystery of identity, for in the words of a perceptive writer on the theme of identity, "Poems, like identities, never have just one interpretation."[60] The poet expresses mystery, avoiding the conventional which ossifies perception and the premature closure which flees from enigma, and (in Lionel Trilling's words) "refusing the commonplaces that the culture treacherously provides for his convenience and comfort."[61] The poet W. S. Merwin observes, "a poem always comes out of what you don't know."[62] A poem is an expression of mystery, for the poet opens him or her self to the divine source of identity. Dostoevsky claims that "The poet, in the transport of inspiration, unriddles God."[63] Ibn al-'Arabī explains this inspiration in terms of imagery received:

> The friend of God witnesses the similitudes struck by God. In that witnessing he sees what it is that brings together the similitude and that for which it is struck. The similitude is identical with the object in respect of the factor that brings them together, but it is not identical in respect of the similitude. The friend of God does not strike similitudes for God. On the contrary, he knows the similitudes God has struck for Himself.[64]

The poet does not reason as a theologian might. William C. Chittick explains that for Ibn al-'Arabī:

> The subject matter of poetry is not something that one thinks about as one might think about a problem in

---

59 Martin Heidegger, *Poetry, Language, Thought* (Harper Perennial, 2001), p. 70
60 Kwame Anthony Appiah, *The Lies That Bind: Rethinking Identity* (Profile Books, 2019), p. 215
61 Lionel Trilling, *Sincerity and Authenticity* (Oxford University Press, 1974), p. 104
62 *Conversations with W. S. Merwin* (The University Press of Mississippi, 2015), p. 159
63 Joseph Frank, *Dostoevsky, A Writer in His Time* (Princeton University Press, 2010), p. 57
64 William C. Chittick, *Imaginal Worlds: Ibn al-'Arabī and the Problem of Religious Diversity* (Suhail Academy, 2001), p. 77

dogmatic theology. Rather it is something that is seen with the inner eye and heard with the inner ear. Only then is it described.[65]

The poet sees with the eye of the heart what God shows "in the things that have been made."[66] Poetic imagery, when it is inspired, might be considered as expressing what God means by His creation. Everything in it says something about Him, but it takes a poet to hear what it is; for the generality of humanity makes do with an account, mostly fashioned by devices and desires unconnected with God, of what is outward, and furthermore second-hand, lacking in the freshness of primordial perception. Whatever something says about God, that is its identity. God, as it were, delegates His uniqueness when He makes something so that it can speak of what it is. The poet Gerard Manley Hopkins expresses how things do this:

> As kingfishers catch fire, dragonflies draw flame;
> As tumbled over rims in roundy wells
> Stones ring; like each tucked string tells, each hung bell's
> Bow swung finds tongue to fling out broad its name;
> Each mortal thing does one thing and the same:
> Deals out that being indoors each one dwells;
> Selves—goes itself; *myself* it speaks, and spells,
> Crying *What I do is me: for that I came.*[67]

God is the source of "that being indoors each one dwells"—this is identity in the sense of sameness, for all that exists has being—but He is also the One who gives the distinctiveness of each thing's self which enables it to say, "What I do is me." That distinctiveness is a reflection of the utterly transcendent distinctiveness of God, given as it were out of His infinite supply. But note this: the creation is not simply a presentation of God as He is, for its showing reverses the two qualities of identity, the sameness and the difference. God is the unique source of all being: being represents Him, so that He is sometimes called "Supreme Being." There is no other source, no other who can be called Supreme Being. That is God's identity in the sense of His unique difference. As Meister Eckhart puts it, God is distinguished by His indistinction: only

---

65 Ibid., p. 70   66 Romans 1.20
67 *The Poems of Gerard Manley Hopkins* (Oxford University Press, 1970), p. 90

He is totally present in each and every thing. So what is the same in us (and all of creation) is unique in God. We all participate in being; only God is the source of being. The corollary is that what is distinct in us is the same in God. That is perhaps less obvious than the fact that we all have being because understanding it requires the metaphysical perspective in which what is distinct to us (for example, mercy and justice) is one in God, but it may be easier to grasp if I remind you that I am utterly unique just like everybody else. God gives uniqueness to all His creation without distinction. So creation manifests the identity of God rather in the manner of a mirror: it is reversed—God's uniqueness is sameness in creation and God's sameness is uniqueness in creation.

Poetry sees the oneness of God in the particulars of creation. This explains why a poet will often use apparently widely contrasting images in a single description: they may seem from a this-worldly perspective to have nothing to do with each other, yet what they have in common shows God's oneness. The juxtaposition in the poem may awaken in the reader an intuition of the divine reality that is manifested in creation which will in some measure correspond to the intuition or inspiration that led the poet to put them together. There is no question of seeing God—no one can see God and live—but rather an intuition that what cannot make sense in terms of this world gives a sense of what is beyond this world. Or, in words of Ibn al-'Arabī cited above, "The most perplexed of the perplexed shows Her most clearly"—shows, that is, the Divine Wisdom: "a spirit that is intelligent, holy, unique, manifold, subtle, mobile, clear, unpolluted, distinct, invulnerable, loving the good, keen, irresistible, beneficent, humane, steadfast, sure, free from anxiety, all-powerful, overseeing all, and penetrating through all spirits that are intelligent and pure and subtlest."[68] Although it is hidden, the poet does not see it except through what is shown, for it is "both what is secret and what is manifest"[69]—secret in itself but manifest in the form that speaks of the uniqueness of which all form is born. It is important to remember, as Ibn al-'Arabī did, that poetry or "similitudes" show us God only in one aspect of His identity, His uniqueness (for all that poetry surveys is unique). It cannot, and does not, show God

---

68 Wisdom 7.22–23   69 Wisdom 7.21

THE MYSTERY OF IDENTITY

in His utter difference. It cannot speak of His being, for the poet cannot be independent of being to contemplate it, on pain of not existing. The poet (like every artist) sees the oneness in all that is and in that oneness glimpses something of the divine oneness but cannot imagine God's distinctiveness for that would require another distinctiveness and who is like God? Only a satanic lie could pretend to this. Reason asserts the utter otherness of God and if this assertion is neglected, then any statement about how creation manifests Him is false. It is also untrue that God refrains from manifesting Himself. It is true that God is both manifest and hidden. If that cannot be squared in the terms we use to deal with this world, those opposites do coincide in God who is utterly beyond this world.

THE NECK OF THE HOURGLASS

There is more to be said, however, about the relation of the identity of creation to the identity of God. In the poem just cited, Hopkins goes on:

> I say more: the just man justices;
> Keeps gráce: thát keeps all his goings graces;
> Acts in God's eye what in God's eye he is—
> Chríst...[70]

That takes us back to what was said above about a universal identity being realized, as in Saint Paul saying it was no longer he who lived but Christ who lived in him. Not everyone achieves this: rather it belongs, as Hopkins indicates, to the just person. The one who keeps in God's grace acts in accordance with His will, as did Christ who said, "My food is to do the will of him who sent me and to accomplish his work."[71] To have Christ living in one's soul giving a sanctity such as Saint Paul's is to participate in God's universality. So what I said about the creation showing God's sameness through its difference and His difference through its sameness needs to be qualified. That reflective pattern can be imaged in two triangles touching at the apex, with the one on top inverted, so that the left hand of the bottom triangle will correspond through a straight line to the right hand of the top

---

70 *The Poems of Gerard Manley Hopkins* (Oxford University Press, 1970), p. 90
71 John 4.34

triangle and the right hand of the bottom triangle will correspond through another straight line to the left hand of the top triangle. So difference is on the left above and on the right below and similarity is on the right above and on the left below. (This relation between above and below is also how the brain is connected to the limbs—the left, characteristically distinguishing, hemisphere linked to the right and the right, characteristically holistic, hemisphere linked to the left.) In the geometrical pattern there is a point where the triangles join and the lines denoting difference and similarity cross over. At this point the direction could either be upwards to where there is difference to the left and sameness to the right or downwards to where there is sameness on the left and difference on the right.

Now, to give substance to this point, imagine it is the neck of an hourglass and sand is slowly falling through it. Above is God, the source of the time falling through the neck of the hourglass; below is creation which time makes what it is. The neck of the hourglass, or the point in the geometric diagram, is the human person whose identity is ambiguous. Either that identity tends upwards, towards God the eternal source of time, or it tends downwards, towards time and space. If its direction is upwards, then it will be tending towards a spiritual identity like God's which, in its distinctive (and—in reading order—first) aspect, will stand out as exceptionally loving and, in its universal aspect, tend to including everyone and everything's distinctness indistinctly in an all-embracing love which never ends. That direction, of course, does not replace the bodily expression of identity in terms of time and space: it is rather a matter of holding one's head high and being governed by what is above. If the direction of a human identity is downwards, then it will be tending towards an identity which is reduced to merely that of a thing of time and space. In its similar (and—in reading order—first) aspect it will be tending to see other people and all of creation as rivals because they also are in time and place, wanting the same resources; in its distinctive aspect it will be aspiring to dominate, fighting everyone and everything to keep its place. It will be divided from others, without fellow feeling. We choose our direction. We can either go upwards, where we find a spiritual identity that is first of all distinctive, and in that spiritual distinctiveness can embrace what is distinctive on a

THE MYSTERY OF IDENTITY

lesser plane (that of created forms) in other people and *a fortiori* can embrace what is distinctive on the same plane in other people, for it is the same, divine, distinction. Alternatively, we can go downwards where we will feel desperately a lack of identity in our earthly sameness to others and struggle to assert one (incomplete because relating only to things of earth) in the teeth of the truth of this lack of identity. That struggle will characterize the years left to us till we and it die. Going upwards is more difficult than going downwards, so the quest for true identity requires effort.

KNOWING GOD

It also requires vision. Without a vision, people perish, for they do not know who they are. To have a true identity, we need in some way to know God, identity's source. We cannot rise above the things of the earth, the bottom of the hourglass, if we have no sense of what is above. Hence scripture says, "This is eternal life, that they know you, the only true God, and Jesus Christ whom you have sent."[72] An identity that does not depend on the limited resources of earth or the approval of its inhabitants is gained through this two-fold knowledge. It is two-fold, for it needs to encompass both God's transcendence and His immanence, His distinctness and His similarity. Simply to know "God" is to know that one does not know, to be in the cloud of unknowing, to enter darkness, for we cannot know God's uniqueness: it is impossible to distinguish Him from anything else which is unique. We can distinguish a hen from a duck because there are different birds which can be compared to each other, but there is no other god. Any unity or uniqueness that we can know is on a lower plane, under Him. So in the darkness of faith, we reach out to God to rise above the multiplicity of the creation, to exchange the fragility of a fragmented identity for the truth of a transcendent identity invulnerable to the vicissitudes of time. Yet if this transcendence is all we hear about, its lack of connection with the world as we perceive it will make it all too easy to forget. We also need to know God as He shows Himself to us, and so the scripture says we also need to know Jesus Christ whom He sent.[73] We need to know God's identity in the world. It is shown to us in a particular way so that we have a bridge from our particular life to God's universal

---

[72] John 17.3   [73] Ibid.

life. And Christ teaches us to know and love Him in everyone. Every distinctness manifests God's sameness: He is there alike in all—all people, but also all things, for it is said of God's Word that "without him was not any thing made that was made."[74] In that saving knowledge we know that true identity is not linked to the argot of our enclave, unlike the denizens of Babel who imagined that only their particular talk could touch the transcendent and so could not understand each other. Distinctness as such images God, for He gives it to all alike so any stranger can speak of the divine to us, can tell us something of the deep identity, an identity that includes all particulars, which God wants us to find, realizing our being made in His image. That deep identity is a mystery, not only because it is the same in every distinctness, not only because it is unknowably above anything this world can show us, but because both aspects of it—identity as distinct and unique and identity as sameness or identification with all—are, in God, simply one. His unique beauty is the final mystery.

Religion teaches us about it; thought clarifies it for us; poetry shows it to us. That does not mean that poets see God: rather their gift—and burden—is not to be trapped in a foreclosed identity. They see not the outward and limited, but the infinite in all things: the whole in the part, eternity in a grain of sand, the Word in what He speaks. Pushkin's poem "The Prophet" tells something about this transformative vocation:

> I wandered in a lonely place;
> my soul's great thirst tormented me—
> and at a crossing of the ways
> a six-winged seraph came to me.
> Like slumber, fingers light and wise
> he laid upon my weary eyes
> and like an eagle's in amaze
> they opened with all-seeing gaze.
> My ears he touched—and noise and sound
> poured into them from all around:
> I heard the heavens in commotion,
> and angel hosts' celestial flight,
> and sea-beasts stirring in the ocean,
> and vines' growth on the valley-side.

---

74 John 1.3

And to my lips he bent, tore out
my tongue, an idle, sinful thing;
with bloody hand, in my numb mouth
he placed a serpent's subtle sting.
And with his sword he clove my breast,
and took my trembling heart entire;
a coal alight with brilliant fire
into my opened breast he thrust.
In that lone place I lay as dead,
and God's voice called to me, and said:
'Prophet, arise, behold and hearken:
over the world, by sea and land,
go, and fulfil my will unshaken,
burn with my Word the heart of man.'[75]

The reference to "a six-winged seraph" alludes to the prophet Isaiah, but the poem also references "traditions concerning the 'heart-cleansing' of the Prophet Muhammad."[76] This is a calling to a universal vision, to an "all-seeing gaze," and to hearing "noise and sound...from all around," and to seeing and hearing the Word, the Divine Essence, in all of it. The speaker's tongue is torn out: he no longer speaks in a limited way about what is outward, but with a serpent's wisdom penetrates to the essence of all. His identity is remade so that it is universal. He is a prophet.

A POET'S IDENTITY

That is not exactly the same thing as a poet, though a poet can be a prophet and vice-versa and a poet shares with the prophet a sense of what is beyond creation. The prophet speaks for God; the Divine Word is central to his life and identity. The poet, rather, is inspired to speak in a way that allows the essence of things and people to be heard. In other words, he or she hears and articulates with a special sensitivity what God says through creation's being, penetrating to its participation in the divine distinctiveness. The craft involves prescinding from the conventional view that sees mainly in more or less tired formulations which ignore the mystery of identity. Receptivity is at its heart and, since knowledge is

---

75   *The Penguin Book of Russian Poetry*, edited by Robert Chandler, Boris Dralyuk and Irina Mashinski, (Penguin, 2015), pp. 72–73
76   Ibid., p. 72, footnote 7

according to the knower, that characteristically means not having a foreclosed identity. We can only see the world in terms of our self and if we have already decided who we are it will not be able to speak its secrets to us. So a poet remains open, tending to defer establishment of personal identity. Keats famously spoke of Shakespeare's "negative capability,"[77] meaning his ability to get out of the way to allow his characters to be fully who they are. The romantic poet knew of what he was speaking. He had this to say about "the poetical character" which was his:

> It is not itself—it has no self—it is every thing and nothing—it has no character—it enjoys light and shade—it lives in gusts, be it foul or fair, high or low, rich or poor, mean or elevated,—it has as much delight in conceiving an Iago as an Imogen. What shocks the virtuous philosopher delights the camelion poet. It does no harm from its relish of the dark side of things, any more than from its taste for the bright one, because they both end in speculation. A poet is the most unpoetical of anything in existence, because he has no identity; he is continually in for, and filling, some other body. The sun, the moon, the sea and men and women, who are creatures of impulse, are poetical, and have about them an unchangeable attribute; the poet has none, no identity. He is certainly the most unpoetical of all God's creatures. If, then, he has no self, and if I am a poet, where is the wonder that I should say I would write no more?

He explains to his correspondent the difficulty he therefore has in speaking for himself:

> It is a wretched thing to confess, but it is a very fact, that not one word I ever utter can be taken for granted as an opinion growing out of my identical nature. How can it, when I have no nature? When I am in a room with people, if I am free from speculating on creations of my own brain, then, not myself goes home to myself, but the identity of every one in the room begins so to press upon me, that I am in a very little time annihilated—not only among men; it would be the same in a nursery of children.

---

77 Letter to George and Tom Keats, www.poetryfoundation.org/articles/69384/selections-from-keatssletters.

He is not even sure whether his motivation to write poetry is his own:

> I feel assured I should write from the mere yearning and fondness I have for the beautiful, even if my night's labours should be burnt every morning, and no eye ever shine upon them. But even now I am perhaps not speaking from myself, but from some character in whose soul I now live.[78]

This is more than an actor receiving temporary identity from a part: it is receiving identity from all that is—the natural world, as well as people. It is as much a universal identity as no identity. It indicates that the zero-sum concept of identity is inadequate: identity is not limited to belonging to one person only, it can be common property. Poets—and dramatists and novelists—can make it accessible to all. Emptiness of self enables them to be full of everybody and everything and transmit this richness. The chameleon poet grows into a fullness of identity, a savoring of the divine distinctness spread through the creation, an enjoyment of the mystery in everybody. In passing on the joy, he or she teaches us that the depths of identity lie not in this or that characteristic, let alone allegiance, but rather in the quality of enjoyment: not in what is perceived but in how it is perceived. Envy is ignorant: we can enjoy others' good as our own. Spiritually—that is to say, here below within the soul and properly in heaven—we can be each other, but each in a different way so that personal individuality is not primarily in a particular life as in a particular enjoyment of all life, not in principle excluding anyone's life. At the deepest level that is sharing God's joy in all that is.

The French poet Rimbaud put this unmooring from a particular life at its most stark. "I is another," he wrote. For him, "The first study of the man who wants to be a poet is his own knowledge," and he takes this to the extreme:

> I say that one has to be a seer, to make oneself a seer. The Poet makes himself a seer by a long, immense and reasoned derangement of all the senses. All the forms of love, suffering, madness he seeks himself; he exhausts in himself all poisons so as to keep only the quintessence

---

78 Letter to Mr Woodhouse, October 27th, 1818, www.john-keats.com/briefe/271018.htm

Universe & Universality

of them—ineffable torture in which he needs all faith, all superhuman strength, in which he becomes the great invalid, the great criminal, the great accursed one—and the supreme Savant—for he arrives at the unknown!

Rimbaud's intuition here is that there is something beyond what the senses tell us, something that is within all experience however extreme or beyond the pale, which is a mystery. This "unknown" is the essence of identity where there is no more partiality. He goes on to write about "horizons where the other has collapsed." These are the vistas he contemplates in asserting, "I is another."[79] The collapse of "the other" suggests the way in which every created distinction is one with every other: sharing in the one and same (for God) divine distinctiveness. The poetic art is born of an openness to this distinction, itself utterly distinct but in everything without distinction between one thing and another. The poet journeys far from even the outlying fields of sterile solipsism to the realm of identity as such, the kingdom of mystery. Here God's utter uniqueness is manifest in the meanest flower that blows; here all things alike speak of their Maker. There is mystery in how they are different if they all have that same distinction, how they exist at all if without God they would be nothing. It is the mystery of creation. It is the mystery of beauty where the manifold is one and poetry articulates silence.

That journey of the poet is an aspect of the spiritual journey as such. In Christ's telling this latter is a journey to the heart of total love of God, and love of one's neighbor as oneself;[80] it is a pilgrimage to the holy place where one is lovingly identified with the unique divine distinctiveness, the essence and heart of creation; it is a walking towards the home where all are housed without distinction. That heart, that holy place, that home is where God's love is or, simply, where God is, for God is love. We love with the love God gives us, love of both ourselves and our neighbor: one and the self-same love. And for God, loving and knowing are the same, and so to love our neighbor as our self with God's love is to know our neighbor as our self, it is for the other to become I and I the other. It is to have an identity that

---

79 Rimbaud à Paul Demeny, Lettre du Voyant, May 15, 1871, www.macval. fr/emoietmoi/spip.php?article57, my translation
80 Matthew 22.37-40

THE MYSTERY OF IDENTITY

transcends our individuality, a knowledge of the essence of all, a love that goes beyond partiality. This is the love from which the saint lives, the love of which poetry whispers.

Robert Browning had a sense of the divine distinctiveness in all things. He wrote:

> No creature's made so mean
> But that, some way, it boasts, could we investigate,
> Its supreme worth: fulfils, by ordinance of fate,
> Its momentary task, gets glory all its own,
> Tastes triumphant in the world, pre-eminent, alone.[81]

Above all Browning had a sense of this distinctiveness in people. His creations were not projections of his own individuality: they were, he said, "so many utterances of so many imaginary persons, not mine."[82] However, as Professor Seamus Perry has argued persuasively, Browning experienced "the lack of anything central or self-sufficing" in himself.[83] His poetic art, involving entering so many and varied identities of others, left him without a clear sense of his own identity, "The poet thwarting hopelessly the Man."[84] He wrote self-disparagingly to the woman who was to be his wife, "I only make men and women speak—give you truth broken into prismatic hues, and fear the pure white light, even if it is in me."[85] Yet, *Men and Women*, as his major collection of poems is called, does witness to "the pure white light" by its very variety. The "white radiance of Eternity"[86]—to return to the poem by Shelley that I quoted in Chapter One—is, outside of a few exceptional events such as the transfiguration of Christ, not visible in our life here below which can, as in Shelley's metaphor, only stain it. What we can see is the "many-colored glass"[87] through which it shines and to see many colors together is to see that light as such. So by not giving his own coloring to the lives of others,

---

81 *London Review of Books*, 3 November 2016, p. 34 (Seamus Perry, "Against the Same-Old Same-Old")   82 Ibid., p. 35
83 Ibid., p. 38
84 Sordello Book Two, ll.659ff., p. 199 in *Browning: Poetical Works*, edited by Ian Jack (Oxford University Press, 1970)
85 *London Review of Books*, 3 November 2016, p. 38 (Seamus Perry, "Against the Same-Old Same-Old")
86 Percy Bysshe Shelley, *Adonais*, stanza 52, *The Norton Anthology of Poetry* (Norton, 1983), p. 636   87 Ibid.

Universe & Universality

Browning avoids partiality and limitation. By seeing their multiple and variegated lives, he sees—and conveys in his poetry—the essence of that difference, the divine distinctiveness that all alike have. The mistake would be to take the coloring of his own life for light as such and he avoids it by seeing the colors of many other people and so not a superficial single identity but identity as such, in the mystery of its divine heart.

His poem "My Star" expresses how he sees the light in more than one color:

> ALL that I know
> Of a certain star
> Is, it can throw
> (Like the angled spar)
> Now a dart of red,
> Now a dart of blue;
> Till my friends have said
> They would fain see, too,
> My star that dartles the red and the blue!
> Then it stops like a bird; like a flower, hangs furled:
> They must solace themselves with the Saturn above it.
> What matter to me if their star is a world?
> Mine has opened its soul to me; therefore I love it.[88]

It stops and closes itself up when his friends want to see it: they must make do with Saturn, a heavy planet. This is "a world" because its very opaqueness allows them to get a handle on it and so pursue their world-related business. To the poet, by contrast, his star opens up: he sees, and loves, the essence from which variegated color comes. He perceives the meaning within beyond the outward, formal and particular. So does the eponymous artist hero of Browning's dramatic monologue, "Fra Lippo Lippi." He sees not opaqueness but meaning in the world:

> This world's no blot for us,
> Nor blank; it means intensely, and means good:
> To find its meaning is my meat and drink.[89]

That, of course, is also the poet's enterprise, and Browning undertakes it through his characterization. Fra Lippo Lippi, like so

---

88 *Browning: Poetical Works*, edited by Ian Jack (Oxford University Press, 1970), pp. 608-9 89 Ibid., p. 576, ll.313-15

THE MYSTERY OF IDENTITY

many other persons in this collection of poems, is ambiguous in his nature. On the one hand he is a former street urchin who has never taken to the ascetic practices of the religious order to which he belongs; on the other he is both immensely vital and able to see the light that shines through the colors of life. He is no blot or blank, no cipher standing for a type, not a person who can be categorized and forgotten.

The eponymous character of "Bishop Blougram's Apology" is similarly ambiguous: ambiguity is the very theme of his discourse, an elaborate defense of his worldly occupation of a role which requires a profession of faith that is not fully his own. He assumes that his interlocutor, an idealistic "literary man"[90] called Mr. Gigadibs, despises him for not having the courage of his lack of convictions, and argues that there would be little profit in being true to his doubt:

> All we have gained then by our unbelief
> Is a life of doubt diversified by faith,
> For one of faith diversified by doubt:
> We called the chess-board white,—we call it black.[91]

The whole context of Bishop Blougram's monologue is ambiguous, for the author says at the end, "he believed, say, half he spoke."[92] We do not know what is really within him, and that is the point: his identity is a mystery. That, too, is the import of these oft-quoted lines in the center of the poem which speak of how we are drawn to what we cannot be sure about, what we cannot put in one definite category or another, what cannot be classified:

> You see one lad o'erstride a chimney-stack;
> Him you must watch—he's sure to fall, yet stands!
> Our interest's on the dangerous edge of things,
> The honest thief, the tender murderer,
> The superstitious atheist, demirep
> That loves and saves her soul in new French books—
> We watch while these in equilibrium keep
> The giddy line midway: one step aside,
> They're classed and done with.[93]

---

90 Ibid., p. 671, l.975
92 Ibid., p. 671, l.980
91 Ibid., p. 651, ll.209-12
93 Ibid., p. 656, ll.395-400

Universe & Universality

Identity cannot be "classed and done with"—it is a mystery, a mystery that poets show us.

Yet not all writing is open to mystery. In fact, even accomplished and entertaining fiction can work to close it up. A literary friend of mine offered this observation:

> The identity of fictional narrators is just about always secular. And that is very persuasive for modern readers, for whom novels often offer a convincing window into the hidden inner lives and unknowable separate identities of others. Hence the growing feeling that we are all really just materialist and secular—that that is our common identity.[94]

She explained how one "well-observed novel" in particular was not true to her experience:

> Not one of the many characters has a 'mysterious' identity—they are all recognisable and predictable. Yet as I get older, other people's characters, no matter what their background, seem more and more of a mystery, so that each person seems not a separate planet, but a separate universe, or separate species.[95]

Each person *is* the whole creation, unlimited knowing, a divine mystery. As they say in Yorkshire, there's nowt so queer as folk. We cannot truly predict the identity of anyone. That includes ourselves. The greatest writers have recognized this. The title (*The Unnamable*) of the final work in Samuel Beckett's great prose trilogy points to that mystery which is so near—almost to the point of being obvious—and yet so utterly beyond our grasp. This narrator does not eschew the mysterious. Every apparent saying of identity has to be unsaid:

> Perhaps it's the door, perhaps I'm at the door, that would surprise me, perhaps it's I, perhaps somewhere or other it was I, I can depart, all this time I've journeyed without knowing it, it's I now at the door, what door, what's a door doing here, it's the last words, the true last, or it's the murmurs, the murmurs are coming, I know that well,

---

[94] Clare Asquith, private communication
[95] Ibid.

THE MYSTERY OF IDENTITY

> no not even that, you talk of murmurs, distant cries, as long as you can talk, you talk of them before and you talk of them after, more lies, it will be the silence.[96]

After more writing hugely suggestive of the truth that our real identity does not lie in time, he concludes:

> I can't go on, you must go on, I'll go on, you must say words, as long as there are any, until they find me, until they say me, strange pain, strange sin, you must go on, perhaps it's done already, perhaps they have said me already, perhaps they have carried me to the threshold of my story, before the door that opens on my story, that would surprise me, if it opens, it will be I, it will be the silence, where I am, I don't know, I'll never know, in the silence you don't know, you must go on, I can't go on, I'll go on.[97]

---

96 Samuel Beckett, *The Grove Centenary Edition, Volume II, Novels* (Grove 2006), pp. 406-7   97 Ibid., p. 407

7
Loss & Love

BIODIVERSITY

In the previous chapter I wrote about losing a narrow, selfish, and limited identity for the sake of finding a universal identity in which all are welcomed in love. Before considering how this is done, I want to look at another kind of loss of identity which can give the illusion of tending towards universality but is in reality moving in the opposite direction: the loss that comes with uniformity. This can come about either because people want to be the same as others or because people want others to be the same as them. In both cases there is likely to be a relatively weak sense of true identity. Either they feel an absence of identity and look to others to supply it, or they want to make a constructed and superficial identity seem stronger than it really is by involving others in it, by enticement or force. This conglomeration of identity works against God-given identity. God gives us both difference and sameness. The difference is in our particular form (God's sameness) and the sameness is in our common being (God's distinctness). The drive towards uniformity inverts this, making the outward form the same and—because if we are all the same in form we can't be different any other way—transposing difference to the level of being. On that level the options are being and not being, so the only way to be different (and that urge is fundamental, as Dostoevsky has so acutely observed) is for some people not to be, leaving triumphantly different the ones that still are. Hence there is cultural hegemony and even genocide. Note that all of this—being the same where God wants us to be different and being different where God wants us to be the same—is usurping the place of God who alone is different in being and the same in His manifestation of form. Concomitantly (and obviously), doing down, making miserable, and killing people who share the same being (in the attempt to be different) is against His holy law. Indifference in identity leads to indifference to life. Lack of true difference, the realization of distinctness given by God to all, tends to the false difference of the attempted division of being with the claim that some have the right to it and others not. That is the agenda of the snake saying that if you eat of the fruit of the tree of good and evil, "You will be like God."[1] This is a diabolic parody of the quest I described in the previous chapter to be like God in a good sense (to be perfect as our heavenly Father is perfect) through rising above merely earthly priorities to find a true and spiritual identity, distinguished by its exceptional love and universal in including everyone and everything's distinctness in that love.

This true and spiritual identity is in somewhat short supply on the earth: if it were not, there would not be so much fighting over lesser, earthly forms of identity. And the creation itself, concomitantly, is getting short of identity: there is a loss of biodiversity. Pope Francis observes in his encyclical letter, *Laudato Si'*:

> Each year sees the disappearance of thousands of plant and animal species which we will never know, which our children will never see, because they have been lost for ever. The great majority become extinct for reasons related to human activity. Because of us, thousands of species will no longer give glory to God by their very existence, nor convey their message to us.[2]

The human depredation of biodiversity is the sacrifice of true identity in favor of the pursuit of false identity. The "message" that Pope Francis writes of is a message of identity: the species that are being lost "give glory to God" by their distinctness which manifests to us what is one and the same in God. They are part of our true identity, for we are made to identify with all that is. Motives of profit destroy them, profit that is characteristically used to boost a sense of identity based on the false supposition that quantity—sway or purchasing power—can replace God's gift in His creation of quality. Pope Francis explains the dynamic:

> A sober look at our world shows that the degree of human intervention, often in the service of business interest and consumerism, is actually making our earth less rich and beautiful, ever more limited and grey, even as technological

---

1 Genesis 3.5
2 Pope Francis, *Laudato Si'* (CTS, 2015), paragraph 33

advances and consumer goods continue to abound limitlessly. We seem to think that we can substitute an irreplaceable and irretrievable beauty with something which we have created ourselves.[3]

The "irreplaceable and irretrievable beauty" is the identity God gives creation, the multi-colored glass staining the white radiance of eternity, an identity which He means us to share through our "dominion over the fish of the sea and over the birds of the heavens and over every living thing that moves on the earth."[4] We properly have dominion in the sense that creation is our domain: it shows us who we are; our milieu nurtures our nature; our estate reflects our identity. The "dominion over the fish of the sea" (for example) is improperly exercised when we turn "the wonderworld of the seas into underwater cemeteries bereft of colour and life"[5] in the mistaken belief that power exercised through technology can provide us with an identity according to our own will, whereas true identity is received from God according to His will. It is contemplated rather than controlled.

The result of this mistaken belief is a homogenization of the world: a tendency towards monoculture reflecting the social tendency to want to be the same as others or to make others the same as oneself. As biodiversity ebbs, the identity of creation begins to fade. Monoculture, whether the culture of the fields or culture *tout court*, becomes a sort of cancer in which replication takes over from hierarchy, order, and beauty. As the creation came from God through His creative act expressing His oneness in its diversity, so creation prepares its apocalyptic return to Him through parodying His oneness by the degeneration of its diversity. Its distance from the primordial moment when everything was fully itself is evidenced in the fading of distinction. Seasonal variety is manipulated by air freight, human beings are less sure than they used to be of their difference from animals, and gender is becoming more fluid. Language is less inflected and less rich: the erosion of the distinctiveness that Latin has and Italian lacks is at work; Shakespeare's mastery of words is not our own.

---

3 Ibid., paragraph 34   4 Genesis 1.28
5 Pope Francis, *Laudato Si'* (CTS, 2015), paragraph 41, citing Catholic Bishops' Conference of the Philippines, Pastoral Letter, *What is Happening to Our Beautiful Land?* (29 January 1988)

Roles are less demarcated: where once there may have been a ruling class, a warrior class, and a religious class, now everybody is expected to be responsible for everything; where once women nurtured life and fostered reconciliation, protecting the identity of sameness of being, and men fought to defend life and drew up demarcations, protecting the identity of distinction, now there is an expectation of universal acquiescence in eschewing any cultural construction of gender identity. Loss of the identity of distinction which is God's gift of a uniqueness like His own and the loss of the identity of sameness, whether that of personal integrity or solidarity with all of humanity and creation, which is God's gift of a sameness like His own, are indicators of a distance not only from the first moment of creation but also from the Creator. The peace of being inwardly united in Him with all He has made and the joy of outwardly showing His uniqueness to the benefit of all are being replaced by the angst of atomization and the fearful anger of the struggle to stand out from sameness.

ONLY A NOBODY CAN BE SOMEBODY

It is hardly surprising therefore that people can be jumpy about their identity. Status indicators, purchasing power, legally established right of recognition are all marshaled in its defense. Yet, with a dramatic irony worthy of the finest fiction, the opposite is the true path. It is precisely by losing anything of this ilk that we find our identity, for the simple reason that this comes from God and He will not give us who we are, our true selves, if we are blocking the gift by preferring the construction of our contriving. The "irreplaceable and irretrievable beauty" of our true identity, which (because it includes them) is like that of all the wonders of the world, is in this preference bartered for a bigger bank balance, or some such leverage, which is no more suitable for finding our identity than a bulldozer is for picking a daisy. The counter-intuitive truth is that we find who we are when we are nothing so that God can be all, for identity comes from Him. Nothingness, of course, makes people feel insecure about their identity, so this way is the road less travelled: it requires great trust. Yet it is easy to see that it has taken people who have gone down it to their destination. Saint Thérèse said that she was happy to be nothing, for if she were something, God would not be everything. Her own life illustrated both that nothingness and the universal identity she found by letting God be everything. Her radiance through space and time is incalculable. When it was already perceptible as she lay on her deathbed, she illustrated the principle by pointing out trees illuminated by the golden sun and explaining that as they would be occluded in darkness without the sunlight so would she radiate nothing without God. The principle is also illustrated by the basilica in Lisieux built in her honor: the crypt underground with pastel-colored mosaics of episodes from her short life corresponds to the nothingness of her obscurity and the great dome above with its golden illustration of her life in the glory of God corresponds to her thaumaturgical renown throughout the world. The whole edifice illustrates the gospel saying carved on its outside wall: he who humbles himself will be exalted. The humble one allows the All-High to be present and we are truly ourselves when He shines through us and He shines through us when we know our nothingness without Him.

We can't listen or see without in a sense being nothing: as soon as we are saying something for ourselves or putting on spectacles tinged with our interests, we stop hearing and seeing clearly. If our identity is what we perceive (and what is knowing but a kind of identification?), then it is who we are when we are nothing. Our identity is nothing; it is everything. It is nothing we can say for ourselves; it is nothing that we can paint upon the world. It is everything we can hear; it is everything that we can see. Indeed, it is also everything we can read. C. S. Lewis made this latter point in his *Experiment in Criticism*, indicating our need for self-transcendence if we are to find our identity:

> In reading great literature I become a thousand men and yet remain myself. Like the night sky in the Greek poem, I see with a myriad eyes, but it is still I who see. Here, as in worship, in love, in moral action, and in knowing, I transcend myself; and am never more myself than when I do.[6]

Our identity is nothing that we bring to bear from ourselves upon our need for it; it is everything that God gives us. It is the

---

6 C. S. Lewis, *An Experiment in Criticism* (Cambridge University Press, 1992), p. 141

THE MYSTERY OF IDENTITY

manifold distinctness of form through which God bestows His sameness on His creation; it is the unique sameness of being through which God bestows His difference on His creation. It is nothing of our own; it is all from God. It is a gift of the best giver who can only give the best gift and what is that but Himself? He radiates His glory through our nothingness to show who we are. Yet what can that nothingness be if it being anything is nothing but a contradiction? Who is contradicting what if not God contradicting what is not? What is creation from nothing if not a transcendence of homogeneity and othering, of sameness and difference, of you and I? Who is so near and so far as God? What is this creation of His which is both blending and separation but love? Where does it come from but from the God who is love? What is it but mystery and miracle?

Our identity is a mystery because it is seen when we are nothing; our identity is a miracle because it is manifest when God lives in us. Our nothing becomes a miracle when—to use an image from Saint Thérèse—it is placed after the One who is God, as zero is placed after a one to give ten, symbol of fullness and life. Something of the mystery and miracle is expressed by the Persian mystical poet Rumi (1207-1273) who records an answer to the question "Who are we?" in his poem entitled "Emptiness":

> Nothing.
> We are
> emptiness.
> When you are with everyone but me,
>   you're with no one.
> When you are with no one but me,
>   You're with everyone.
> Instead of being so bound up *with* everyone,
>   *Be* everyone.
> When you become that many, you're nothing,
>   Empty.[7]

Here he starts with the outcome Peer Gynt found when he saw nothing in the onion he peeled, but in the emptiness a divine voice speaks to his heart. It tells him that when he is with Him alone God shares His universal presence with him so that he is

---

[7] Rumi, *Selected Poems*, translated by Coleman Banks (Penguin Classics), p. 28

with, and identified with, everyone. In that fullness, he is empty of self. God is his life, giving him a universal identity. That identity cannot be seen, still less grasped: it is the reward of trust, not mastery of information; the result of self-forgetfulness, not self-assertion; the fruit of surrender, not control. It is in God's eternal truth, not in the empty shell of its mortal frame.

"Man is a limited being who is himself limitless"[8] is Pope Francis's characterization of the contrast between this mortal frame and our identity in God. The limitation comes from time and space, the limitlessness from God for whom everything is possible. The former can only give identity in a negative sense, an identity which is what is left when everything that is not it is excluded. In Buddhist tradition, this residue is known by the Sanskrit term *anātman*, meaning non-self.[9] The realization of *anātman* comes with the awareness of identification with everything else, which is enlightenment. This corresponds to the total unselfishness of a Christian saint realizing she is nothing and God everything, and also to the linking of emptiness to being (or identifying with) everybody in Rumi's poem. In simply logical terms, this could be presented as the practical assessment that an individual is not everything else and so in his or her self virtually nothing. In God, by contrast, a human person is virtually everything. Each contains as it were a little dot of its opposite: a speck of true, celestial identity in the outward earthly life and a speck of earthly insubstantiality in the fully realized, heavenly identity. Only the Creator is absolutely and transcendentally pure: everything created contains at least in seed an aspect of its opposite. That connection makes it possible for the earthly and limited to be a means of reaching the heavenly and unlimited.

It can only be so, however, in the realization that of itself the earthly and limited is nothing. People who think, for example, that the extent of their possessions is the mark of who they are mistake the false for the true: mere egoism projected onto wealth is not a true and enduring identity. It is of course possible to have things without being egotistical and, indeed, to use them

---

8 Pope Francis, *Fratelli Tutti* (CTS, 2020), paragraph 150, p. 73, citing Georg Simmel

9 Florian Coulmas, *Identity, A Very Short Introduction* (Oxford University Press, 2019), p. 25

THE MYSTERY OF IDENTITY

unselfishly, but such is the help that poverty gives to avoiding the illusion that one is of oneself somehow something in this world that people seeking their true life will, after the manner of Saint Francis, wed her. This dynamic of less being more relates to more than possessions: weakness and limitation in general are an advantage for realizing one's nothingness and for the realization that everything comes from God and, therefore, for enjoying it all. In terms of the narrative of mundane human striving this is a plot reversal and, like a denouement in a story, it explains a lot. It makes sense of why saints at whose word miracles of healing were and are performed themselves suffered illness and incapacity and—above all—how the Son of the omnipotent God underwent abject and humiliating suffering and death. Saint Paul summed up the principle when he wrote, "When I am weak, then I am strong."[10] A malady is leverage, a disability can be weaponized: not in the sense of gaining sympathy or social concessions, but in the struggle against (to borrow again the phrasing of an author quoted in the previous chapter) the cosmic illusion that makes us identify with our body, our ego, our thoughts and our desires. Any interruption of somatic power, any paralysis of action, can help to wean us from the milk of flattery of our nothingness so that we get our teeth into the vivifying truth that God is all in all. This does not mean that we should not take care of our health and that of others, for this life is precious since in it grows our eternal identity, but it does mean that anything which redirects us from sublunary preoccupations to God as our goal can be gratefully welcomed and that indeed "for those who love God all things work together for good."[11] The saints have known this secret, known that in the limited is contained the gift of the universal, known that we find our true identity through losing the illusory.

LOSING IS FINDING

These principles have been proclaimed by Jesus:

> And he said to all, "If anyone would come after me, let him deny himself and take up his cross daily and follow me. For whoever would save his life will lose it, but whoever loses his life for my sake will save it. For what does

---

10 2 Corinthians 12.10   11 Romans 8.28

Loss & Love

it profit a man if he gains the whole world and loses or forfeits himself?"[12]

The daily cross is every limitation that tells us that we do not have absolute power, every frustration of our desires, every reminder that we cannot be all in all. Taking it up may in some cases mean preferring some such loss to doing something wrong, but in all cases it means receiving it sweetly without cursing or bitterness. That can be a process rather than immediate: if the cross is heavy there can to begin with be an almost involuntary bitterness and then that very bitterness will be a cross to be accepted. The essential is to understand that it can work for good by helping us to escape an illusory sense of where our true life is to be found. In this, we are "looking to Jesus, the founder and perfecter of our faith, who for the joy that was set before him endured the cross, despising the shame, and is seated at the right hand of the throne of God."[13] The joy in question is that of an unlimited life, found by following Him through being willing to let go of limited life. The word "life" (in the passage about losing and finding it) translates the Greek word that gives us our word "psyche" and which means both life and soul. These two are near to being synonyms if we take "life" in the sense of the whole of what we live and experience: in other words they point to who we are, to our identity. If we do try to home in on our identity, clinging to whatever in the world we consider as marking it, we become turned in on ourselves and lose our true identity which is found in loving openness. Ultimately it is found in universal love, that love which Christ has for all, which is why He enjoins us to let go of the limited life for His sake. His life, which He invites us to share, is universal and is our true life. Rowan Williams puts it like this: "What and who we are is essentially defined by the gratuitous invitation from an unimaginable other into shared life."[14] If we win through in taking up our cross, Christ offers us, as I wrote at the end of Chapter Four, His "own new name"[15]—He invites us to share in the identity which has triumphed over limitation and death. That is the pearl of great price for which the whole of this

---

12 Luke 9.23-25   13 Hebrews 12.2
14 Rowan Williams, *Looking East in Winter: Contemporary Thought and the Eastern Christian Tradition* (Bloomsbury, London, 2021), p. 153
15 Revelation 3.12

world is but a profitless substitute. If our psychic energy, and so our sense of self, is invested in what passes, the loss of this may seem like mere annihilation, but Saint John of the Cross reminds us, "To be what you are not you must go by a way in which you are not."[16] That way, of losing one's life to find it, is integral to the Christian spiritual path as evidenced, for example, in the *Rule of Saint Benedict*, which says that the monk should not even have his body and will as his own.[17] Loss is the only way to finding. As the Second Vatican Council teaches, "Man can fully discover his true self only in a sincere giving of himself."[18] That giving identifies us with Christ, who said, "Greater love has no one than this, that someone lay down his life for his friends."[19]

These truths do not belong to Christians alone. Ibn al-'Arabī, using the language of the Koran, refers to what has been discussed above in terms of limitation and loss, as being God's "servant." This state, in its emptiness and poverty, realizes the human person's utter nothingness without God. To reach it is to find one's true identity for, in Ibn al-'Arabī's words, "The servant necessarily becomes manifest in the form of the Real when he makes manifest his servanthood, which is activity in conformity with what God has prescribed."[20] The "nothing" of the servant becomes the "no thing" of God, who cannot be limited to any particular. It corresponds to the void of Buddhism, to enter which is to gain universal compassion. In the Hindu tradition, the loss of *nāmā-rūpa*—the name and form of a limited identity—has been compared to "water sprinkled on a boiling hot stone which evaporates so that it can no longer be seen. It then expands beyond all limits, having actually achieved its full potential."[21] It is universally true that self-transcendence

---

16 *The Collected Works of St. John of the Cross*, translated by Kieran Kavanaugh, O. C. D. and Otilo Rodriguez, O. C. D. (Institute of Carmelite Studies, 1979), p. 67
17 *Rule of Saint Benedict*, Chapter 58
18 *Gaudium et Spes* in *Vatican Council II: The Conciliar and Post Conciliar Documents* (Fowler Wright, 1980), p. 925
19 John 15.13
20 William C. Chittick, *Imaginal Worlds: Ibn al-'Arabī and the Problem of Religious Diversity* (Suhail Academy, 2001), p. 170
21 Dominique Wohlschlag, *The Queen and the Avatar* (originally *La Reine et l'avatar: mythologie de Krishna*), translated by Deborah Bell (Matheson Trust, 2017), p. 108

is the way to true life and identity. Being stripped of a partial, limited identity allows the real person to be known.

LEAR UNDOES THE COSMIC ILLUSION

Shakespeare dramatizes this in *King Lear*, a tragedy of a man who does not know his true identity until the bitterest of circumstances reveal it to him. In a central scene, Lear contemplates a man who has in fact made himself nothing: Edgar, who to escape malicious pursuit has disguised himself as a witless beggar. Having taken "the basest and most poorest shape/ That ever penury, in contempt of man,/ Brought near to beast," he can say, "Edgar I nothing am."[22] They are exposed to the elements in the midst of a terrible storm and Lear says to him:

> Thou wert better in a grave than to answer with thy uncover'd body this extremity of the skies. Is man no more than this? Consider him well. Thou ow'st the worm no silk, the beast no hide, the sheep no wool, the cat no perfume. Ha? here's three on's are sophisticated. Thou art the thing itself: unaccommodated man is no more but such a poor, bare, fork'd animal as thou art. Off, off, you lendings! Come, unbutton here. [*Tearing off his clothes.*][23]

As one of his two companions says shortly afterwards, "his wits begin t'unsettle,"[24] yet spiritually this is a turning point for him. Tearing off his clothes enacts his leaving behind his limited and essentially false identity, so that he has only the bare minimum for his life in this world: his body. The silk, the hide, the wool, the perfume—all of these, especially in the context of court life which he has just left, denote the falsification of a spurious identity: one that is "sophisticated" or adulterated. His clothes are "lendings" because they are taken from animals, but also because they give him a status or persona that is not truly his. Essentially, he is "unaccommodated man"—a person without the additions that mark social identity—he is "the thing itself," no different from the beggar who has given rise to these reflections.

It is significant that this rejection of his old, limited identity is presented alongside the glimmer of a sense of universal compassion

---

22 Act 2, scene iii, ll.7–9 & 21   23 Act 3, scene iv, ll.101–9
24 Act 3, scene iv, l.162

THE MYSTERY OF IDENTITY

which is the seed of his new and truer self. Shortly before he tears off his clothes, he is reminded by the storm of the poor:

> Poor naked wretches, whereso'er you are,
> That bide the pelting of this pitiless storm,
> How shall your houseless heads and unfed sides,
> Your loop'd and window'd raggedness, defend you
> From seasons such as these? O, I have ta'en
> Too little care of this![25]

It is the beginning of a change of heart, a move from the false to the true. The enormity of the change will become clear if we look at how he is first presented to us and then trace his journey through this pivotal point of realization to becoming the man he is at the end of the play. At the start of the play, he is very much under the cosmic illusion that makes him identify with his ego, thoughts, and desires. Although he acts with extraordinary rashness at this point, "He hath ever but slenderly known himself,"[26] as one of his daughters observes. This lack of awareness of his true identity makes him vulnerable to those who:

> Smooth every passion
> That in the natures of their lord rebel,
> Bring oil to fire, snow to the colder moods;
> Renege, affirm, and turn their halcyon beaks
> With every gale and vary of their masters,
> Knowing nought (like dogs) but following.[27]

These are the words of his follower, Kent, and they describe exactly how those surrounding someone in power keep him in thrall to the illusion identifying him with his thoughts and desires. Kent confronts Lear with truth and is banished for his pains. Yet the seed of Lear's awakening to truth is in the very folly that Kent has objected to: Lear's supposing that he can keep "the name, and all th' addition to a king" while giving away "the sway, revenue, execution of the rest."[28] This abdication of power undercuts social investment in the false identity of his thoughts and desires. In fact, it leads to the collapse of social meaning and order and, provoked by the reaction to his own insistence that he should

---

25   Act 3, scene iv, ll.28–33
27   Act 2, scene ii, ll.75–80
26   Act 1, scene i, ll.293–94
28   Act 1, scene i, ll.136–37

have that attendance which would affirm this false identity, to his departure from both society and shelter. Without them, losing his false identity, he goes mad, but nature shows him where he has gone wrong. He enters "crowned with weeds and flowers"[29] and, so identified with nature, realizes what has happened:

> They flatter'd me like a dog, and told me I had the white hairs in my beard ere the black ones were there. To say "ay" and "no" to everything that I said! "Ay" and "no" too, was no good divinity. When the rain came to wet me once, and the wind to make me chatter, when the thunder would not peace at my bidding, there I found 'em, there I smelt 'em out. Go to, they are not men o' their words: they told me I was every thing. 'Tis a lie, I am not ague-proof.[30]

He was told that he had the wisdom of "the white hairs" of age before he had the good sense of the "beard" of manhood. The bad theology of affirming his thoughts and desires as though they were the voice of God telling him the truth about himself is shown up by nature—the rain, wind and thunder—not doing his bidding. The weakness of his body, subject to illness, collapses the cosmic illusion that his ego is all.

Yet from the very beginning of the drama he has been told the truth as well as being lied to. When he blatantly offers to sell his kingdom for professions of love—in effect affirmations of his false self—from his daughters, Cordelia, his youngest (and, when he was more balanced, his best loved) lacks the "glib and oily art/ To speak and purpose not"[31] of her sisters Goneril and Regan who flatter him to gain their share of his kingdom and power. Her refusal to affirm his worldly identity very eloquently tells him exactly what it amounts to. Asked what she can say to get a bigger share than her sisters, she says "Nothing, my lord." The dialogue continues:

> *Lear.* Nothing?
> *Cordelia.* Nothing.
> *Lear.* Nothing will come of nothing, speak again.
> *Cordelia.* Unhappy that I am, I cannot heave
> My heart into my mouth. I love your Majesty
> According to my bond, no more nor less.[32]

---

29 Act 4, scene vi, l.80
30 Act 4, scene vi, ll.96–105
31 Act 1, scene i, ll.224–25
32 Act 1, scene i, ll.87–93

THE MYSTERY OF IDENTITY

If Lear could accept the truth that his partial, limited, socially established self is nothing, which is in effect what Cordelia says through her refusal to affirm it, he would be like Saint Thérèse, happy to be nothing and therefore radiant with God, or like Rumi, knowing his emptiness and so identifying with everyone, or like one who has realized *anātman* and is enlightened. He cannot, and banishes her from his affections. Ultimately the five times repeated "nothing" in their dialogue becomes the five times repeated "never" as, in the final act, he holds her body in his arms and laments that he will not see her alive again.[33] It is as though he is banishing Christ who calls himself "the way, and the truth, and the life."[34] She has shown him the way to enlightenment by telling him the truth and in the end his life ends with hers.

There is another character who tells him the truth: the Fool, who also echoes Christ through the ancient tradition of being a fool for His sake. As Neil McEwan has argued cogently, in Shakespeare's time the fool may well have been played by the same actor as played Cordelia.[35] And as the Russian poet Marina Boroditskaya wittily observes in a poem, "Cordelia, you are a fool! Would it have been/ that hard to yield to the old man? ... And now he's dead, you too, everyone's dead."[36] They are linked, too, by affection: one of Lear's knights observes that following Cordelia's departure "the Fool hath much pin'd away."[37] Together, Cordelia and the fool speak the truth, echo Christ. The Fool makes it clear to Lear that he thinks he acted foolishly in giving his lands and their revenue away to Regan and Goneril. When Lear asks if he is calling him a fool, he replies, "All thy other titles thou hast given away, that thou wast born with."[38] The "titles" are what construct his socially validated identity: without them it begins to unravel. Lear's first question about his identity is addressed to Goneril's steward, Oswald, whom he has noticed treating him with a lack of respect to which he is not accustomed. "Who am I, sir?" he asks and receives the reply, "My lady's father."[39] This enrages him: as

---

33   Act 5, scene iii, l.309   34   John 14.6
35   Neil McEwan, "The Lost Childhood of Lear's Fool" in *Essays in Criticism*, Volume XXVI, Issue 3, July 1976, pp. 209-217
36   *The Penguin Book of Russian Poetry* (Penguin, 2015), edited by Robert Chandler, Boris Dralyuk and Irina Mashinski, p. 514
37   Act 1, scene iv, l.74   38   Act 1, scene iv, ll.149-150
39   Act 1, scene iv, ll.78-79

king he is used to being attributed a central identity, not one that is relative to that of another person. He has become, in the Fool's words, "an O without a figure."[40] That of course is spiritually the truth about the identity of every person: we are, as Saint Thérèse realized, only somebody when our nothing comes after the One of God; yet for Lear, who at this point is still expecting to receive his glory from people, it means he is merely nothing. The Fool speaks the truth to him when he says, "I am better than thou art now, I am a Fool, thou art nothing."[41] In the absence of the affirmation he expects from Goneril, he enters an identity crisis whose questions become more acute:

> Does any here know me? This is not Lear.
> Does Lear walk thus? speak thus? Where are his eyes?
> Either his notion weakens, his discernings
> Are lethargied—Ha! waking? 'T is not so.
> Who is it that can tell me who I am?[42]

He no longer recognizes himself: neither his body, nor his mind ("notion"), nor his senses ("discernings") seem able to tell him who he is and he wonders if he is dreaming. He can only appeal to others to tell him. The Fool answers, "Lear's shadow."[43] He is indeed only the shadow of the man he was in terms of a socially established identity. On the spiritual level, he is being confronted with the truth that of himself he is nothing but the negation of all that he is not, a shadow where the light which contains all possibilities does not fall, someone who cannot be who he truly is until he transcends the self in which is trapped. He has, in fact, ever depended on others to tell him who he is; and when he does not get the recognition he expects from his daughter Goneril, the loss of identity is so complete that he bitterly refuses to recognize her, asking, "Your name, fair gentlewoman?"[44] It is as though the whole system of social recognition of identity is some giant Ponzi scheme whose currency of credit has collapsed.

He bears considerable responsibility for this collapse. When Lear goes mad his first words are, "No, they cannot touch me for coining, I am the King himself,"[45] meaning that he cannot be

---

40 Act 4, scene iv, ll.192–93   41 Act 1, scene iv, ll.193–94
42 Act 1, scene iv, ll.226–30   43 Act 1, scene iv, l.231
44 Act 1, scene iv, l.236   45 Act 4, scene vi, ll.83–84

THE MYSTERY OF IDENTITY

accused of counterfeiting currency since the monarch gives money its legitimacy; yet his disconnection from reality is apparent here in two respects: he has given away his kingly title and he has in fact been dealing in false currency. He has accepted the counterfeit speeches of love of his two elder daughters—as when Regan says, "I am made of that self metal as my sister"[46] and tried (unsuccessfully) to get his youngest daughter to give him false coin. In doing this he has abdicated his responsibility as king to be the source of true social recognition which he can only be if he is humble—to the point of knowing himself as nothing—before God, or simply before reality as such. He has misused kingly power, whose function is to channel truth, to foster flattery. He has bought into false social credit for the support of an unreal identity whose disintegration is to have tragic consequences.

These unfold as he refuses to disinvest. Although he begins to get a sense of proportion about Cordelia's refusal to make the speech he wanted, he still looks to Regan to give him the affirmation and comfort that he has not received from Goneril, whom he tells:

> I have another daughter,
> Who I am sure is kind and comfortable.
> When she shall hear this of thee, with her nails
> She'll flea thy wolfish visage.[47]

This is highly unrealistic as the Fool tells him: "She will taste as like this as a crab does to a crab,"[48] meaning that the bitterness common to crab apples is common to these two daughters. And, indeed, Regan takes Goneril by the hand and proposes that Lear go back to her with half of his hundred knights dismissed, telling him she can accommodate only twenty-five. His response is to say to Goneril, whom he has so recently cursed:

> I'll go with thee,
> Thy fifty yet doth double five and twenty,
> And thou art twice her love.[49]

This is a double misunderstanding of love: it is a quality, not a quantity, sharing in the oneness of God, and it is an expression of truth not a gratification of particular desires, such as that of

---

46 Act 1, scene i, l.69
48 Act 1, scene v, ll.18-19
47 Act 1, scene iv, ll.305-8
49 Act 2, scene iv, ll.257-60

having attendant knights. If the idea of currency as a metaphor for social recognition of identity ever worked, here it breaks down completely. It means nothing in this context, and the delusion that such quantified recognition can give true identity is here exposed. When the two sisters agree that neither of them will take any attendant knights but only Lear himself, he takes his response to this bitter truth to a logical extreme: he abandons all kinship and society and goes out into the harshest of weather on his own.

In this weather, nature strips him of false identity. This pivotal action, which I began this reflection on the play by considering, is the prologue to finding a true identity, finally free from the cosmic illusion. Again, nature helps. First, however, the illusion has one final counter-attack: it drives him to a madness in which he imagines that what troubles his ego—that his two older daughters have been unkind to him—is a universal description of reality. He assumes that Edgar, disguised as a madman, is in the condition he is because he gave all to his daughters, that Goneril and Regan are present to undergo trial, and that an old man is "Goneril with a white beard."[50] Yet truth, in the person of Cordelia, is also present. In his saner moments, Lear is aware that a reunion with her is proposed, and, as his loyal servant Kent says, the truth speaks in his conscience:

> A sovereign shame so elbows him: his own unkindness,
> That stripp'd her from his benediction, turn'd her
> To foreign casualties, gave her dear rights
> To his dog-hearted daughters—these things sting
> His mind so venomously, that burning shame
> Detains him from Cordelia.[51]

Cordelia herself asks a doctor what can be done to restore him to sanity and he answers, "Our foster-nurse of nature is repose,/ The which he lacks" and assures her that there are many medicines which "will close the eye of anguish."[52]

Such are administered to Lear, and after sleeping he awakens to the sound of Cordelia's voice, to the truth and to a true sense of who he is. His first awareness is of a purgatorial cleansing from his faults:

---

50   Act 4, scene vi, l.96   51   Act 4, scene iii, ll.42–47
52   Act 4, scene iv, ll.12–15

THE MYSTERY OF IDENTITY

> I am bound
> Upon a wheel of fire, that mine own tears
> Do scald like molten lead.[53]

The second is an exploratory awareness of his own body:

> I will not swear these are my hands. Let's see,
> I feel this pin prick. Would I were assur'd
> Of my condition![54]

He finds this assurance of his condition in dialogue with Cordelia. His relationship with her is of that positive kind which I discussed towards the end of Chapter Three. It is, in Saint Aelred's phrase, "perfected in Christ."[55] It is free, to quote Robert Bolton's words again, "from being a part of the cosmic illusion," so that there can "be no question of self-identification with anything of a lower nature than that of the real self."[56] Cordelia is, like Christ in Alyosha Karamazov's dream, the other through whom and in relation to whom Lear finds his identity. Cordelia asks for his blessing, but he kneels to her and speaks the simple truth about who he is:

> I am a very foolish, fond old man,
> Fourscore and upward, not an hour more or less;
> And to deal plainly,
> I fear I am not in my perfect mind.[57]

In the most moving dialogue in the play, their true relationship is established:

> *Lear.* Do not laugh at me,
> For (as I am a man) I think this lady
> To be my child Cordelia.
> *Cordelia.* And so I am, I am.
> *Lear.* Be your tears wet? Yes, faith. I pray weep not.[58]

Lear has one further stripping to undergo before he enters eternity in utter nakedness of spirit: this relationship is taken away from him through Cordelia's death. He survives this for

---

[53] Act 4, scene vii, ll.45-47   [54] Act 4, scene vii, ll.54-56
[55] Aelred of Rievaulx, *Spiritual Friendship*, translated by Lawrence C. Braceland (Liturgical Press, 2010), p. 75
[56] Robert Bolton, *Self and Spirit* (Sophia Perennis, 2005), pp. 41-42
[57] Act 4, scene vii, ll.59-62   [58] Act 4, scene vii, ll.67-70

only a few moments. His condition recalls that of Saint Thérèse who, a few months before her death from a terrible and wasting illness, wrote a poem that compared her heart to a rose stripped of its petals.[59] The nun who had commissioned it thought it ought to have a final couplet about God gathering up the petals at her death to remake of them a beautiful rose which would shine for all eternity. Thérèse responded, "I'm not at all inspired to compose it. My desire is to be stripped of petals for ever, to give joy to God. That's all."[60] She was, simply, a joy to God. Like Lear, like Thérèse, each of us is in our ultimate identity stripped of everything: of every pretense, of every possession, of every claim and are only what we always have been—a joy to God.

THE DOOR OPENED WIDE

That final stripping is in the normal course of things death, which removes every false identity. Yet it is possible to die spiritually—that is, for the false identity to die—before one dies physically, in accord with the words of Jesus about losing one's life to find it. All authentic spiritual traditions speak of this in one way or another and give guidance about reaching it. The one who has so died can be a guide to others. There is a third possibility in addition to finding this life-giving death, either before or at the moment of one's physical death: that is to let go of one's false identity after death, purged by the fire of God's love. Those in this state, often termed purgatory, are dependent on the prayers of others for it is only in this vale of soul-making that we can parent the person we are to be for all eternity. They cannot directly guide others, as can those who have lost their lives to find them in this world. However, people nearing their end—even if the losing and finding is only to happen with their last breath—have something spiritually precious to offer. This is a sacred time of life and traditionally what is spoken at this moment is especially worthy of attention. There is a closeness to God, who is about to be met, and a natural openness to truth: the truth of a person's whole life which is sometimes said to run through one's mind at the moment of death, and the truth of God in the light of which it is about to be seen. It is a moment of meaning

---

59 *Une Rose effeuillée*, pp. 744-45 in *Thérèse de Lisieux, Oeuvres Complètes* (Cerf, 1992)   60 Ibid., p. 1395

THE MYSTERY OF IDENTITY

but also of mystery, and so not fully subject to logical analysis.

Yet poetry can suggest something about it. Here, from the end of his life and issued posthumously, are some words of a lifelong Jewish seeker[61] which are both poem and song:

> I can't make the hills
> The system is shot
> I'm living on pills
> For which I thank God

"The hills" (the title of the song) denote the spiritual heights which cannot be reached. Spiritual realization involves accepting one's powerless and turning to God, which is why Saint Paul wrote, "I have the desire to do what is right, but not the ability to carry it out"[62] and another time was told by the Lord, "My power is made perfect in weakness."[63] That "the system is shot" indicates the end of bodily life which is postponed only by the gratefully received pills, a metonym for a life given by God. The struggle continues:

> My animal howls
> My angel's upset
> But I'm not allowed
> A trace of regret

There is still a precarious balance between flesh and spirit. Both are troubled, but this is accepted as God's will, for there will be a resolution:

> For someone will you
> The thing I could not be
> My heart will be heard
> Impersonally

The ego will be transcended: what "I" cannot be for all its struggles "you" will be. This evokes Rimbaud's "I is another" but also points to how identity is realized in relationship, as in Peter Pomerantsev's father's observation (cited towards the end of Chapter Two) that "identity only appears when it recognizes the presence of someone else" and his encounter with another in which, "We do not say 'you' to each other but 'I'." Further, it suggests that it is the divine "You" that gives true identity, that which the ego struggles

---

61   Leonard Cohen   62   Romans 7.18
63   2 Corinthians 12.9

but fails to attain. That identity is in its essence in the "heart." It will be "heard"—that is, known—in a context that transcends personal boundaries, even those of a mortal life. That hearing will also be the receiving of a spiritual teaching, the life-giving word, by another who hears it through this heart:

> She'll step on the path
> She'll see what I mean
> My will cut in half
> And freedom between

"She" here is richly ambiguous. First of all, it is the heart which finds the spiritual way ("the path") and true identity ("what I mean"), but it is also the one who comes after and through awareness of this particular finding is able to make it her own. Above all, she is *Shekinah*, the Divine Presence which alone can give true meaning to identity and guide the individual to its finding. Ultimately, identity is revealed.

The last two lines—"My will cut in half/ And freedom between"—allude to the fifteenth chapter of the book of Genesis, a foundational passage about revelation in the Jewish (and Christian) scriptures. It concerns God's covenant with Abram, who is to be given the identity of "Abraham ...the father of a multitude of nations."[64] His spiritual descendants include those of all three monotheistic faiths, the peoples of the book. He is told, "Look toward heaven, and number the stars, if you are able to number them.... So shall your offspring be."[65] God explains His purpose and how Abram is to know it to him:

> And he said to him, "I am the LORD who brought you out from Ur of the Chaldeans to give you this land to possess." But he said, "O Lord GOD, how am I to know that I shall possess it?" He said to him, "Bring me a heifer three years old, a female goat three years old, a ram three years old, a turtledove, and a young pigeon." And he brought him all these, cut them in half, and laid each half over against the other. But he did not cut the birds in half. And when birds of prey came down on the carcasses, Abram drove them away.[66]

---

64 Genesis 17.4-5   65 Genesis 15.5
66 Genesis 15.7-11

THE MYSTERY OF IDENTITY

This sacrifice is Abram's "will cut in half"—it is essentially the sacrifice of his will to God. His descendants in the Jewish tradition will receive a codification of this will in the law; those in the Christian tradition will seek to follow their Master who said in the Garden of Gethsemane, "Not my will, but yours, be done,"[67] and pray for this in the prayer He gave them; those in the Islamic tradition will seek to practice submission to God. The animals cut in two are the will of the flesh subject to the will of God; the birds are not cut in two for they denote the Spirit. The birds of prey are driven away for there must be no spoiling by predatory self-interest of the sacrifice of Abram's will, which is to be tested to the extreme. He then becomes detached from his surroundings:

> As the sun was going down, a deep sleep fell on Abram. And behold, dreadful and great darkness fell upon him.[68]

Darkness is a prerequisite for receiving revelation: only in absolute unknowing can the unknown absolute speak. Any pretension to knowing violates the silence in which God makes Himself known. Abram, in deep sleep and darkness, is no longer bound in time and place and can be told of the destiny of both his offspring and himself. This is ratified by the divine presence, the *Shekinah*:

> When the sun had gone down and it was dark, behold, a smoking fire pot and a flaming torch passed between these pieces.[69]

This presence is the "freedom between" of the song: Abram's will cut in two allows the presence of God's will which alone has perfect freedom. Making it his own gives Abram that freedom, together with his legacy. The fire and flame, the divine light in the human darkness, testify to the particular terrestrial identity of Abram's descendants:

> On that day the LORD made a covenant with Abram, saying, "To your offspring I give this land, from the river of Egypt to the great river, the river Euphrates, the land of the Kenites, the Kenizzites, the Kadmonites, the Hittites,

---

67 Luke 22.42
68 Genesis 15.12
69 Genesis 15.17

the Perizzites, the Rephaim, the Amorites, the Canaanites, the Girgashites and the Jebusites."[70]

The unique place of his people is established by covenant. Through Abram, they have a special calling, but it is paradigmatic of the particular calling of each people and of each person. If the Jewish people are identified as unique, it is to show and to teach all people the uniqueness that God shares with them in the distinction they receive from Him. It is through revelation that the culture of a spiritual tradition is received and in the symbols and language of that culture that identity is expressed: it is God-given.

This revelation and this culture, which forms terrestrial identity, is for the sake of a celestial identity, as the seed is for the sake of the plant, the flower for the sake of the fruit, the caterpillar for the sake of the butterfly. And the Jewish poet goes on to sing of this:

> For less than a second
> Our lives will collide
> The endless suspended
> The door opened wide

The instantaneous contact between the ego and the other, the self and the *Shekinah*, opens the heart to infinite truth: the eternal God alive in this particular identity—"The endless suspended." This line can also be heard as "the end is suspended," in which case it indicates going beyond the limit of death to an unlimited life, "The door opened wide." It is the moment of which Beckett's narrator in *The Unnamable* is on the threshold and we might ask with him, "What's a door doing here?" It is always a surprise to receive from God like this and always a surprise to realize we need never have left the door closed to the One who says, "Behold, I stand at the door and knock."[71] It is the door to life, to who we truly are.

SPIRITUAL NAKEDNESS

Crossing this threshold involves dispossession, whether of power and title as with King Lear or of a properly functioning bodily system as in the song, and an acceptance of that dispossession. The reality is that we are not ours at all: we belong to God. The work of realizing our true identity is that of abandoning ourselves to

---

70 Genesis 15.18-21   71 Revelation 3.20

THE MYSTERY OF IDENTITY

God and coming to the state here described by Meister Eckhart:

> When you have completely stripped yourself of your own self, and all things and every kind of attachment, and have transferred, made over and abandoned yourself to God in utter faith and perfect love, then *whatever* is born in you or touches you, within or without, joyful or sorrowful, sour or sweet, that is no longer yours, it is altogether your God's to whom you have abandoned yourself.[72]

Eckhart uses the comparison of things having different colors because of light from the sun shining on them to explain how various impulses such as good intent, charity or gratitude come from God and are all His, just as the light is the sun's. The imperative is: "you must lay claim to nothing!"[73] That stripping of all pretensions of ownership goes very deep for those who truly belong to God. It goes much further than pooling resources for the family budget or common ownership of things in a community. It involves falling on the ground with Job and worshipping in his words, "Naked I came from my mother's womb, and naked shall I return."[74] I have already touched on this theme in Chapter Five in relation to disidentification and (in Ferrucci's phrase) "a state of psychological nudity" and in relation to the teaching of Saint John of the Cross about the nakedness in which the spirit finds its rest; but I come back to it now because between that chapter and this I have explored the universal nature of identity and the way it is not confined to a particular religious tradition. The consequence of this is that full spiritual nakedness involves not only being divested of the obvious things such as pretensions to position and status, not only abandoning any prideful claim to personal virtue, but also not resting in the very form of faith itself. This is as far as it can be from a shallow, uncommitted eclecticism. It is, rather, entering into faith so deeply and with such commitment that one comes to what faith is given to us for: complete spiritual nakedness. Faith is the packaging, not what the parcel contains; it is the outward silver plating, not the inner gold; it is the clothing of the spiritual man, not his body. This

---

72 Meister Eckhart, *Sermons & Treatises, Volume 1*, translated and edited by M. O'C. Walshe (Element Books, 1987), p. 32
73 Ibid. 74 Job 1.21

spiritual nakedness is not a loss of faith in the sense of no longer bothering to worship or no longer caring how one behaves, but it is a loss of the feeling of meaning. It is, simply, a dispossession. One has no longer the comfort of owning it; the sense of being defined by it; the familiarity of existing within known contours. It is an awareness of the stark truth that identity does not belong to us: it belongs to God. Further on in the song cited above are the words:

> I know she is coming
> And I know she will look
> That is the longing
> And this is the who

This could refer just to a disciple who seeks and finds the path, but it has the ambiguity of the earlier lines that suggest also the divine presence. The conviction and the longing is that this will come and that this is "the who"—identity itself. God's presence is our identity, is the identity of everyone, as the light of the sun is every color under the sun.

For that light (the light of Christ who said, "I am the light of the world"[75]) to illuminate us we have to be in complete darkness, what Saint John of the Cross called the dark night of the spirit. His spiritual daughter Saint Thérèse of Lisieux entered this and wrote about how fogs suddenly penetrated and enveloped her soul so that the idea of heaven, so sweet for her, suddenly disappeared.[76] The veil of faith became "a wall going right up to the heavens and covering the firmament with its stars."[77] It seemed to her that mocking voices said that eternal possession of the Creator was a dream and that death would give her not what she hoped for but "a yet deeper night, the night of nothingness."[78] Later, in her final illness, she said, "My soul is exiled, heaven is shut for me,"[79] and in the month before she died reflected that one might say that God was "deluding her into thinking that there is no heaven!"[80] The reality was that God was denuding her: when a sister told her of a thought she had had about heaven, Thérèse

---

75   John 8.12
76   *Thérèse de Lisieux, Oeuvres Complètes* (Cerf, 1992), p. 242
77   Ibid., p. 244   78   Ibid., p. 243
79   Ibid., p. 1019   80   Ibid., p. 1092

replied, "For my part, I only have light to see my little nothing."[81] Her darkness was a true light, showing her that her real life, her true identity was in God.

Saint Teresa of Calcutta, who was named for Saint Thérèse, also experienced this dark night of the spirit and loved Jesus and His poor in the dark. Neither of them had even a spiritual identity of their own: everything belonged to God. Saint John of the Cross, the great teacher of this path of darkness, explains what happens during this night by reference to a text in the book of Exodus where:

> God, desiring to humble the children of Israel and make them know themselves, ordered them to remove their festive garments and adornments which they were ordinarily wearing in the desert: *From now on leave aside your festive ornaments and put on common working garments that you may be aware of the treatment you deserve.* This was like saying: Since the clothing you wear, being of festivity and mirth, is an occasion for your not feeling as lowly as you in fact are, put it aside, so that seeing the foulness of your dress you may know yourself and your deserts.
>
> As a result the soul recognizes the truth about its misery, of which it was formerly ignorant. When it was walking in festivity, gratification, consolation, and support in God, it was more content, believing that it was serving God in some way. Though this idea of serving God may not be explicitly formed in a person's mind, at least some notion of it is deeply embedded within him owing to the satisfaction he derives from his spiritual exercises. Now that the soul is clothed in these other garments of labor, dryness and desolation, and its former lights have been darkened, it possesses more authentic lights in this most excellent and necessary virtue of self-knowledge.[82]

Naked before God, glad rags removed, we know who we truly are: only what God gives us to be. He alone knows us from inside; in Him alone is the mystery of our identity. Our identity in this

---

81 Ibid., p. 1091
82 *The Collected Works of St. John of the Cross*, translated by Kieran Kavanaugh, O. C. D. and Otilo Rodriguez, O. C. D. (Institute of Carmelite Studies, 1979), p. 321

world is a gift of a sharing in His sameness manifested as our uniqueness; our identity in the world to come is a sharing in His uniqueness manifested as our sameness—our enduring and eternal life. These two are wonderfully one, as the absolute sameness and the absolute difference of God are one: a single Identity, which is both sameness and difference.

WHO AM I, REALLY?

Gentle reader, thank you for coming this far with me. As we approach the final pages of this book, in view of the quest I have undertaken you may feel entitled to ask me a personal question: "Who do you think you are?" or even, "Who (a couple of intensifying words) do you think you are, writing a book like this?" There are, of course, many possible answers. One would be simply to say I get my identity from my ancestors, as—for example—the people of Israel are named for their forefather and patriarch Israel. An early memory I have is being in bed with a book and playing at being like my father (who had many books) putting it onto an imaginary shelf and then taking it off again as though it were another book. *The Boys' Book of Magic*, for that it was, then contained all books for me rather as, in a different way, the Bible does now. I still do this—though no longer in an imaginary way—which my father did: he lives on in me. Then again, I could say that who I am contains all epochs of my life, not just the one I am in now, and so I am who I am when I am asleep and in my dreams people and places from all the times in my life can pop up—and, indeed, from time to time events from the future, too. Certainly you could find those who would characterize me as one who sleeps. Or I could go for an obvious answer and say I am a writer, though I would prefer to be known as a reader—one who listens, rather than talks. On the other hand, I could go back to ancestry and say that I am identified by religion: after all, my mother was religiously minded and my grandfather wanted to be a monk and I sometimes think he is being a monk through me. Yet if religion is what makes me who I am, the sacred character of the priesthood with its duties and privileges is surely particularly significant.

What if it is none of the above, but simply who I am when I feel most fully alive—in the dark of the early morning, swimming in the sea (symbol of eternity), enjoying the cold and the exercise, living in my body, looking at the sky and the stars (symbol of heaven), forgetting myself and blending with the cosmos, the time so perfect and the scene so beautiful that when as I walk back from the sea the dawn comes it is a disappointment? Or am I only dust which will return to dust? Or am I the manner of my knowing and the quality of my love: what I see with my eyes, keep in my heart, and speak with my voice? Or am I rather the way I am known and loved? Am I the joy of another in me?

You have been a wonderful reader, whether you have made your way through explorations of upwards of eighty thousand words or were just judicious enough to look first of all for my conclusion at the end of the book, so I owe you more than questions. Here then is an answer, to the last of these questions. Yes, I am the joy of Christ: that is my primary identity. If my love for God gives me any identity, that is a reflection—like the light of the moon by which I walk through the woods on the way back from the sea. If my body gives me any identity, that is because it is God's joy that I exist in this world. If the culture I grew up in and what I inherited from those who went before me gives me any identity, that is because those who formed it and my parents too were—and are—God's joy. Utterly irrespective of any merit or deserving, I, too, am God's joy, made known through His creating Word, Christ. My identity is not my own; I cannot even see my identity any more than I can see my seeing. It belongs to and is known by God, for whom it is a joy: that joy makes it what it is. That joy is the joy of Christ shared with His Father in the joy of the Holy Spirit. The joy of Christ is the purest of joy and it is at work to purify me so that I may be who I truly am. The joy of the Holy Spirit is the most loving joy and it is at work to draw me to the Father. The joy of the Father is the most welcoming of joy and it is at work to draw me to His embrace. I am the joy of Christ.

You, too, are the joy of Christ.

EXILE

We are living through many changes and many obscurities, but they will pass and light will come. In the end the source will be known. It is simply the bliss of God. His loving bliss keeps us in being; His eternal bliss gives us an enduring identity; His boundless bliss is the balm for our sore eyes and He calls us to the seeing and sharing of it. We cannot bear that sight now, but we can know this: identity is God's joyful bliss in His creation. That bliss is the amniotic fluid in the womb of time. We are afloat in it, but do not yet know the birth to which we shall be brought. That bliss is the bright shining sun. We stand in it, but see the shadow that our figures cast. That bliss is our home and our heritage. We long for it, but for a time we are exiles. In our earthly life our true identity is hidden from us.

This must be so because it is not yet complete. It comprises the whole of our lives, the whole of who we are. The husk of it, which we know now, is a unique pattern of place-time combinations or—more accurately—a dance with other identities. The kernel of it is our hidden destiny, revealed when the husk is broken open. So we cannot say in any absolute sense that we are—for example—an old person or a young person. This may be useful for the purposes of getting a free bus pass or student rail card, but our true identity remains mysterious. We change and we are the same: the change belongs to the husk; the sameness to the kernel held in God's loving hand. Only His glance, His judgment scanning the whole of our lives, gives us final identity in which it is revealed if we honored the indwelling sameness in God bestowing our difference from others and honored the transcendent difference in God giving us our sameness with others. At the very moment when what seems outwardly to be our identity is taken away and dissolved into dust, we find who we truly are. Death is losing limitation, entering eternity. Then we shall know in full, now we know in part.

And the truest part is hidden, so we manifest our identity most truly in a sort of hiddenness. This has always been integral to the monastic quest for purity of heart—seeking identity only in relation to God. The cloistered life is a hidden one. Saint Thérèse observed that it was the greatest wisdom to want to be unknown. That is the way to avoid falsity, flattery and pretense. Outside the cloister, people who are not flashy—acting to show off or make an impression—are recognizable as having an integrity lacking in those who are. In the long term, seeking and receiving recognition are opposites. Hermits, who are also outside the cloister, bear witness to an identity that depends on God, not people. And, as the lives

THE MYSTERY OF IDENTITY

of Saint Antony of the desert and Julian of Norwich show, their counsel and teaching is therefore sought. Of all these folk it can be said that their "life is hidden with Christ in God."[83] Perhaps the most emphatic identity statement in this line is the custom of Carthusian monks being buried without any identification at all—their identity is wholly in God.

DIVINE AND HUMAN LOVE

So I come back to what I wrote in the first chapter about the mystery of identity being the mystery of God. His identity is hidden in the Jewish tradition that His name, the Tetragrammaton, is not to be pronounced and even ordinary reference to Him will be written "G-d" in reverent acknowledgment of the sacredness of the mystery. If Christ has a name, He is also "above every name that is named, not only in this age but also in the one to come."[84] God *is* identity; creatures *have* identity. God is the identity (the oneness) of every opposite *and* the identity of utter uniqueness. Our identity is simply God's gift of Himself to us. The deepest mystery is that He gets out of the way in order to let us be. It is the mystery of an infinitely courteous love. God is love, identifying with us in all that we are, but also in letting us be who we are. There is a reflection of this love in that of parents who totally support their offspring in their chosen way of life but do not force them to take any particular direction. God hides so that we may appear; He empties Himself so that we may be full; He loves so that we may be. That love is His bliss; we are His bliss; our bliss is His bliss in us, our identity.

So what is God's identity? It is both being the same and different: one God in three persons. The mystery of the Trinity is the mystery of identity, in the sense of being the same and in the sense of being different. The Father, the Son, and the Holy Spirit are the same God and they are different persons. The sameness and the difference are the sameness and difference of love: the love that is totally present to the other to the point of complete identification and also totally absent to allow the other to be totally different. This is the mystery of unity and diversity; the mystery of indistinction and distinction; the mystery of the many and the one—the mystery of identity.

---

83 Colossians 3.3   84 Ephesians 1.21

This mystery is present in divine love and reflected in human love. Shakespeare gives both extraordinary brilliance of expression in his poem, *The Phoenix and Turtle*. This presents love in which there is distinction but not division, love which transcends arithmetic:

> So they loved as love in twain
> Had the essence but in one,
> Two distinct, division none:
> Number there in love was slain.

Those who love are the same and distinct: in other words they have identity in both the sense of being identical and in the sense of being unique. They are one and two: they are the death of counting. Quality replaces quantity. This quality of love transcends quantity in the latter's instantiation as space:

> Hearts remote, yet not asunder;
> Distance and no space was seen
> 'Twixt this Turtle and his queen:
> But in them it were a wonder.

Love is the exchange of identity:

> So between them love did shine,
> That the Turtle saw his right
> Flaming in the Phoenix' sight;
> Either was the other's mine.

What belongs to the Turtle ("his right") is in the eyes ("sight") of the Phoenix and what belongs to each ("mine") is "the other's." The idea of identity being proper to an individual is transcended:

> Property was thus appalled,
> That the self was not the same;
> Single nature's double name
> Neither two nor one was called.

The splitting of the word "selfsame" into "self" and "not the same" enacts the destruction of ownership of identity. Love reveals the reality of God's creation: "single" in its being and "double" in its distinctness; neither differentiated nor the same. This is a challenge to the reasoning mind which works by differentiation and identification:

THE MYSTERY OF IDENTITY

> Reason, in itself confounded,
> Saw division grow together,
> To themselves yet either neither,
> Simple were so well compounded:
>
> That it cried, "How true a twain
> Seemeth this concordant one!
> Love hath reason, Reason none,
> If what parts, can so remain."[85]

The excluded middle is itself excluded: the reality is not one or the other but both either and neither. Reason gives way to love as being more reasonable in its understanding of how what is parted can remain one. It is humble before the mystery of love, identity's heart. For identity is God's love among us, in the double sense of God giving us love and of us giving that love to one another. The two senses are distinct but there is no division in them: they are the same love. It is a love that transcends time as well as space: it is an eternal love. It is the eternal life that the phoenix, with its legendary ability to be reborn from its ashes, symbolizes. It is the life of Christ, risen from the dead. That is our life and our mystery.

APORIA

Dear reader, please do not think I am trying to tell you who you are; I don't even know who I am; it is all a mystery. I make my own Meister Eckhart's aporia: "None can find the soul's true name, although mighty tomes have been written about this."[86] I shall give the last word to Dostoevsky, who wrote "Man is an enigma ... and if you spend all your life at it, don't say you have wasted your time; I occupy myself with this enigma because I wish to be a man."[87] That is why I have written this book, and I hope you do not feel that you have wasted your time reading it. I began with the reflection of one of Dostoevsky's characters about monks; I end with one of his depictions of a monk, Makar Ivanovich (the

---

85 *The Phoenix and Turtle*, ll.25-48
86 Meister Eckhart, *Sermons & Treatises, Volume 1*, translated and edited by M. O'C. Walshe (Element Books, 1987) p. 218
87 Joseph Frank, *Dostoevsky, A Writer in His Time* (Princeton University Press, 2010), p. 50

Loss & Love

adoptive father of Arkady the eponymous narrator of *The Adolescent*), who has left his home to follow this calling. Arkady is surprised to find him in a room adjoining his sick chamber. Makar speaks affectionately to him of a pilgrimage to a monastery:

> It's good in the world, my dear! If I mended a bit, I'd go again in the spring. And that it's a mystery makes it even better; your heart fears and wonders, and this fear gladdens the heart: "All is in thee, Lord, and I am in thee, and so receive me!" Do not murmur, young one; it's all the more beautiful that it's a mystery.[88]

Everything is in His Lord and he, too, is in Him. He prays that he may be kept in Him, kept in the mystery of the beauty of God's creation. He teaches his young disciple that:

> Everything is mystery, my friend, there is God's mystery in everything. Every tree, every blade of grass contains this same mystery. Whether it's a small bird singing, or the whole host of stars shining in the sky at night—it's all one mystery, the same one.[89]

Seeing a recurrent sight that hitherto he had viewed with loathing, Arkady finds it transformed: "it was as if my whole soul leaped up and a new light penetrated my heart."[90] This is greater than the mystery that can be seen through a microscope. It cannot be nailed down by science. Yet there is a still greater mystery:

> The greatest mystery of all is what awaits the human soul of man in the other world.[91]

Our identity is a mystery not simply because it is informed by God; our identity is a mystery because it belongs properly to a world beyond this one; our identity is a mystery whose full beauty is yet to be revealed. And that beauty will only make it more mysterious.

---

88 Fyodor Dostoevsky, *The Adolescent*, translated by Richard Pevear and Larissa Volokhonsky (Everyman's Library, 2003), p. 358
89 Ibid., p. 355   90 Ibid., pp. 359–60
91 Ibid., p. 355

BIBLIOGRAPHY

These are the principal works referred to in the text. Editions are those cited.

PHILOSOPHY
Derek Parfit, *Reasons and Persons* (Oxford University Press, 1984)
Robert Bolton, *Person, Soul and Identity* (Minerva Press, 1994)
Robert Bolton, *Self and Spirit* (Sophia Perennis, 2005)
Robert Bolton, *The One and the Many* (Sophia Perennis, 2008)
Gottfried Leibniz, *The Monadology and Other Philosophical Writings*, translated with introduction and notes by Robert Latta (Oxford University Press, 1898)
Florian Coulmas, *Identity, A Very Short Introduction* (Oxford University Press, 2019)
Martin Buber, *I and Thou*, translated by Ronald Gregor Smith (T. & T. Clark, 1966)

LITERARY CRITICISM
Yuri Corrigan, *Dostoevsky and the Riddle of the Self* (Northwestern University Press, 2017)
Rowan Williams, *Dostoevsky: Language, Faith and Fiction* (Continuum, 2008)
Joseph Frank, *Dostoevsky, A Writer in His Time* (Princeton University Press, 2010)
Lionel Trilling, *Sincerity and Authenticity* (Oxford University Press, 1974)
Samuel Beckett, *Proust* (Grove Press, 1957)

LITERATURE
William Shakespeare, *Hamlet, Othello, King Lear, The Two Gentlemen of Verona, Coriolanus, The Phoenix and Turtle* in *The Riverside Shakespeare* (Houghton Mifflin, 1974)
Fyodor Dostoevsky, *The Double and The Gambler*, translated by Richard Pevear and Larissa Volokhonsky (Everyman's Library, 2005)
Fyodor Dostoevsky, *The Idiot*, translated by Richard Pevear and Larissa Volokhonsky (Everyman's Library, 2002)
Fyodor Dostoevsky, *Demons*, translated by Richard Pevear and Larissa Volokhonsky (Vintage, 2006)
Fyodor Dostoevsky, *The Brothers Karamazov*, translated by Richard Pevear and Larissa Volokhonsky (Everyman's Library, 1997)
Fyodor Dostoevsky, *The Adolescent*, translated by Richard Pevear and Larissa Volokhonsky (Everyman's Library, 2003)

THE MYSTERY OF IDENTITY

Fyodor Dostoevsky, *Notes from Underground*, translated by Richard Pevear and Larissa Volokhonsky (Everyman's Library, 2004)
John Milton, *Paradise Regained* in *Milton: Complete Shorter Poems*, edited by John Carey (Longman, 1971)
Browning: Poetical Works, edited by Ian Jack (Oxford University Press, 1970)
The Poems of Gerard Manley Hopkins (Oxford University Press, 1970)
Henrik Ibsen, *Peer Gynt and Brand: Verse Translations by Geoffrey Hill* (Penguin, 2016)
Samuel Beckett, *Not I* in *The Complete Dramatic Works* (Faber, 2006)
Samuel Beckett, *The Unnamable* in *Samuel Beckett, The Grove Centenary Edition, Volume II, Novels* (Grove, 2006)
The Penguin Book of Russian Poetry, edited by Robert Chandler, Boris Dralyuk and Irina Mashinski (Penguin, 2015)
Kazuo Ishiguro, *When We Were Orphans* (Faber and Faber, 2001)
Kazuo Ishiguro, *Klara and the Sun* (Faber, 2021)

POLITICS

Barack Obama, *Dreams from My Father* (Canongate Books, 2004)
Peter Pomerantsev, *Nothing is True and Everything is Possible: Adventures in Modern Russia* (Faber, 2017)
Francis Fukuyama, *Identity: Contemporary Identity Politics and the Struggle for Recognition* (Profile Books, 2018)
Kwame Anthony Appiah, *The Lies That Bind: Rethinking Identity* (Profile Books, 2019)
Peter Pomerantsev, *This is Not Propaganda: Adventures in the War Against Reality* (Faber, 2019)
Julia Ebner, *Going Dark: The Secret Social Lives of Extremists* (Bloomsbury, 2020)

PSYCHOLOGY

Erik Erikson, *Identity, Youth and Crisis* (Norton, 1994)
Piero Ferrucci, *What We May Be: The Vision and Techniques of Psychosynthesis* (HarperCollins, 1990)
Sister Marie Thérèse of the Cross, *The Silent Struggle* (Redemptorist Publications, 2008)

RELIGION

The Augustine Bible: English Standard Version, Catholic Edition (Augustine Institute, 2019)
The Desert Fathers: Sayings of Early Christian Monks, translated by Benedicta Ward (Penguin, 2003)
Athanasius, *The Life of Antony and the Letter to Marcellinus*, translated by Robert C. Gregg (Paulist Press, 1980)

Bibliography

Aelred of Riveaulx, *Spiritual Friendship*, translated by Lawrence C. Braceland (Liturgical Press, 2010)

Meister Eckhart, *Sermons & Treatises, Volume 1*, translated and edited by M. O'C. Walshe (Element Books, 1987)

The Collected Works of St. John of the Cross, translated by Kieran Kavanaugh, O.C.D. and Otilo Rodriguez, O.C.D. (Institute of Carmelite Studies, 1979)

Thomas Traherne, *Centuries of Meditation* (Faith Press, 1969)

Thérèse de Lisieux, *Oeuvres Complètes* (Cerf, 1992)

Rowan Williams, *On Augustine* (Bloomsbury, 2016)

Rowan Williams, *Looking East in Winter: Contemporary Thought and the Eastern Christian Tradition* (Bloomsbury, 2021)

Pope Francis, *Fratelli Tutti* (CTS, 2020)

Pope Francis, *Laudato Si'* (CTS, 2015)

The Jātakas: Birth Stories of the Bodhisatta, translated by Sarah Shaw (Penguin Books, 2006)

Dominique Wohlschlag, *The Queen and the Avatar*, translated by Deborah Bell (Matheson Trust, 2017)

William C. Chittick, *Imaginal Worlds: Ibn al 'Arabī and the Problem of Religious Diversity* (Suhail Academy, 2001)

'Abd al-Karîm al-Jîlî, *De l'Homme Universel, extraits du livre Al-insân Al-kâmil*, traduit de l'arabe et commentés par Titus Burkhardt (Dervy-Livres, 1975)

Tom Holland, *Dominion: The Making of the Western Mind* (Little, Brown, 2019)